TERRY KOTTMAN

Play Therapy:
Basics and Beyond

AMERICAN
COUNSELING
ASSOCIATION

5999 Stevenson Avenue
Alexandria, VA 22304-3300

Play Therapy: Basics and Beyond

10   9   8   7   6   5

American Counseling Association
5999 Stevenson Avenue
Alexandria, VA 22304

Director of Publications
Carolyn C. Baker

Production Manager
Bonny E. Gaston

Copy Editor
Sharon Doyle

Cover art by Donna Coleman

Cover design by Martha Woolsey

Library of Congress Cataloging-in-Publication Data
Kottman, Terry
  Play therapy: basics and beyond/by Terry Kottman.
    p. cm.
Includes bibliographical references.
  ISBN 10: 1-55620-186-9 (alk. paper)
  ISBN 13: 978-1-55620-186-8
  1. Play therapy. 2. Psychotherapy. I. Title.

RJ505.P6K643   2001
615.8′5153—dc21   00-069456

For Jacob, who teaches me
what being a kid is all about—every day—
whether I want to learn or not.

TABLE OF CONTENTS

ACKNOWLEDGMENTS

A s usual, I want to thank my husband, Rick, who is my first and last reader—gentle, but firm, in telling me what makes sense and what doesn't, what can stay and what needs to go.

I also wish to thank a small band of dedicated play therapists who read the first (or was it the seventh?) draft of this book and gave me feedback about how I could make it more coherent and (hopefully) more helpful to practitioners and future practitioners: Kathie Barry, Clare Dickey, Jenny Gringer Richards, and Nancy Richards.

I am also grateful to the expert play therapists who were willing to fill out the survey I sent to representative play therapists for each of the theoretical orientations:

Helen E. Benedict, PhD, RPT-S, Licensed Psychologist; Professor of Psychology, Baylor University; Thematic play therapy (object-relations/cognitive)

Lois Carey, MSW, RPT-S; President, NYAPT, Inc.; Jungian/analytic play therapy

Diane E. Frey, PhD, RPT-S; Professor of Counseling, Wright State University; eclectic prescriptive play therapy

Louise Guerney, PhD, RPT-S; client-centered play therapy and filial therapy

Susan Knell, PhD; Meridia Behavioral Medicine—Cleveland Clinic Health System; Department of Psychology, Case Western Reserve University; cognitive–behavioral play therapy

Garry L. Landreth, EdD; Regents Professor in the Department of Counseling, Development, and Higher Education; Director of the Center for Play Therapy at the University of North Texas; child-centered play therapy

John Paul Lilly, MS, LCSW, RPT-S; Jungian/analytic play therapy

Violet Oaklander, PhD; Gestalt play therapy

Kevin O'Connor, PhD, RPT-S; Professor/Clinical Psychologist, California School of Professional Psychology, Alliant University; ecosystemic play therapy

Lessie Perry, PhD, RPT-S, LPC; Private Practice; Adjunct Professor, University of North Texas; child-centered play therapy

Chris Ruma-Cullen, cognitive–behavioral play therapy

Charles Schaefer, PhD; Professor of Psychology, Fairleigh Dickinson University; eclectic prescriptive play therapy

Risë VanFleet, PhD, RPT-S; Director of the Family Enhancement and Play Therapy Center; Past President of the Association for Play Therapy; filial therapy and child-centered play therapy

JoAnna White, EdD, LPC, NCC, RPT-S; Professor and Chair, Department of Counseling and Psychological Services, Georgia State University; Adlerian play therapy

PREFACE

Over the past 10 years, the demand for mental health professionals and school counselors who have training and expertise in using play as a therapeutic modality in working with children has increased tremendously. In response to this demand for trained play therapists, several professional organizations have begun the process of registering qualified professionals who have the required training and experience. One of the primary difficulties encountered by candidates for registration has been the limited number of play therapy training programs. In response to this increased desire for didactic training in play therapy, many colleges and universities have added introductory play therapy courses or have added play therapy units to existing courses.

I designed *Play Therapy: Basics and Beyond* to provide an introduction to the different skills used in play therapy combined with an atheoretical orientation to the basic concepts involved in play therapy. This book is a practical introduction to play therapy concepts and skills. I have stressed the application of various play therapy strategies across a wide range of theoretical orientations.

The primary intended audience for this book is students enrolled in introductory play therapy courses and introductory child counseling courses. Because the book provides information about many different theoretical orientations, it can be helpful no matter what the theoretical orientation of the professor, the student, or the program. I also wrote this book for clinicians who would like to have more knowledge and understanding of play therapy but who do not have access to formal training in the field.

With these two audiences in mind, I made some assumptions about the backgrounds of those using the book as their entry to the world of play therapy. I assumed that the reader has some basic background in counseling, psychology, social work, or some other related field—many of the terms and concepts used in this book are borrowed from other mental health-related arenas. Two other assumptions were that the reader has some knowledge and exposure to children and at least a sketchy understanding of child development.

Plan of the Book

Chapters 1 through 3 compose Part 1, Basic Concepts. In chapter 1, "Introduction to Play Therapy," I provide several definitions and rationales for play therapy, descriptions of the therapeutic powers of play, information about appropriate clients for play therapy, descriptions of characteristics and experiences needed by therapists who want to use play as a treatment modality, and an explanation of the paradigm shift necessary to move from talk as therapy to play as therapy. In chapter 2, "History of Play Therapy," the reader will learn about the evolution of play therapy. Chapter 3, "Theoretical Approaches to Play Therapy," contains detailed descriptions of seven selected contemporary approaches to play therapy, focusing on the theoretical constructs, the stages of play therapy, the role of the therapist, goals of therapy, approaches to working with parents, and distinctive features of each approach.

Chapters 4 through 11 compose Part 2, Basic Skills. In chapter 4, "Logistical Aspects of Play Therapy," the reader will learn about setting up a space for play therapy, choosing and arranging toys, explaining the play therapy process to parents and children, handling the initial session, assessing children's play behavior, dealing with paperwork, ending a session, and terminating the therapy process. There are several basic play therapy skills that are used in most approaches to play therapy: (a) tracking behavior, (b) restating content, (c) reflecting feelings, (d) limiting, (e) returning responsibility to the child, and (f) dealing with questions. The application of these skills varies depending on the theoretical orientation of the therapist and the stage of therapy, but at one time or another, most play therapists use them. In chapters 5 through 10, I define each of these skills, delineate the purpose for its use in the play therapy process, and explain how the skills can be applied in various situations in play therapy. To make each of the skills more concrete and accessible to the reader, I provide examples of the application of the skill and invite the reader to practice the skill using exercises tailored to demonstrate various situations in which the skills would be appropriate. At the end of each chapter, the reader can find practice exercises designed to hone the application of the targeted skill. I believe that all play therapists need to look at their own thoughts, feelings, attitudes, and personal issues to become truly skillful in working with children. The "Questions to Ponder" at the end of each chapter are my attempt to facilitate this self-examination process.

In chapter 5, "Tracking," the reader will learn about using tracking to establish a relationship with the child. Building rapport is also the focus in chapter 6, "Restating Content." The reader can explore strategies for reflecting feelings to help the child learn to understand his or her emotions in chapter 7, "Reflecting Feelings." In chapter 8, "Setting Limits," I provide the reader with several different techniques for limiting inappropriate behavior in the playroom. In chapter 9, "Returning Responsibility to the Child," a rationale and description of methods for returning responsibility to the child will help the reader explore this important skill. Because all children in the playroom ask questions, the reader will learn how to understand possible meanings and how to handle queries in chapter 10, "Dealing With Questions."

In chapter 11, "Integration of Basic Skills: The Art of Play Therapy," I provide an explanation of and practice in methods for deciding which skill to use when and for integrating several different skills together to create a combined intervention that works more smoothly and more efficaciously than an isolated skill would. The reader will also explore the need for blending the therapist's personality and interactional style with play therapy skills to present a more natural flow of interaction with the child.

Chapters 12 through 14 compose Part 3, Advanced Skills and Concepts. Much of the communication that takes place in play therapy comes in the form of metaphors. Chapter 12, "Recognizing and Communicating Through Metaphors," contains descriptions of strategies and practice exercises for learning to understand possible meanings of children's metaphors. The reader will also learn and practice ways to use metaphors created by children to facilitate communication with them in their own natural language.

Chapter 13, "Advanced Play Therapy Skills," includes information on using metacommunication, therapeutic metaphors, mutual storytelling, and role-playing/playing with children in play therapy. In this chapter, the reader can find examples of the application of each of these advanced skills and exercises that provide guided practice in their use.

Because play therapy is an emerging profession, it is essential that individuals interested in the field stay informed about professional issues that can have an impact on the field. To facilitate this process, in chapter 14, "Professional Issues in Play Therapy," I include information on the following issues: (a) public awareness of play therapy, (b) managed health care, (c) research support for play therapy, (d) interventions for specific children, (e) cultural awareness and sensitivity, and (f) professional identity.

Becoming a Trained Play Therapist

Reading this book will not be sufficient to transform the reader into a trained play therapist. To become a play therapist, it is essential to thoroughly study the concepts and information in this text, explore specific theoretical approaches in more depth, learn more about both beginning and advanced-level play therapy skills, and gain experience working with children using play therapy interventions under the supervision of a play therapy professional. I believe that an introductory play therapy class should require the students to conduct multiple play therapy sessions for which they receive feedback from experienced play therapists before venturing to begin to conduct other play therapy sessions (also under the supervision of a trained and experienced play therapy supervisor). I also believe that an individual who wishes to become a play therapist must continue to work on his or her own personal issues.

ABOUT THE AUTHOR

Terry Kottman, PhD, RPT-S, NCC, LMHC, recently founded The Encouragement Zone, a training center for play therapists and other counselors. Before her "retirement," she was a professor of counselor education at the University of Northern Iowa and the University of North Texas. She is a Registered Play Therapist–Supervisor and maintains a small private practice, working with children and families. Dr. Kottman developed Adlerian play therapy, an approach to counseling children that combines the ideas and techniques of Individual Psychology and play therapy. She regularly presents workshops on play therapy, activity-based counseling, counseling children, and school counseling. Dr. Kottman is the author of *Partners in Play: An*

Adlerian Approach to Play Therapy. She is the coauthor (with J. Muro) of *Guidance and Counseling in the Elementary and Middle Schools,* co-author (with J. Ashby and D. DeGraaf) of *Adventures in Guidance: How to Integrate Fun Into Your Guidance Program,* and coeditor (with C. Schaefer) of *Play Therapy in Action: A Casebook for Practitioners.*

Part 1
Basic Concepts

Chapter 1

Introduction to Play Therapy

*M*aurice walks into a room in which there is an assortment of toys on the shelves and on the floor—puppets, a dollhouse and dolls, cars, trucks, a wooden stove and refrigerator, plastic snakes and spiders, and many other play materials. He looks around the room, picks up a family of rabbits, and starts telling a story about the little rabbit that always gets into trouble and believes that no one cares about him. A woman who is sitting with him talks to him about his play—reflects the feelings of the little bunny, makes comments about what is happening between the little bunny and the rest of the bunny family, and stops him when he tries to throw the rabbit out of the window. This is play therapy.

Sally comes into a room with no toys at all. A man there tells her that they are going to play with one another and brings out several different hats, and they both try on the hats, making faces at a mirror. This is play therapy.

Khalid comes into a room with a few cars and trucks. A woman sitting at a table in the room suggests that Khalid use the cars and trucks to show her what happened when a car broadsided the truck in which he and his family were riding to the store. This is play therapy.

Play therapy is an approach to counseling young children in which the counselor uses toys, art supplies, games, and other play media to communicate with clients using the "language" of children—the "language" of play. Because children under the age of 12 have relatively limited ability to verbalize their feelings and thoughts and to use abstract verbal reasoning, most of them lack the ability to come into a counseling session, sit down, and use words to tell the therapist about their problems. They tend to lack the introspective and interactional skills required to take full advantage of "the talking cure." Children can come into a session and use toys, art, stories, and other playful tools to communicate with the therapist.

This ability to use play as a natural form of reasoning and communication makes play an appropriate modality for therapeutic intervention with young children (Landreth, 1991). In play therapy, the play can be a means for (a) establishing rapport with children; (b) helping counselors understand children and their interactions and relationships; (c) helping children reveal feelings that they have not been able to verbalize; (d) constructively acting out feelings of anxiety, tension, or hostility; (e) teaching socialization skills; and (f) providing an environment in which children can test limits, gain insight about their own behavior and motivation, explore alternatives, and learn about consequences (Thompson & Rudolph, 2000).

Therapeutic Powers of Play

Play therapy is the "systematic use of a theoretical model to establish an interpersonal process in which trained play therapists use the therapeutic powers of play to help clients prevent or resolve psychosocial difficulties and achieve optimal growth and development" (Association for Play Therapy, 1997, p. 4). According to this definition, play therapy is an approach to counseling clients using the "therapeutic powers of play." Schaefer (1993) outlined a list of 14 therapeutic powers of play, suggesting that each of these factors has specific beneficial outcomes for clients. These therapeutic factors are (a) overcoming resistance, (b) communication, (c) competence, (d) creative thinking, (e) catharsis, (f) abreaction, (g) role-play, (h) fantasy/visualization, (i) metaphoric teaching, (j) attachment formation, (k) relationship enhancement, (l) positive emotion, (m) mastering developmental fears, and (n) game play.

Overcoming Resistance

Many children who come to therapy are reluctant, usually because it is not their choice to seek counseling. They may also be resistant because their being the "identified patient" labels them as "the problem," which is a rather intimidating prospect. By using play as the basis for interaction with the child, the play therapist will usually be able to overcome the child's resistance to the therapeutic process. Play can be a relatively easy and fun way to establish a working alliance with a client without seeming threatening or scary.

The following scenario illustrates how the play therapist can use play to help overcome a client's resistance: *When Mr. and Mrs. Jarvis bring Jacob (8) to play therapy, they decide that the only way to get him into the building is to carry him. He does not want to come to counseling and is terribly unhappy with his parents for bringing him into the playroom. Jacob tells the play therapist that he is not going to talk to her or do anything else in the room because he "is not the one with the problem, no matter what anyone else thinks." The play therapist does not try to force him to play or even to talk to Jacob. Instead, the therapist plays by himself in the sandbox, draws pictures on the marker board, and makes small figures with the clay. After a while, Jacob comes over to look over his shoulder and see what he is doing. Jacob picks up a piece of clay and starts making a figure—the play therapy has started without him even realizing it.*

Communication

Because play is the usual mode of communication for the child, therapeutically using play can help to quickly and smoothly develop a sense of understanding between the child and the therapist. In addition, the therapist's willingness and ability to "speak" in the child's language can convey a respect for the child that he or she may never have experienced previously. By watching how the child plays, what toys he or she chooses, and when he or she switches from one activity to another, the therapist can receive multifaceted messages from the child.

The following scenario illustrates how the play therapist can use play to communicate with the child: *Levi's (4) parents are very excited because Mrs. Waldman is going to have a baby. They are a little worried because Levi has not expressed any interest, curiosity, or enthusiasm about the coming child. Levi comes into the playroom and picks up a baby doll and puts it in the trash can. He then proceeds to take all of the other "baby things"—the bottles, the doll clothes, the doll blanket—and stuffs them all into the trash can. He looks around for other items connected with the baby doll, doesn't see anything else, smiles, and goes over and begins to play with some blocks. Levi has now communicated through the play how he feels about having a new sibling.*

Competence

Many of the children who come into play therapy lack a sense of competence, which negatively affects the development of positive self-esteem. They frequently feel as though they are not capable people. One of the jobs of a play therapist is to provide opportunities for children to prove to themselves that they have the potential to be successful. Play is an excellent avenue for helping children practice doing things that they can do well. The therapist can encourage children to try activities that they would not usually try because they are afraid of failing. It is also helpful to point out children's efforts. By acknowledging children when they are working hard and when they are making progress, rather than waiting for them to be 100% successful, the therapist will build their feelings of competence (Kottman, 1995). This process is also reinforced by not doing things for them that they can do for themselves. By returning the responsibility for making decisions and getting things done in the playroom to children, the therapist can help improve their self-confidence and self-reliance.

The following scenario illustrates how the play therapist can use play to increase a child's sense of competence: *Luis (5) wants to play with the toy soldiers because "these are toys for boys—they are strong." He tells the play therapist to open the jar with the toy soldiers in it for him. The play therapist has seen Luis open this jar in previous sessions and tells him that she thinks he can do it for himself. He frowns and says, "I am not a man yet, so I am not big or strong." The play therapist reassures Luis that he can open the jar. He tries, looks pitiful,*

and tries again. He gets it open and smiles, saying, "I really can do it for myself.
I guess I am pretty strong. I will be a strong man."

Creative Thinking

Play is a creative process in and of itself. To play, children must generate ideas from their imaginations to fuel the action. In play therapy, children continually use creative thinking to solve problems in innovative and constructive ways. By not making decisions or providing solutions to difficult situations and by not telling the child how to play, the therapist can encourage creative thought.

The following scenario illustrates how the play therapist can use play as a method to encourage a child to think creatively: *Jacqueline (6) uses construction paper to make "magic glasses" for herself. She laughs and tells the play therapist that the glasses will restore her diminishing vision . She says, "I figured out how to do this all by myself even though I didn't really know how to do it. I can make my eyes better again, just like magic."*

Catharsis

Catharsis involves the expression of powerful feelings, resulting in emotional release. Because the play therapist is a caring and empathic adult who will continue to accept the children no matter what emotions they express, many children take advantage of the freedom of the play therapy setting to express strong emotions (both positive and negative) that they might not ordinarily be willing or able to communicate. The sense of release that follows the expression of powerful feelings, especially those that might not be acceptable to many other people, can be a growthful experience for children.

The following scenario illustrates how the play therapy process can facilitate catharsis: *T'Keesah (8) reports that she has gotten in trouble with the principal at her school, "again." She grabs a foam bat and starts hitting the punching bag, yelling, "I hate her! I hate her! I hate her!" She dissolves into tears, crying and saying, "She doesn't like me just because I'm Black! She thinks my hair is kinky and my skin is too dark! I hate her."*

Abreaction

Abreaction allows children to relive (symbolically) stressful or traumatic events and reexperience the feelings associated with those events. The purpose of abreaction is to provide children with a vehicle through which they can release some of the negative thoughts and emotions attached to painful experiences. In play therapy, children can reenact "bad stuff" over and over again if need be. This process helps them gain a sense of mastery over their own negative experiences and interactions, which may assist them with their adjustment to past traumas.

The following scenario illustrates how play therapy can trigger and facilitate a child's abreactive response: *Duncan (5) uses the figures of a doctor, a nurse, and several ambulance attendants to depict his recent hospitalization for an operation to correct a congenital heart defect. Initially, when he does this play, he is very tense and agitated, almost tearful. As he plays the surgery and other hospital scenes over and over, he seems to gradually become more relaxed, even smiling as he repeats comments made by his doctors and the nurses who cared for him.*

Role-Play

Through role-play, children can express their perceptions of family and peer relationships and enhance their level of empathy for others. In play therapy, children many times act out events in their lives in a metaphoric way. Role-playing can be helpful in assisting children to learn and practice new skills for interacting with others and constructively solving interpersonal problems. Using the fantasy aspect of role-playing, children can also generate and perfect solutions to problems in their lives without having to actually "own" those problems.

The following scenario illustrates how a play therapist can use role-playing to help a child: *Siobhan (8) tells the play therapist, "You be the baby, and I will be the mother. I will feed you bad food. You need to spit it out, but I will keep on trying to make you eat it. Don't do it—don't eat the bad food, no matter what I do to try to make you eat it." She proceeds to put sand on a plate and tries to make the play therapist "eat" it. Every time the play therapist refuses to eat the food, Siobhan smiles but pretends she is angry, yelling at the therapist in an angry voice: "Just eat that food, you nasty kid!! If you don't, the priest will come and get you and you will burn in hell!"*

Fantasy/Visualization

Many times, children who come to play therapy do not really think that their lives can get better in the future. They have had negative experiences and interactions in the past, leaving them with little or no evidence that the future will be more positive for them. Fantasy and visualization in the play therapy process can help children experiment with the possibility that they can change their lives and their interactions with others. By encouraging children to imagine themselves as strong, powerful, and proactive through fantasy interludes in the playroom, the play therapist can provide them with an experience that is completely different from the rest of their lives. For some children, this experience can instill hope for the future.

The following scenario illustrates how a child can use fantasy/visualization in the play therapy process: *Randy (5) picks up a magic wand and waves it over his head. He puts on a cape and twirls around, whispering, "This is going to make my parents like everyone else's parents—they will be able to hear, and I won't have to use my hands to talk to them and tell them what other people are saying, and my teacher won't always ask me what they are doing with their hands."*

Metaphoric Teaching

Metaphoric teaching is a method of exposing resistant clients to new insights, perspectives, and coping strategies without evoking their defensive reactions. By using stories, playing, and artwork to explore issues and present different ways of looking at situations, the play therapist can help children examine their cognitive and affective patterns and teach them new skills and attitudes in a way that short-circuits resistance.

The following scenario illustrates how the play therapist can use play to metaphorically teach problem-solving skills: *Miranda (4) and Jeremy (7) are playing in the sandbox with a family of plastic lizards. Jeremy uses one of the bigger lizards to hit one of the smaller lizards held by Miranda, saying, "Get out of my way. I want to go through here." Miranda starts crying—partially in pretending that her lizard is crying and partially in complaint that her brother is bothering her. The play therapist says to the bigger lizard, "You need to work out a way to let the smaller lizards know what you want without hitting them," and says to the smaller lizard, "Can you use words instead of crying to let the big lizard know how you feel when he hits you?"*

Attachment Formation

Some of the children who come to play therapy have limited attachment to other human beings. The process of play therapy provides several avenues for increasing these children's connectedness to others. In play therapy, through shared fun, children frequently grow to feel affection and a sense of attachment to the therapist. By using role-playing and fantasy play, the therapist can begin to build children's empathic responses, which can potentially generalize to stronger attachment to other people. It is sometimes helpful to include an additional child in several play therapy sessions or to involve the child with attachment difficulties in a group to maximize the transfer of attachment to peers. The play therapist can also work with parents to help them learn strategies for forming attachment with their children.

The following scenario illustrates how the play therapy process can be the basis for beginning to set the stage for the formation of an attachment between the therapist and a child: *Hilda (5) has been in a series of foster families, moving sometimes as many as three or four times a year. These moves are usually triggered by her own inappropriate behavior but sometimes by circumstances beyond her control. She comes to play therapy and plays completely by herself for the first 17 sessions, making little eye contact and seldom smiling at the play therapist. At the beginning of her 18th session, she tosses a ball to the therapist and gives her a small smile. When the therapist tosses the ball back, she again smiles but goes back to playing by herself. She does the same thing in her 19th and 20th sessions. At the end of the 21st session, she asks the therapist, "Want to play ball?" in a very serious voice. When the therapist agrees, Hilda begins by tossing the ball over the therapist's head but gradually starts tossing it to him.*

Relationship Enhancement

Because many children referred for play therapy have not experienced success in building relationships with others, the opportunities inherent in the process can prove invaluable. Because the play therapist consistently demonstrates a caring, supportive attitude toward the children, the children begin to believe that perhaps they are worthy of love and positive attention. Some play therapists actually teach social skills and other strategies for building positive social relationships, either in group or in individual modalities.

The following scenario illustrates using play to enhance the relationship between the therapist and a child: *Keeton (4) comes into his third session and asks if the play therapist wants to play a game with him. When she replies that she would be delighted, Keeton says, "I have never had a friend like you."*

Positive Emotion

Playing together is fun, and play therapy can provide children with an experience of laughing and having a good time in an accepting environment. Because quite a few of the children who come to play therapy have not had the opportunity to experience or express positive emotions, the play therapy process can be a revelation to them.

The following scenario illustrates how play can promote positive feelings in the therapeutic relationship: *Mei (7) puts on a puppet show for her play therapist. She tells knock–knock jokes, laughs, and rolls on the floor of the playroom. She tells the play therapist, "My grandmother never lets me do anything like all this stuff. She is always busy or mad and never has time to listen to me like you do."*

Mastering Developmental Fears

As a natural function of growing up, children experience certain fears—of the dark, of being alone, and so forth. In certain cultures, there are objects or concepts that typically evoke anxiety in individuals, (e.g., several Native American tribes such as the Navaho believe that they must not speak of the dead for fear that evil spirits or witches will harm them). In play therapy, children can express and sometimes master these fears by interacting with the toys, art supplies, and play media in a way that lets them experience fear and recognize that they have the skills for coping with fear and taking care of themselves.

The following scenario illustrates how play therapy can help children learn to express and cope with their fears: *Joseph Leaphorn (8) sees the ghost puppet and starts to cry. Looking very nervous, he uses a bat to push it toward the door of the playroom. The play therapist says, "You seem really scared about that and want it out of the room." In a whisper, the play therapist asks, "What do you want to happen next?" Without acknowledging the question or the play therapist, Joseph whispers, "I wish someone would take it away from here." Because the play therapist knows that in Joseph's culture a person might be con-*

sidered contaminated by touching a dead person, he opens the door to the play-room and uses a bat to push the ghost puppet out the door and down the hall out of sight. When the play therapist comes back into the room, Joseph seems much calmer.

Game Play

Playing games helps children enhance their social skills, increase communication strategies, and practice rule-governed behavior. This is true whether children are playing a casual game of pitch and catch; a simple game based on luck, such as "Chutes and Ladders"; or a highly structured game that requires advanced skill, such as chess. Specially designed therapeutic games, such as "Feelings Bingo" and the "Talking, Thinking, and Doing Game" (Gardner, 1973), can provide children with these opportunities and also expand their skills and insights in other ways related to their particular therapeutic goals.

The following scenario illustrates how a play therapist can use game play to help a child practice social skills and rule-governed behavior: *Lucy (9) has difficulty sitting still and taking turns. The play therapist suggests that they play one of the games available in the playroom to help her practice taking turns and following rules. Lucy chooses the game "Don't Break the Ice," and they proceed to play. To win the game, Lucy must pay attention to the arrangement of the blocks of ice and to where the little man sits on the ice. She must also alternate knocking the ice blocks out of the holder—paying attention to whose turn comes next and where the pieces connect with one another.*

What Personal Qualities Does a Play Therapist Need?

The personal characteristics and personality traits of the therapist are key elements in the play therapy process (Barnes, 1996; Landreth, 1991; Schaefer & Greenberg, 1997). An effective play therapist should (a) like children and treat them with kindness and respect, (b) have a sense of humor and be willing to laugh at himself or herself, (c) be playful and fun-loving, (d) be self-confident and not dependent on the positive regard of others for a sense of self-worth, (e) be open and honest, (f) be flexible and able to deal with a certain level of ambiguity, (g) be accepting of others' perceptions of reality without feeling threatened or judgmental, (h) be willing to use play and metaphors to communicate, (i) be comfortable with children and have experience interacting with them, (j) be able to firmly and kindly set limits and maintain personal boundaries, and (k) be self-aware and open to taking interpersonal risks and exploring his or her own personal issues.

Personality and personal history will have a tremendous influence on play therapists' interaction with children in the playroom. As part of the process of learning more about play therapy, therapists need to learn more about themselves—their own personal characteristics, their strengths and weaknesses, their likes and dislikes, and their own psychological and emotional issues. This knowledge can help play therapists to understand their own reactions to children in the playroom and to avoid letting their own personalities or issues interfere with their ability to interact effectively with children.

Who Is an Appropriate Client for Play Therapy?

Although there are play therapists who work with adults (Frey, 1993; Ledyard, 1999; Peyton, 1986), most play therapy clients are children between the ages of 3 and 11 years, depending on the developmental level and abstract verbal-reasoning skills of the child. Children who have experienced trauma may be appropriate candidates for play therapy at earlier ages (as young as 2 years) or later ages (11–14 or 15 years) (Gil, 1991; Terr, 1983, 1990).

With many preadolescent and younger adolescent children, it is appropriate to ask whether they would be more comfortable sitting and talking to the therapist or more comfortable playing with the toys. By adding toys aimed at older children, such as craft supplies, carpentry tools, office supplies and equipment, and more sophisticated games or games designed for therapeutic purposes, the therapist may be able to extend the usual age range and include some activity therapy in his or her repertoire (James, 1997; Kottman, Strother, & Deniger, 1987).

Anderson and Richards (1995) outlined a structured method for deciding whether a client is appropriate for intervention through play therapy. This method involves considering questions related to the child and questions related to the therapist. First, the therapist should consider the following questions related to the child:

1. Can the child tolerate/form/utilize a relationship with an adult?
2. Can the child tolerate/accept a protective environment?
3. Does the child have the capacity for learning new methods of dealing with the presenting problem?

4. Does the child have the capacity for insight into his or her behavior and motivation and into the behavior and motivation of others?
5. Does the child have the capacity for sufficient attention and/or cognitive organization to engage in therapeutic activities?
6. Is play therapy an effective/efficient way to address this child's problems?
7. Are there conditions in the child's environment over which the therapist will not have control that will have a negative impact on the therapy process?

If the answers to Questions 1 through 6 are "no," then play therapy may not be the optimal intervention strategy for this particular child. If the answer to Question 7 is "no," the therapist must consider how handicapping the conditions that might have a negative impact on the therapeutic process will be. If he or she believes that these obstacles will effectively sabotage the process, play therapy will probably not be the best intervention for this child.

Anderson and Richards (1995) further suggested that the decision whether to use play therapy with a specific child depends on the answers to the following questions related to the therapist:

1. Do I have the necessary skills to work with this child? Is there consultation or supervision available if I need it?
2. Can I effectively treat this child in my current practice setting (e.g., appropriate space, funding issues, and length of treatment allowed)?
3. If effective therapy for this child will involve working with other professionals, can I work within the necessary framework?
4. Is my current energy/stress level such that I can fully commit to working with this particular child?
5. Have I resolved any personal issues that will interfere with my capacity to work with this child and his or her family?

If the answer to any of these questions is "no," the therapist should seriously consider avoiding play therapy as an intervention strategy for that particular child.

A meta-analysis of play therapy research by LeBlanc and Ritchie (1999) suggested that play therapy was effective regardless of the presenting problem of the child. The results of this study found that only two variables affected the efficacy of play therapy—the involvement of parents in the play therapy process and the number of therapy sessions. Those children whose parents were active participants in the process and those who had participated in 30–35 therapy sessions were more likely to have positive results than those children whose parents did not actively participate and those who had less than 30 sessions or more than 35 sessions.

Bratton and Ray (2000) synthesized the results of more than 100 case studies documenting the effectiveness of play therapy as an intervention. In these case studies, the participants demonstrated elevated levels of positive behavior and decreased levels of symptomatic behavior after play therapy interventions. These authors also summarized the findings of 82 articles representing experimental research related to play therapy, ranging from the 1940s to the present. They found that these studies provided support for the efficacy of play therapy as a treatment modality for children with the following issues: social maladjustment, conduct disorder, problematic school behavior, emotional maladjustment, anxiety/fear, negative self-concept, "mental challenges," or physical or learning disabilities.

Reading the available research studies and anecdotal reports would suggest that certain diagnoses and life situations seem to be more amenable to play therapy intervention than other diagnoses and life situations. Considering this body of professional literature, there seem to be four distinct categories into which children with specific presenting problems or diagnoses can fit: (a) play therapy (regardless of the approach) would be the treatment of choice, (b) certain approaches to play therapy have been useful in treating these children, (c) play therapy can be an effective intervention when combined with other interventions, and (d) play therapy would not be the treatment of choice (see Table 1.1). In the space available in this text, it is impossible to thoroughly discuss each of these populations. For more specific information about working with a particular population, the reader should explore the books, articles, and book chapters related to each presenting problem or diagnosis.

On the basis of anecdotal case studies and empirical research, play therapy (regardless of the approach) would seem to be the treatment of choice for children with a diagnosis of Adjustment Disorder, Posttraumatic Stress Disorder, Dissociative Disorder, depressive episodes, or specific fears and phobias. Play therapy can also be an effective intervention for children struggling with aggressive, acting-out behavior; anxiety and withdrawn behavior; abuse and neglect; divorce of parents; family violence; grief issues; issues

Table 1.1

**Play therapy (regardless of the approach)
would be the treatment of choice**

Adjustment Disorder	Anderson & Richards, 1995
Posttraumatic Stress Disorder	Allan & Lawton-Speert, 1993 Auerbach-Walker & Bolkavatz, 1988 Bevin, 1999 Gil, 1991 Hall, 1997 Marvasti, 1993, 1994 B. Mills & Allan, 1992 Strand, 1999 Van de Putte, 1995
Dissociative Disorder	Anderson & Richards, 1995 J. Klein & Landreth, 1993
Depressive Episodes	Briesmeister, 1997
Specific Fears and Phobias	S. Cooper & Blitz, 1985 Lyness-Richard, 1997 Milos & Reiss, 1982 Sugar, 1988
Aggressive, Acting-Out Behavior	Bleck & Bleck, 1982 Kottman, 1993 O'Connor, 1986 Smith & Herman, 1994
Anxiety and Withdrawn Behavior	Barlow, Strother, & Landreth, 1985 B. Mills & Allan, 1992
Abuse and/or Neglect	Allan & Lawton-Speert, 1993 Auerbach-Walker & Bolkavatz, 1988 Cockle & Allan, 1996 Doyle & Stoop, 1999 Gil, 1991 Hall, 1997 Marvasti, 1993, 1994 B. Mills & Allan, 1992 Pelcovitz, 1999 Strand, 1999 Tonning, 1999 Van de Putte, 1995
Divorce of Parents	Berg, 1989 Cangelosi, 1997 Faust, 1993 Hellendoorn & DeVroom, 1993 Mendell, 1983

Divorce of Parents	O'Connor, 1993
	Price, 1991
	Robinson, 1999
Family Violence and Other Family Problems	Hammond-Newman, 1994
	Nisivoccia & Lynn, 1999
	VanFleet, Lilly, & Kaduson, 1999
	N. B. Webb, 1999
Grief Issues	Bluestone, 1999
	Carter, 1987
	LeVieux, 1994
	Masur, 1991
	Perry, 1993
	Saravay, 1991
	Tait & Depta, 1994
Adoption and Foster Care-Related Issues	Kottman, 1997b
	Van Fleet, 1994a
Hospitalization	Alger, Linn, & Beardslee, 1985
	Brunskill, 1984
	Ellerton, Caty, & Ritchie, 1985
	Golden, 1983
	Kaplan, 1999
	Shapiro, 1995
	J. Webb, 1995
	Wojtasik & Sanborn, 1991
Severe Trauma (e.g., earthquake, car wreck, war, or kidnapping)	Fornari, 1999
	Hofmann & Rogers, 1991
	Joyner, 1991
	Shelby, 1997
	N. B. Webb, 1991
	N. B. Webb, 1999
	Williams-Gray, 1999
Chronic or Terminal Illness	Bertoia & Allan, 1988
	Boley, Ammen, O'Connor, & Miller, 1996
	Boley, Peterson, Miller, & Ammen, 1996
	Glazer-Waldman, Zimmerman, Landreth, & Norton, 1992
	Goodman, 1999
	Kaplan, 1999
	Landreth, 1988
	LeVieux, 1990
	Ridder, 1999
	VanFleet, 2000b

Certain approaches to play therapy have been useful in treating these children

Attachment Disorder (Theraplay and Thematic Play)	Benedict & Mongoven, 1997 Jernberg, 1979 Jernberg & Booth, 1999
Selective Mutism (Cognitive–Behavioral Play Therapy and Client-Centered Play Therapy)	Barlow, Strother, & Landreth, 1986 Cook, 1997 Knell, 1993b
Moderate to Severe Behavior Problems (Filial Therapy, Adlerian Play Therapy, and Ecosystemic Play Therapy)	Bleck & Bleck, 1982 Cabe, 1997 L. Guerney, 1991 Kottman, 1993 O'Connor, 1986 Reid, 1993 Smith & Herman, 1994

Play therapy can be an effective intervention when combined with other interventions

Attention Deficit Hyperactivity Disorder	Kaduson, 1997 Kaduson & Finnerty, 1995
Major Depressive Disorder	Briesmeister, 1997
Separation Anxiety Disorder	Anderson & Richards, 1995
Enuresis or Encopresis	Knell & Moore, 1990
Learning Disabilities	L. Guerney, 1983b Kale & Landreth, 1999
Mental Retardation	Ginsberg, 1984 Hellendoorn, 1994 Leland, 1983 O'Doherty, 1989
Physical Handicaps	Palumbo, 1988 Salomon, 1983 Williams & Lair, 1991

Play therapy would not be the treatment of choice for these children

Severe Conduct Disorder	Anderson & Richards, 1995
Severe Attachment Disorder	Anderson & Richards, 1995
Manifest Signs of Psychosis	Anderson & Richards, 1995

related to adoption and foster care; hospitalization; severe trauma (e.g., earthquakes, car wrecks, war, or kidnapping); or chronic or terminal illness.

Specific approaches to play therapy seem to be effective in treating certain groups of children. Theraplay and Thematic Play therapy are reported to be particularly effective with children diagnosed as having Attachment Disorder. For children with selective mutism, therapists using cognitive–behavioral play therapy and client-centered play therapy have reported success. Filial therapy, Adlerian play therapy, and ecosystemic play therapy seem helpful to children manifesting moderate to severe behavior problems.

Children who have been diagnosed with Attention Deficit Hyperactivity Disorder (ADHD), Major Depressive Disorder, or Separation Anxiety Disorder may be appropriate candidates for play therapy if it is combined with other treatment strategies. This also seems to be the case with clients who are enuretic or encopretic and those who have learning disabilities, mental retardation, or physical handicaps. With these diagnoses, a combination of play therapy with medication, other interventions with the children, and collateral work with parents and other family members has been an effective treatment plan.

Play therapy is probably not the treatment of choice for children with severe conduct disorder or severe Attachment Disorder or for children who manifest signs of psychosis (Anderson & Richards, 1995). These children usually need interventions that are more medical, behavioral, and/or systemic than the typical play therapist can provide.

No matter what the child's presenting problem, the therapist must clearly define his or her goals for play therapy with a child and communicate these goals to parents. For instance, although play therapy does not reduce impulsivity and distractibility in children with ADHD, it does help them deal with feelings of discouragement and failure and low self-esteem. Depending on the theoretical orientation of the play therapy approach, the play therapist may decide that children with ADHD should also learn needed skills (e.g., social skills and anger management tactics) in play therapy. For children with more severe pathology or problems with organic components, play therapy will not eliminate symptoms. However, it may help them with quality-of-life concerns. The essential task of the play therapist is to be clear with parents about specific goals and about what play therapy can and cannot do.

Paradigm Shift From Talk to Play

Therapists who wish to learn play therapy must make a cognitive leap across a chasm. On one side of the canyon is the practice of using conversation, verbal skills, and the "talking cure" as the primary vehicle for communication and for change in the process of therapy. On the other side of the canyon is the practice of using play, toys, and metaphor as the primary vehicle for communication and for change in the process of therapy.

On the face of it, this change seems simple to make—just stop focusing on words as communication and start focusing on toys. In reality, the transition from doing talk therapy to play therapy involves an extremely complex conceptual paradigm shift that can be difficult for adults to make. Play therapists look at themselves, children, and the world from a different perspective than talk therapists do. Before they can begin to acquire the skills involved in using play to communicate with children, potential play therapists must learn a completely different way of understanding communication—to a symbolic, action-oriented model in which actions of puppets and animal figures are important pieces of information and in which a shrug, a smile, or a turned back can be an entire "conversation."

Practice Exercises

Making the paradigm shift from talk to play as the primary tool for communication in therapy can be a difficult process. To begin this transformation, you will need to consider the following issues:

1. What do you believe about the way people communicate their thoughts and attitudes? What do you believe about the way people communicate their feelings?
2. What do you believe about the way children communicate their thoughts and attitudes? What do you believe about the way children communicate their feelings? What are the differences between the way children and adults communicate? What do you believe is the best way to communicate with children?
3. How do you build rapport with adults? How do you express yourself to adults?
4. What are your strengths in communicating with adults? What are the weak areas in the way you communicate with adults?

5. How do you usually build rapport with children? How would this fit into the play therapy modality?

6. How do you usually express yourself to children? How do children usually express themselves to you?

7. What are the strengths in the way you communicate with children? What are the weak areas in the way you communicate with children?

8. Think about how you could make a shift from thinking about talk as communication to thinking about play as communication. What do you think would be involved for you to begin to make this paradigm shift?

9. Begin to observe the ways children naturally relate to others—both peers and adults. What do you notice about patterns in the ways they interact and the ways they express their thoughts, attitudes, and feelings?

10. As you observe children, focus on the potential for play being metaphoric. What have you observed about the metaphors present in children's play and communication?

Questions to Ponder

1. As you think about the therapeutic powers of play described in this chapter, which ones have value to you in your life? Which ones have you observed in the lives of other adults and children?

2. Which of these therapeutic powers of play do you think would be most helpful with clients? Explain your thoughts.

3. With which of the therapeutic powers of play do you think you would be most comfortable? Explain your thoughts.

4. With which of the therapeutic powers of play do you think you would be uncomfortable? What would the sources of that discomfort be?

5. As you think about children with whom you have worked in the past and other children of your acquaintance, are there certain problem situations or diagnoses with which you think you would want to work? What are they? What draws you to these children?

6. As you think about children with whom you have worked in the past and other children of your acquaintance, are there certain problem situations or diagnoses with which you think you would not want to work? What are they? What are the sources of your discomfort?

7. How would you describe the process of play therapy to a friend or a colleague?

Chapter 2

History of Play Therapy

The historical progression in the development of play therapy in many ways parallels the history of the development of psychology and reflects the zeitgeist of the society (Richards, 1996). However, because many approaches to play therapy evolved simultaneously, it is difficult to present them in a linear fashion. Although I attempt to follow chronological order, the more recent developments in play therapy occurred at the same time, without a clear pattern of how they evolved.

Because this is not a book on the history of play therapy, the descriptions of each approach to play therapy presented in this chapter are necessarily brief. In chapter 3, "Theoretical Approaches to Play Therapy," I go into more detail about selected contemporary approaches to play therapy. I encourage you to continue your exploration of the various theoretical orientations by reading the original sources by the experts who have pioneered each of them.

Psychoanalytic/Psychodynamic Play Therapy

The first report in the professional literature of play as having a role in a psychological intervention was a description of the work of Sigmund Freud (1909/1955) in his treatment of "Little Hans," a child who was experiencing a phobic reaction. Freud did not work directly with Hans but had Hans's father describe the child's play. On the basis of the information he gathered from Hans's father, Freud provided interpretations of the underlying conflicts and made suggestions for how Hans's father could intervene directly with Hans. Freud believed that play is a repetition of unconscious concerns and conflicts. He suggested that play has a role in the process of mastery and abreaction.

Hug-Hellmuth (1921) was the first psychoanalytic therapist to directly use play with children in therapy. She visited children's homes and watched and participated in their natural play without directing it in any way. Although no specific play techniques are mentioned in her writings, Hug-Hellmuth believed that the therapist can use the material present in the child's play to understand intrapsychic conflict and personality structures explored in the process of child analysis.

Anna Freud (1928, 1946) also worked directly with children. She used the observation of children's play as a tool for building a relationship with these clients. Although Freud suggested that play was an appropriate way for establishing communication with children, she did not actually use the play in a therapeutic way because she did not believe behaviors in play were necessarily symbolic or metaphoric. After she had used the play to establish rapport, Freud switched to the more traditional forms of therapeutic dialogue, such as history taking, dream interpretation, free association, and drawing.

M. Klein (1932), who was also a psychodynamic therapist, had a totally different understanding of the function that play can serve in therapy. She believed that play is children's natural medium of expression and should be considered as a direct substitute for the verbal expression that takes place in adult therapy. Klein suggested that spontaneous play is the equivalent of free association in adults, full of important information about subconscious processes. Rather than simply storing the information gathered through the play and making interpretations to parents or crafting a conceptualization of the client for the sole purposes of the therapist's understanding, Klein advocated interpreting play behavior using psychodynamic concepts to the children themselves.

Structured Play Therapy

Based on psychodynamic conceptualizations of clients, combined with a more structured, goal-oriented practice of interacting with children, structured play therapy stems from a belief in the cathartic value of play (James, 1997; Richards, 1996). In all of the structured approaches to play therapy, the therapist plays an active role in determining the focus and goals of therapy. Levy (1938), Solomon (1938), and Hambridge (1955) were well-known practitioners of structured play therapy.

Levy (1938) developed Release Therapy to treat children under the age of 10 years who had experienced some specific trauma. He provided specially chosen toys that he believed would facilitate clients' focusing on the traumatic event. He did not direct them to play with the toys in a certain way nor did he interpret their play. On the basis of Sigmund Freud's (1938) concept of repetition compulsion theory, Levy believed that clients would resolve problems through catharsis if given the appropriate setting and toys. Levy suggested that children would act out various scenarios that would help them discharge painful memories, thoughts, and emotions so that they no longer threatened their emotional or mental well-being.

Solomon (1938) developed "active play therapy" to work with impulsive, acting-out children. On the basis of Sigmund Freud's (1938) concept of abreactive effect, he advocated encouraging children to express their negative feelings, inappropriate impulses, and regressive tendencies in play therapy sessions, in which they would not get the usual expected negative or judgmental reaction from the therapist. Solomon believed that experiencing a nonjudgmental, accepting attitude from an adult, even when they were expressing themselves in ways that usually evoked negative reactions, could be transformational for these children. Through abreaction, they could resolve any traumatic effects from their past and experiment with more socially appropriate behaviors.

Hambridge (1955), building on the ideas of Levy (1938), used an even more directive approach to play therapy. After having established a relationship with children, he asked them to play out specific situations similar to stressful experiences or relationships in their lives. On the basis of the idea that repetition would first provide a cathartic experience and then help them resolve any issues connected with the trauma, Hambridge believed that, by exactly reenacting a traumatic experience, children would learn to cope more effectively with any aftermath that lingered subsequent to the event.

Relationship Play Therapy

In a shift away from psychodynamic ideas about psychology, Rank (1936) suggested that the relationship between the therapist and the client in the here and now was the primary vehicle for change in clients. Taft (1933), Allen (1942), and Moustakas (1959) based their work with children on this concept.

Taft (1933) believed that the essence of therapy with children was the examination of the real relationship between the therapist and the client and of the client's functioning in the here and now. He stressed the process of building a relationship with the child and the use of time in therapy. Because he believed that the ending of each therapy session and the final termination of therapy are parallel to the process of birth—with the trauma experienced being similar—Taft set the date for termination at the beginning of therapy. Taft made a connection between successful separation from the therapist and successful resolution of the trauma resulting from the original separation from the child's mother.

Allen (1942) also focused on the child–therapist relationship, with an emphasis on the autonomy and self-actualizing ability of the child. Allen believed that the primary task in therapy is for the child to learn to function in relationships and everyday life.

Moustakas (1959) "should be credited with framing the major portion of theory and technique that is used in many of the current approaches to play therapy" (James, 1997, p. 140). Moustakas focused on using the secure therapeutic relationship as the basis for the child to explore interpersonal interactions and move toward individuation. He stressed the need for the growth process to be mutual, in that the therapist must continue to grow with the child in both self-awareness and awareness of others. The therapist must convey unconditional acceptance and faith in the child's ability to move in a positive direction without guidance or interference. The emphasis in the interaction with the child is on the child's feelings, without interpretation on the therapist's part. Moustakas also believed that the therapist must be an active participant in the play if invited by the child to do so.

Nondirective, Client-Centered Play Therapy

Axline (1947, 1969, 1971) combined Carl Rogers's (1951) client-centered therapy for adults with many of the ideas from relationship play therapy when she developed nondirective, client-centered play therapy. She believed that children naturally move toward positive growth if they are provided with a relationship in which they experience unconditional acceptance and safety (Axline, 1947). Axline (1969) believed that change in the child occurs as a result of the relationship with the therapist, not as a result of the application of specific techniques. She suggested that it is not appropriate to interpret the child's play or to praise his or her behavior.

Landreth (1978, 1991) expanded on Axline's (1947, 1969) work, combining many of her ideas with concepts described by Ginott (1959) and Moustakas (1953, 1959), to develop his own approach to play therapy, child-centered play therapy. According to Landreth (1991), the play therapy relationship and the play therapy setting must be different from any other relationship or setting that the child has experienced. When this happens, the child begins to actuate his or her innate potential for development and growth. Landreth suggested that the therapist must serve primarily as a mirror for the child and the child's feelings. This belief precludes the therapist from actively interacting with the child or taking responsibility for making decisions in the playroom.

Bernard Guerney (1964) and Louise Guerney (1983a) adapted many of the ideas inherent in nondirective, client-centered play therapy to teaching parents to work directly with their children using "filial therapy." The Guerneys developed strategies for training parents in nondirective play therapy techniques they can use in specifically designated "play sessions" designed to build the parent–child relationship and enhance children's self-esteem. The primary techniques taught in filial therapy training are tracking, restating content, reflecting feelings, and setting limits.

Limit-Setting Therapy

Bixler (1949) and Ginott (1959) contended that the development and enforcement of limits are the primary vehicles of change in therapy sessions. Bixler (1949) stated that "limits are therapy" (p. 1). He believed that the therapist must set limits in the playroom to maintain an unconditionally accepting attitude toward clients and to establish that this relationship is different than other relationships. Bixler contended that setting limits in the playroom communicates to the child that the relationship is grounded in a sense of integrity and responsibility. He defined the basic types of limits necessary in play therapy as those that ensure safety to people, property, and play materials.

Ginott (1959) believed that limits are a key component in play therapy with children who have experienced inconsistent reactions from adults and consequently feel that they must constantly test their relationships with adults with acting-out behavior. He suggested that the therapist, by carefully and consistently applying limits, could reestablish these children's view of themselves as people who are protected and supported by adults. According to Ginott, by setting limits on aggressive or acting-out behavior, the therapist is much more likely to maintain a positive attitude toward children in therapy.

Theories Designed for Working With Children Who Have Attachment Issues

In the 1970s, there was much interest in helping children who were struggling with attachment. Jernberg (1979) developed Theraplay and Brody (1978) designed Developmental Play Therapy as strategies for using play to work with this population.

Theraplay

Theraplay therapists use intrusive methods to duplicate the interactions typically present in parent–infant interactions to improve impaired parent–child relationships (Jernberg, 1979; Jernberg & Booth, 1999; Munns, 2000). They design each of the limited sessions to include the following dimensions: structure, challenge, intrusion, nurturing, and playfulness. In Theraplay, children have one or two therapists focusing on them, while in another part of the treatment room, the parents have a therapist who works with them—first explaining what is happening with the children and then helping them integrate themselves into the session as cotherapists.

Developmental Play Therapy

In another directive approach designed to improve the attachment in parent–child relationships, Developmental Play Therapy, the emphasis is on the developmental processes (Brody, 1978, 1997). Practitioners of Developmental Play Therapy evaluate the developmental stage of clients, adapting the therapeutic approach to provide the elements of nurturing missed by children in their early attachment to their parents. Brody stressed the need for children to experience touching as they grow to adequately attach to parental figures. The developmental play therapist holds, strokes, and rocks children in an attempt to provide children with experiences vital to the development of infants, in hopes that this remedial nurturing will help children move forward in the developmental process.

Play Therapy Approaches Based on Theories Developed to Work With Adults

One of the trends in the more recent history of play therapy is for practitioners to develop approaches to play therapy derived from theoretical orientations that have traditionally placed an emphasis on understanding and working with adult clients. These approaches include cognitive–behavioral play therapy, Adlerian play therapy, Gestalt play therapy, and Jungian play therapy.

Cognitive–Behavioral Play Therapy

Drawing from the work of early behaviorists and cognitive–behaviorists such as Ellis (1971), Beck (1976), and Bandura (1977), Knell (1993a, 1993b) incorporated cognitive and behavioral interventions within a play therapy paradigm in cognitive–behavioral play therapy. This approach is structured, directive, and goal-oriented. Cognitive–behavioral play therapists use behavioral techniques and cognitive strategies couched in play to teach children new ways of thinking about themselves, their relationships, and problem situations. They set up play scenarios that parallel the behavioral and emotional dilemmas experienced by children so as to help children learn new coping skills and practice alternative appropriate behaviors.

Gestalt Play Therapy

Oaklander (1978/1992, 1993) based her conceptualization of child clients and her work in the playroom on the ideas of Perls (1973), founder of Gestalt therapy. She focused on the relationship between the therapist and children; the concept of organismic self-regulation; children's boundaries and sense of self; and the therapeutic role of awareness, experience, and resistance (Oaklander, 1994).

Gestalt play therapy combines elements of directive and nondirective play therapy approaches. At times, the therapist controls the session by asking children to participate in experiences and experiments, and at times, the therapist follows the lead of clients in the playroom.

Jungian Play Therapy

Several therapists (Allan, 1988, 1994; Bradway, 1979; Carey, 1990; Kalff, 1971; Lowenfeld, 1950) based their approach to play therapy on Jungian principles. Lowenfeld asked children to choose miniatures to represent various aspects of their world. She developed a system called "The World" for understanding the symbolism of each object available to the children. Kalff expanded the work of Lowenfeld, with the therapist choosing special miniatures for each client and asking the client to arrange the miniatures in a sand tray and develop a narrative that described the scenes created this way. Bradway used the sand tray and miniatures but did not encourage a great deal of verbalization on the part of the child. She photographed each sand tray scenario to look for patterns and themes in the child's worldview. Carey, in her work with sand tray therapy, suggested that the most important element of the play is the exploration of the child's expression of the collective unconscious—in both the verbal and nonverbal communication of the child.

Allan (1988, 1994) expanded the use of techniques in Jungian play therapy. In addition to sand tray work, he also used art and play strategies to help children explore the ego, the self, and the collective unconscious. Allan believed that by establishing a nondirective relationship with the child, the therapist could provide an environment in which the child could feel safe to do the work necessary for him or her to move along the natural path of individuation and healing.

Adlerian Play Therapy

Adlerian play therapy is an approach to play therapy that combines the theoretical principles and strategies of Individual Psychology with the treatment modality of play therapy (Kottman, 1993, 1994, 1995). The therapist integrates nondirective and directive interaction with clients, depending on how the process of play therapy unfolds. The Adlerian play therapist also works with parents to help them make shifts in the ways they perceive their children and learn additional parenting strategies and (when appropriate) with teachers to help them learn new ways of interacting with children to reduce emotional and behavioral problems that can interfere with instruction.

Play Therapy Approaches Based on Integrating Several Different Theories

Another trend that has developed in the past 10–20 years is the evolution of approaches to play therapy that have integrated multiple theoretical conceptualizations and therapeutic strategies usually used with adults and families. These approaches to play therapy include ecosystemic play therapy, Thematic Play Therapy, family play therapy, and Dynamic Play Therapy.

Ecosystemic Play Therapy

In ecosystemic play therapy, O'Connor (2000) proposed that play therapists shift their focus away from the individual facets of children's lives and consider the multiple spheres of the many subsystems that have an effect on them. These subsystems include the family, the school, and the peer group. According to this approach, only by considering the impact of each system in which children take part can the therapist truly understand clients and their struggles.

In a systematic fashion, the ecosystemic play therapist uses several evaluative tools to assess the developmental level of children in each of the following areas: cognitive, physical, social, emotional, and processing of life experiences (O'Connor, 2000). On the basis of this assessment, the therapist plans therapeutic experiences designed to remediate the deficits in children's development, either in a group or in an individual context. The therapy process is extremely structured and directive, with the therapist controlling the setting, the materials, and the activities.

Thematic Play Therapy

Thematic Play Therapy is an approach to play therapy based on object relations theory and cognitive therapy that is especially effective with children with attachment disorders (Benedict & Mongoven, 1997; Benedict & Narcavage, 1997). In Thematic Play Therapy, the therapist first works to establish a trusting relationship with the child. By providing a totally different experience in play therapy than any previous experiences the child has had, the therapist begins to modify the way the child conceptualizes the world—shifting the child's internal working model of the world and relationships. When the child's worldview has changed enough for the child to believe that some people can be trusted, the therapist works to teach him or her how to discriminate between those who are trustworthy and those who are not.

Family Play Therapy

In a parallel to family therapy, the therapist in family play therapy must make a paradigm shift to conceptualizing difficulties as system problems, rather than problems of a specific individual. Instead of an identified client who needs help, the family play therapist thinks of the entire family as the client (Gil, 1994; Kottman, 1997b; Schaefer & Carey, 1994). By combining elements of various play therapy techniques with family therapy strategies and conceptualizations, the practitioner of family play therapy acts as an educator, play facilitator, role model, and directive therapist to help parents and children make changes in the way they see themselves and one another and in the way they interact with one another.

Dynamic Play Therapy

Harvey (1993, 1994) integrated expressive arts therapies (including art therapy, dance therapy, and drama therapy) and play therapy into Dynamic Play Therapy—a form of family play therapy that may include movement, dramatic play, art, and video expression. Harvey suggested that the therapist use the play process to identify family interactive patterns and metaphors. The therapist uses the understanding of these themes and metaphors to develop and prescribe the creation of new family metaphors and to coach the family in practicing more appropriate ways of interacting with one another and resolving conflicts.

Short-Term, Time-Limited Play Therapy

Given the current focus on brief therapy in the field of mental health, it is not surprising that there is a trend toward developing short-term, time-limited approaches to play therapy (Kaduson & Schaefer, 2000). One of these models, developed by Sloves and Peterlin (1993, 1994), is based on psychodynamic conceptualization of client problems, but with a central theme that is used to organize the therapy process. The time-limited play therapist uses a highly structured, very directive method of interacting with children to help them work toward the resolution of this central theme, which is a reenactment of the separation–individuation process. The therapist works to maximize the child's development of a positive transference and a sense of mastery while attempting to minimize regression, dependency, and feelings of helplessness. The time-limited play therapist (a) assesses whether the client and the client's family are appropriate for this approach; (b) works to establish positive transference; (c) helps the child move toward understanding and resolution of the central theme of separation–individuation; and (d) helps the child to "internalize the therapist as a positive replacement or substitute for earlier ambivalent objects, thereby making separation a genuine maturational event" (Sloves & Peterlin, 1994, p. 54). The therapist also works with the rest of the child's family in several family sessions to help them learn new ways of supporting the child's separation–individuation process in other relationships outside of the therapy process.

Other practitioners have described short-term play therapy applications with individual children using cognitive–behavioral play therapy (Knell, 2000), Gestalt play therapy (Oaklander, 2000), and child-centered play therapy (Mader, 2000). VanFleet (2000b), Booth and Lindaman (2000), and McNeil, Bahl, and Herschell (2000) have described ways for play therapists to work with children and their parents in family play therapy using a short-term model.

Eclectic Prescriptive Play Therapy

Schaefer (1993), Faust (1993), and Kaduson, Cangelosi, and Schaefer (1997) have suggested that the strict adherence to one particular approach to play therapy is outdated. These authors believe that the more appropriate method for working with children is for the therapist to choose from an array of theories and techniques based on the individual client and his or her presenting problems, specific personality traits, and particular situation. They believe that play therapy can be a much more effective intervention strategy if therapists are willing to tailor the treatment to the individual client and his or her family. Although the proponents of eclectic prescriptive play therapy acknowledge that this approach will necessitate knowledgeable therapists with training and experience in many different treatment modalities and ways of conceptualizing problems, they believe that clients will be best served by this method of individualizing treatment.

Questions to Ponder

1. What are your thoughts about how the zeitgeist of society influences psychology/play therapy? How is the current situation in society affecting the profession? What changes do you project for the next 20 years?
2. What is your reaction to Sigmund Freud's technique of using the reports of Hans's father as the basis for his intervention with Hans? What would be the advantages of working directly with the parents and not with the child? What would be the disadvantages?
3. What is your reaction to Hug-Hellmuth's method of working with children in their homes rather than in an office?
4. What is your reaction to M. Klein's strategy of making psychodynamic interpretations directly to children as a way of helping them gain insight into their issues?
5. If you were going to conduct play sessions using a structured play therapy approach, would you prefer Levy's method of providing children with the toys they would need to reenact a traumatic event or Hambridge's method of directively encouraging children to reenact a traumatic event? Explain your reasoning.

6. What is your reaction to Taft's idea that it is more therapeutic for children to enter therapy with the termination date already set? How would this practice affect the process of therapy?

7. What is your reaction to Moustakas's assertion that the therapist must be an active participant in the play if invited by the child to do so?

8. What is your reaction to Axline's contention that children will naturally move toward positive growth if they are provided with a relationship in which they experience unconditional acceptance and safety? Do you believe that the provision of these core conditions is sufficient to move children toward adequate functioning and resolution of their problems? Explain your reasoning.

9. What is your reaction to Bixler's contention that "limits are therapy"?

10. What is your reaction to Brody's contention that children must be physically touched for therapy to be effective?

11. What is your reaction to the contention of family play therapy practitioners that the child is not the client, the entire family system is the client?

12. What is your reaction to the concept of short-term, time-limited play therapy?

13. What factors would limit your ability to practice eclectic prescriptive play therapy?

Chapter 3

Theoretical Approaches to Play Therapy

Because this book is an introduction to play therapy, rather than an in-depth study of the different approaches, an examination of each theoretical orientation is impossible. To give the reader a "feel" for some of the approaches to play therapy currently used by practitioners in the field, I have chosen to provide an overview of Adlerian play therapy, child-centered play therapy, cognitive–behavioral play therapy, ecosystemic play therapy, Gestalt play therapy, psychodynamic play therapy, and Theraplay. I also very briefly describe eclectic prescriptive play therapy.

For each of the theoretical orientations in this chapter (except eclectic prescriptive, which by its very nature requires special treatment), I provide a brief synopsis of the following topics: (a) important theoretical constructs, (b) phases of the counseling process, (c) role of the therapist, (d) goals of therapy, (e) approach to working with parents, and (f) distinctive features. These components are not equally important in every approach, so some sections are significantly longer than others. Because of the limited space in an overview of several different theories, I would suggest that you seek out more in-depth coverage of the orientations that interest you. (See Appendix A for a list of recommended readings.)

My decision to include these approaches was based on three factors: (a) recent surveys of practitioners regarding their theoretical orientation toward play therapy (Kranz, Kottman, & Lund, 1998; Phillips & Landreth, 1995), (b) the predominance of certain theories in recent play therapy literature (articles, books, and book chapters), and (c) the number of presentations at play therapy conferences devoted to particular orientations. I do not mean to imply that the approaches that are omitted are less valuable or less important than the approaches that are included. Instead, the omitted approaches have not yet attained the same contemporary level of exposure as those that are included, they have not maintained their widespread use over the years, or there is not yet enough information in the literature to present a coherent picture of the application of those approaches. In addition to material gathered from the play therapy literature, I have included information from a survey I conducted to garner opinions of experts in the field about current practices in the different approaches to play therapy.

Adlerian Play Therapy

Adlerian play therapy (Kottman, 1993, 1994, 1995, 1997a) combines the concepts and strategies of Individual Psychology with the basic idea and many techniques drawn from play therapy. The therapist conceptualizes clients from an Adlerian perspective while using toys and play materials to communicate with clients.

Important Theoretical Constructs

Adlerian play therapists base their work on the belief that all people are unique and creative (Kottman, 1995). They believe that people are born with an innate capacity to connect with others (social interest) but must learn how to make those connections in constructive and useful ways.

People are always striving to move from a position of inferiority to a position of confidence. Some overcompensate and move toward a superiority complex, trying to prove that they are better than others. Some give up the struggle and are overpowered by a sense of discouragement and despair. Others use their feelings of inferiority as a challenge to live life in the most effective way they know how.

Adlerians believe that all behavior is purposeful. Dreikurs and Soltz (1964) suggested that there are four basic goals involved in children's misbehavior: attention, power, revenge, and proof of inadequacy. When the therapist discovers the goal of children's misbehavior, he or she can help them learn to strive toward more appropriate goals. Lew and Bettner (2000) delineated several positive goals (the "Crucial Cs") toward which the therapist can help clients move: feeling connected, feeling capable, feeling like they count, and developing courage. Kottman (1999b) suggested several different methods for helping children move toward enhancing their Crucial Cs in play therapy.

An important theoretical construct in Adlerian theory is the lifestyle, which is the individual's unique approach to life (Kottman, 1995). Each individual develops his or her lifestyle before the age of 8 years, based on observations of others, their interactions and relationships, their treatment from others, and so forth. From these observations, the individual formulates perceptions of self, others, and the world, and his or her behavior is predicated on the idea that these perceptions are accurate. However, because children tend to be excellent at watching others but may be weak in their interpretation of situations and relationships, the conclusions drawn and perceptions formed may be inaccurate. The therapist's job, then, is to gather enough information in the therapy process to understand what the client's lifestyle is; learn about the conclusions the client drew at an early age; begin to explore the accuracy and efficacy of these conclusions; and help the client make new decisions about self, others, and the world and formulate new strategies for approaching problems and interacting with others.

Phases of the Counseling Process

Adlerian play therapy has four phases: (a) building an egalitarian relationship with the client, (b) exploring the client's lifestyle, (c) helping the client gain insight into his or her lifestyle, and (d) providing reorientation and reeducation for the client when necessary (Kottman, 1993, 1994, 1995). In the first phase, the play therapist uses tracking, restatement of content, reflection of feelings, returning responsibility to the child, encouragement, limiting, answering questions, asking questions, and cleaning the room together to build an equal partnership with the child. In the second phase, the therapist uses drawing techniques; questioning strategies; investigation of goals of behavior, Crucial Cs, family constellation, and family atmosphere; and solicitation of early recollections to gather enough information to be able to formulate hypotheses about the child's lifestyle. During the third phase, the Adlerian therapist uses metacommunication, metaphors, "spitting in the soup" (a technique in which the therapist points out situations in which the child is acting as if self-defeating beliefs about self, others, and the world are true), and drawing techniques to help the child gain a better understanding of his or her lifestyle and make some decisions about whether or not to begin making changes in parts of it. The fourth phase, reorientation and reeducation, involves teaching the child new skills and attitudes and helping him or her practice those new skills so that they will be useful in relationships and situations outside the play therapy setting. Both encouragement for improvement and effort and teaching are crucial skills used in this phase. The boundaries between the four phases are not rigid. For instance, Adlerian play therapists are constantly working on the relationship, and they may decide to help a child gain insight to part of his or her lifestyle before they finish completely exploring his or her views on self, others, and the world.

Role of the Therapist

In Adlerian play therapy, the role of the therapist flexes according to the phase of counseling (Kottman, 1995). In the first phase, the therapist is both partner and encourager. The therapist is usually relatively nondirective, sharing power in most sessions with the client. One aspect of the therapist's job during this phase is to use encouragement to help the client gain self-confidence and a sense of competence.

During the second phase, the therapist is an active, relatively directive detective, ferreting out information about the child's attitudes, perceptions, thinking processes, feelings, and so forth. This process is important because all subsequent interventions depend on the therapist's formulation of lifestyle hypotheses, which are based on the data gathered during the investigation in the second phase.

In the third phase, the role of the therapist is again a partner, but one with essential information to communicate. At times during this phase, the therapist will be nondirective and supportive. At other times, the therapist will be challenging long-held self-defeating beliefs about self, others, and the world. This is also when the therapist delivers the initial invitation for the child to decide to make some changes in his or her perceptions and behavior.

The reorientation and reeducation phase requires the therapist to be an active teacher and encourager—helping the child learn and practice new skills and incorporate new attitudes and perceptions into his or her way of looking at life. The therapist may provide training and experience in assertiveness skills, negotiation skills, social skills, or other useful strategies for getting along with others and coping with problem situations.

Goals of Therapy

The goals of Adlerian play therapy are parallel to the phases of the process. The first goal is for the child to develop a relationship with the therapist in which these two parties can share power and work together as partners (Kottman, 1995, 1997a). The second goal is for the therapist to understand the child's lifestyle well enough to comprehend the underlying issues related to the presenting problem. The third goal is for the child to gain a cognitive understanding of his or her lifestyle and to decide to make necessary changes—emotional, attitudinal, and behavioral. The fourth goal is to help the child learn any new skills necessary to effect these changes outside the playroom. As part of this process, the therapist hopes to move the child from destructive goals and misbehavior toward constructive goals; enhance attainment of the Crucial Cs; increase the child's social interest; adjust self-defeating perceptions in the child's beliefs about self, others, and the world; reduce discouragement; and help the child to understand and "own" his or her personal assets.

Approach to Working With Parents

In Adlerian play therapy, there is a special emphasis on working with parents (Kottman, 1995). Because Adlerians believe that all people are socially embedded and cannot be understood without comprehending their social system (which starts with the family), whenever possible, they work simultaneously with children and their parents. Most Adlerians divide their sessions between play therapy with the child and consultation with the parents.

In the parent consultations, the process goes through phases very similar to those in the play therapy (Kottman, 1995). First, the Adlerian play therapist uses basic counseling skills to build a relationship with the parents. Next, the therapist uses Adlerian exploration strategies to gain insight into the parents and, on the basis of an understanding of the parents' personality priorities and other aspects of their lifestyles, the therapist custom-designs suggestions to parents so as to avoid evoking defensive responses (Kottman & Ashby, 1999). The therapist gathers information from the parents about the child's lifestyle, social interests, goals of behavior, and so forth and about the parents' lifestyle, social interests, goals of behavior, and so forth. In the third phase, the therapist works to help the parents gain insight into the child and into themselves so that they will have a better basis for making decisions about which parenting strategies to use and how to implement them. Teaching parenting skills is the primary focus of the fourth phase with parents—using Adlerian parenting resources such as *The Parent's Handbook: Systematic Training for Effective Parenting* (*STEP;* Dinkmeyer & McKay, 1989), *Raising Kids Who Can* (Bettner & Lew, 1996), *A Parent's Guide to Understanding and Motivating Children* (Lew & Bettner, 2000), and *Active Parenting Today* (Popkin, 1993).

Distinctive Features

Adlerians set limits differently from other orientations by using a four-step process in which the therapist does not redirect the child's behavior but engages the child in redirecting his or her own behavior (Kottman, 1995). They also set up logical consequences as an integral part of the limiting process.

The focus of the information gathered in the second phase of Adlerian play therapy is somewhat different from other approaches to play therapy. The aim of the therapist is to understand how the child is making decisions and incorporating perceptions into his or her lifestyle. The therapist asks questions, observes play, and engages the child in art activities designed to gather information about family constellation (birth order), family atmosphere, and goals of behavior. The therapist may also ask the child to draw or describe a series of early memories, which will provide clues about the child's lifestyle.

The process of cleaning the room as a team (Kottman, 1995) seems to be unique in the play therapy literature. Although other play therapists do ask children to pick up toys and materials, the Adlerian approach is very structured and specific, designed to promote teamwork (see chapter 4, "Logistical Aspects of Play Therapy").

The specific emphasis on encouragement also seems to be unique to Adlerian play therapists (Kottman, 1995). They use strategies designed to point out children's assets and focus on effort and improvement in order to improve children's sense of self-efficacy and reduce discouragement.

Child-Centered Play Therapy

Virginia Axline (1947, 1969, 1971) applied the basic concepts of client-centered therapy (Rogers, 1959) to work with children when she developed nondirective, child-centered play therapy. Contemporary experts such as Garry Landreth (1991; Landreth & Sweeney, 1997), Louise Guerney (1983a; Guerney & Welsh, 1993), Lessie Perry (1993), and Risë VanFleet (1994a, 1994b) have continued to refine the ideas and strategies of child-centered play therapy in their work with children. According to several recent surveys (Kranz et al., 1998; Phillips & Landreth, 1995, 1998), the majority of practitioners using play therapy as a treatment modality subscribe to the nondirective child-centered approach.

Important Theoretical Constructs

Child-centered play therapists believe that human personality structure consists of (a) the person, (b) the phenomenological field, and (c) the self (Landreth & Sweeney, 1997; Rogers, 1951). The person consists of the individual's thoughts, feelings, behaviors, and physical being, all of which are constantly changing and developing. The person is a balanced system, so when one aspect of the person changes, the other aspects change as well, moving toward actualizing the self (Landreth & Sweeney, 1997). This faith that all people have an innate tendency to move in a positive direction, striving toward self-actualization and constructive growth, is a key concept in child-centered play therapy (Landreth & Sweeney, 1997).

As part of this process toward self-actualization, each person must attempt to satisfy his or her needs as experienced in the phenomenological field, which is the sum total of all of the person's experiences (Landreth & Sweeney, 1997; Perry, 1993). Each individual's perception of his or her experiences is the reality of that person. Because of the phenomenological view of reality, the child-centered play therapist must try to understand each client from that child's perspective (Landreth, 1991).

As children grow up, they begin to organize some of their perceptions into a concept of "me"—the self. Initially, these perceptions are filtered through the child's organismic valuing system, an innate process in which the child attaches positive significance to experiences seen as self-enhancing and negative significance to experiences seen as threatening or self-defeating (Landreth & Sweeney, 1997; Perry, 1993; Rogers, 1951).

As time passes, however, on the basis of children's experience of being conditionally accepted and judged by others, children begin to introject the ideas and evaluations of others and discount their own organismic valuing (Landreth & Sweeney, 1997; Perry, 1993; Rogers, 1951). Children incorporate these experiences into their perceptions of the self, resulting in feelings of self-doubt and insecurity. They may also begin to distort the way they interpret the phenomenological field and begin to experience reality in ways that are inconsistent with their own true perceptions. A gap may appear between their "real" self—the self based on their organismic valuing—and the "ideal" self—the self based on their introjection of the attitudes and values of others. This incongruity frequently leads to maladjustment.

To remediate this problem and restore children to the path toward self-actualization, Axline (1969) outlined eight basic principles of nondirective client-centered play therapy.

1. The therapist must build a warm, friendly, genuine relationship with the child client that will facilitate a strong therapeutic rapport.
2. The therapist must be completely accepting of the child, without desiring the child to change in any way.
3. The therapist must develop and maintain an environment of permissiveness so that the child can feel free to completely explore and express his or her feelings.
4. The therapist must pay constant attention to the child's feelings and reflect them in a manner that encourages the child to gain insight and enhance his or her understanding of self.

5. The therapist must always be respectful of the child's capacity for solving his or her own problems if given the opportunity and resources necessary. The child must be solely responsible for his or her own decisions and must be able to freely choose whether and when to make changes.
6. The therapist must not take the lead in therapy. This responsibility and privilege belong to the child. The therapist always follows the lead of the child.
7. The therapist must never attempt to hasten the course of therapy. Play therapy is a slow and gradual process dependent on the child's pace, not the therapist's.
8. The therapist must only set limits that are essential for anchoring therapy to reality and to return responsibility for his or her role in the therapeutic process back to the child.

Phases of the Counseling Process

Moustakas (1955, as cited in Landreth & Sweeney, 1997) suggested that the therapy process in child-centered play therapy has five distinct stages. The descriptions of these stages focus on the child's feelings and attitudes, rather than the interaction between the therapist and the child or the child's behavior.

In the first stage, children express diffuse negative feelings in every aspect of their play. During the second stage, they primarily manifest ambivalent feelings, usually anxiety or hostility. The third stage again features mostly negative feelings, but in this stage these feelings are expressed directly toward parents, siblings, or the therapist or are expressed through regressive behaviors. In the fourth stage, ambivalent feelings (positive and negative) resurface, but in this stage they are focused on parents, siblings, the therapist, and others. In the final stage of play therapy, children express primarily positive feelings, with realistic negative attitudes expressed appropriately and without ambivalence.

Role of the Therapist

"The therapist maintains an active role in the process of play therapy, not in the sense of directing or managing the experience, but by being directly involved and genuinely interested in all of the child's feelings, actions, and decisions" (Landreth, 1991, p. 99). In child-centered play therapy, the primary role of the therapist is to provide the child with the key core conditions of unconditional positive regard, empathic understanding, and genuineness. By accepting the child and believing in the child's ability to solve his or her own problems and make any changes necessary for optimal living, the therapist frees the child to grow in positive directions.

Child-centered play therapists fulfill this role by using nondirective skills—tracking, restating content, reflecting feelings, returning responsibility to the child, and setting necessary limits. They do not use skills that would involve leading the child in any way, so they avoid interpreting, designing therapeutic metaphors, and using bibliotherapy and other techniques that take the child somewhere the child would not naturally go.

Goals of Therapy

The goals of child-centered play therapy are very broad and general. The therapist does not set specific individual goals for each child, but rather works to provide a positive experience in which the child moves in a positive direction and discovers his or her own personal strengths (Landreth, 1991; Landreth & Sweeney, 1997). Landreth (1991) listed the following objectives in child-centered play therapy:

1. Help the child enhance his or her positive self-concept.
2. Help the child move to accepting more responsibility for self.
3. Help the child reach enhanced levels of self-acceptance, self-reliance, and self-direction.
4. Help the child practice self-directed decision making.
5. Help the child feel more in control.
6. Help the child increase his or her awareness of the process of coping.
7. Help the child develop an internal locus of evaluation.
8. Help the child learn to trust himself or herself more.

Within this framework, the child may choose to work on specific issues or problems (Landreth & Sweeney, 1997). However, the therapist does not lead or direct the child's attention or efforts to particular issues, such as a presenting problem described by parents or teachers. The child-centered play therapist does not even really try to explore specifically (either through making conversation or through making guesses about the meaning of play) what it is that the child wishes to establish as a goal and may not even really know what the child's goals are. Believing in the child's ability to set his or her own goals and direction, the therapist has faith that the child is working on whatever he or she needs resolved.

Approach to Working With Parents

The most widely accepted approach to working with parents among child-centered play therapists is filial therapy (L. Guerney, 1997; Kraft & Landreth, 1998; VanFleet, 1994a, 1994b, 2000a). Filial therapy is a strategy for teaching parents the skills involved in child-centered play therapy. These skills were defined by VanFleet (1994a, 1994b, 2000a) as (a) structuring skills, (b) empathic listening skills, (c) child-centered imaginary play skills, and (d) limit-setting skills. Through lectures, demonstrations, modeling, role-playing, skills exercises, feedback, supervised play sessions, and reinforcement, the filial therapist teaches parents how to use these skills in weekly half-hour sessions with their children. The goals of filial therapy are to reduce problem behaviors in children, help parents learn skills they can apply in daily interactions with their children, and improve parent–child relationships (L. Guerney, 1997). This training can take place in group situations or in individual families. The therapist can deliver the training as a formal structured program or can teach individual skills as needed by specific parents.

Not all child-centered play therapists have the training to use filial therapy. Those who do seem to focus most of their interactions with parents on teaching parents to use the filial skills to enhance their relationships with their children (L. Guerney, personal communication, October 1997; R. VanFleet, personal communication, October 1997). Other child-centered play therapists may not work with parents at all or may spend a brief period of time each session consulting with parents about parenting skills and family interactions (Landreth, 1991; L. Perry, personal communication, October 1997).

Distinctive Features

The primary distinctive feature of child-centered play therapy is the absolute faith that children can work out their own problems with minimal intervention or interference from adults. In most other approaches to play therapy (and other kinds of counseling for children), there is an underlying belief that one or more adults must intervene in children's lives to help them get back on track. The play therapists surveyed who focus exclusively on child-centered therapy do not believe this, and their faith that each child has the capacity for self-healing and for self-actualizing is their unique contribution to the world of child therapy.

Cognitive–Behavioral Play Therapy

Developed by Susan Knell (1993a, 1993b, 1994, 1997, 2000), cognitive–behavioral play therapy incorporates cognitive and behavioral strategies within a play therapy delivery system. It is based on cognitive and behavioral theories of emotional development and psychopathology. Cognitive–behavioral play therapists use interventions derived from these two theories, combining play activities with verbal and nonverbal communication.

Important Theoretical Constructs

Cognitive–behavioral play therapy integrates ideas from behavior therapy, cognitive therapy, and cognitive–behavioral therapy. Knell (1993a, 1993b, 1994, 1997) borrowed constructs from each of these schools of thought in formulating the theoretical basis for cognitive–behavioral play therapy.

From behavior therapy, Knell (1993a) took the concept that all behavior is learned. A key component in behavior therapy is discovering factors that reinforce and maintain behavior that is deemed inappropriate. By changing these factors, the therapist can alter the child's behavior. A cognitive–behavioral play therapist might use behavioral techniques directly with a child client or might teach parents and/or teachers behavioral intervention strategies.

Neither cognitive therapy nor cognitive–behavioral therapy has a theory of personality development. Instead, the focus is on psychopathology and the factors that lead to difficulties in emotional development (Knell, 1997). According to this model of emotional disorders, behavior is mediated through verbal and cognitive processes. The three key ideas in cognitive therapy are (a) thoughts influence emotions and behavior; (b) beliefs and assumptions influence perceptions and interpretations of events; and (c) most individuals who are having psychological problems have errors in logic, irrational thinking, or cognitive distortions (Beck, 1976; Knell, 1997).

Knell (1994) listed six specific properties important to an understanding of cognitive–behavioral play therapy.

1. In cognitive–behavioral play therapy, the child is involved in treatment through the play. The child is an active participant in the therapy process.
2. In cognitive–behavioral play therapy, the therapist deals with the thoughts, feelings, fantasies, and environment of the child. The therapy is problem-focused rather than client-focused.
3. In cognitive–behavioral play therapy, the emphasis is on developing new, more adaptive thoughts and behaviors and developing more helpful coping strategies for dealing with problems.
4. The cognitive–behavioral play therapy process is structured, directive, and goal-oriented.
5. In cognitive–behavioral play therapy, the therapist uses behavioral and cognitive techniques that have empirical evidence that supports their efficacy.
6. In cognitive–behavioral play therapy, the therapist has many opportunities to empirically examine the effectiveness of specific treatments for specific problems.

Phases of the Counseling Process

The process of cognitive–behavioral play therapy has several distinct stages: (a) assessment, (b) introduction/orientation to play therapy, (c) middle stages, and (d) termination (Knell, 1993a, 1994, 2000). During the assessment stage, the therapist uses various assessment tools to gather information about the child's current level of functioning, the child's development, the presenting problem, the child's perception or understanding of the problem, and the parents' perspective on the child and the problem (Knell, 1994). The therapist can use parent-report inventories, clinical interviews, play observation, formal cognitive/developmental instruments, projective tests, drawings, and therapist-created measures to gather information about the child and his or her thoughts, feelings, attitudes, perceptions, and behaviors (Knell, 1993a, 1994).

During the introduction/orientation to play therapy, the therapist and/or parents need to give children a clear, nonjudgmental explanation of their perception of the presenting problem and a description of the play therapy process. Knell (1994) suggested bibliotherapy using *A Child's First Book*

About Play Therapy (Nemiroff & Annunziata, 1990) as one way to facilitate this process. During this stage, the therapist meets with the parents of the child to give feedback on the initial evaluation of the child and to develop a treatment plan, including treatment modality and goals for the therapy (Knell, 1993a, 1994). One part of this process is deciding on the role of the parents in the process.

In the middle stages of therapy, the therapist focuses on using specific cognitive and behavioral intervention strategies to teach children new adaptive responses to cope with specific situations, problems, issues, or stressors (Knell, 1993a, 1994). The therapist also tries to help children transfer what they have learned in the playroom with the therapist to other situations and settings. Built into their interactions during this stage are interventions designed to teach children coping strategies for avoiding relapses after therapy is finished.

During the final stage, the therapist prepares children for termination by gradually phasing therapy out over a period of time (Knell, 1994). During this stage, the therapist and the child talk about the child's plans for handling situations after termination. The therapist reinforces changes the child has made in thoughts, feelings, and behaviors and arranges for practice in generalizing learning from the play therapy setting to other settings.

Role of the Therapist

The role of the therapist in cognitive–behavioral play therapy is extremely active and directive. First, the therapist uses formal and informal instruments to assess the current functioning of the child and his or her parents. After this baseline measurement is complete, the therapist actively engages the parents (and sometimes the child, depending on cognitive ability and developmental age) in generating a treatment plan, with concrete, measurable goals for changes in behavior, feelings, attitudes, and beliefs. Part of this treatment plan is the consideration of the wide variety of available cognitive and behavioral intervention techniques and deciding which of these strategies might prove most effective with this particular child and his or her specific difficulties. The therapist then implements the plan, usually using some form of modeling, role-playing, or behavioral contingency to implement changes in the child (Knell, 1993b). These interventions can be used directly with the child or taught to teachers and/or parents who then use them directly with the child. The therapist constantly monitors change, comparing current functioning with the functioning at the beginning of the therapy process and checking for the attainment of the goals delineated during the initial stage of therapy. The attainment of these goals is a major part of the decision to terminate.

Goals of Therapy

In cognitive–behavioral play therapy, there are some global goals in addition to the individual and specific goals of each child and his or her family (Knell, 1993a, 1997). In general, the therapist tries to increase the child's ability to cope with problem situations and stressors and decrease irrational, faulty thinking patterns.

Specifically, each child has behavioral and cognitive goals to work toward that are tailored to his or her particular situation. These goals may include increasing the child's ability to express feelings, decreasing maladaptive thoughts and perceptions, increasing adaptive and realistic assessments of relationships, increasing positive self-talk, increasing appropriate use of problem-solving skills, and so forth. The parents of the child may also have specific goals designed especially for them—these goals are usually related to parenting issues or to personal issues that interfere with their ability to optimally parent.

Approach to Working With Parents

In cognitive–behavioral play therapy, there is a clear mandate to involve parents in the process—whether as active participants in change or as helpers in supporting change in children (Knell, 1993a, 1997). Parents are always active partners in the development of the treatment plan. Part of the process of developing this plan is deciding whether the therapy involves primarily cognitive–behavioral play therapy with the child, direct work with the parents, or some combination of cognitive–behavioral play therapy with the child and direct work with the parents. If the child needs minimal help implementing a treatment plan outside of therapy, the primary focus is working directly with the child. If the parents need a lot of work changing their interactions and relationship with the child, the emphasis is on working mostly with the parents. If the child needs a great deal of help implementing a treatment plan outside of therapy, the focus is shared between working with the child and working with the parents.

Even if parents do not need a lot of help, the cognitive–behavioral play therapist must still meet with them on a regular basis (Knell, 1997). The therapist uses these meetings to gather information about the child, to monitor the interaction between the parents and the child, to help parents learn new skills to support the child, and to provide reinforcement for the parents' efforts.

Distinctive Features

Most of the interventions in cognitive–behavioral play therapy are delivered by modeling (using a puppet, stuffed animal, or doll to demonstrate the desired behavior to the child), role-playing (using the child–therapist interaction to practice specific behaviors within the session), or behavioral contingencies (providing rewards to the child for acquiring new skills). The cognitive–behavioral therapist has a wide range of behavioral and cognitive strategies available for implementation in the play therapy process (Knell, 1993a, 1994, 2000). The behavioral techniques include systematic desensitization, contingency management (e.g., positive reinforcement, shaping, stimulus fading, extinction and differential reinforcement of other behavior, and time-out), self-monitoring, and activity scheduling. The cognitive techniques include recording of dysfunctional thoughts, cognitive change strategies, positive-coping self-statements, and bibliotherapy. Depending on the developmental level of the child, these tactics can be adapted to use more toys and play media or to use more verbal communication.

One other unique aspect of cognitive–behavioral play therapy is the emphasis on gathering empirical data—for specific intervention strategies and for cognitive–behavioral play therapy in general (Knell, 1993a, 1994). The beginning baseline assessment process encourages the play therapist to gather concrete information about current functioning, and the specifically delineated treatment goals allow for close monitoring of progress and change. This process is unusual in a field that has not traditionally lent itself to empirical measurement (Phillips, 1985).

Ecosystemic Play Therapy

Ecosystemic play therapy is a "hybrid model that derives from an integration of biological science concepts, multiple models of child psychotherapy, and developmental theory" (O'Connor, 1994, p. 61). Rather than focusing primarily on the functioning of the child, the ecosystemic play therapist tries to optimize the child's functioning in the context of his or her ecosystem (world) (O'Connor, 1991, 1994, 1997, 2000; O'Connor & Ammen, 1997). The therapy is very structured and directive—with the therapist making many of the decisions about the materials and activities used in any one session.

Important Theoretical Constructs

O'Connor (2000) emphasized that certain aspects of ecosystemic play therapy theory are "structure" (elements of the approach that are consistent and stable across practitioners) and other aspects are "fill" (elements of the approach that are variable, depending on individual practitioners). Because O'Connor purposely kept the structural elements to a minimum to optimize theoretical adaptability and flexibility, sometimes it is difficult to describe the "typical" method of conceptualizing clients or doing play therapy from an ecosystemic model. Each ecosystemic play therapist develops his or her own fill elements to complete the theory.

The most important of these fill elements is a personal counseling theory that fits the therapist's experiences and view of the world. O'Connor (2000) contended that the actual content of the therapist's personal theory is unimportant because there is no evidence that any one theory is more helpful than any other theory. However, it is essential that the theory is internally consistent. The therapist must understand his or her theory well enough that it can provide a vehicle for clearly and consistently developing and communicating an understanding of each client's functioning and transactions with the world.

Given this context, there are still several theoretical constructs that could be helpful in gaining an understanding of ecosystemic play therapy. These constructs include the ecosystemic model and O'Connor's (1991, 1994) personal theory of psychotherapy.

Ecosystemic model. Probably the most important theoretical concept in ecosystemic play therapy is that of the ecosystem and its function in the theory (O'Connor, 2000; O'Connor & Ammen, 1997). To understand what is happening with any particular child, the therapist must take into consideration all the various levels of the ecosystem that can be simultaneously having an effect on that child and his or her world.

> The play therapist will use this ecosystemic view to conceptualize the difficulties the child is experiencing, to anticipate the support and interference each system will generate as the child begins to change with treatment, and to facilitate the generalization and maintenance of those changes over time. At the same time, the play therapist should be committed to preserving and valuing differences whenever and wherever possible. (O'Connor, 1994, p. 65)

O'Connor's personal theory. According to O'Connor (1991, 1994), his personal theory, which provided the basis for ecosystemic play therapy, includes elements from psychoanalytic play therapy (A. Freud, 1928; M. Klein, 1932), humanistic play therapy (Axline, 1947; Landreth, 1991), behaviorally oriented play therapy (Leland, 1983), Theraplay (Jernberg, 1979), and Reality Therapy (Glasser, 1975). He integrated these models with several different approaches to child development, including those of Piaget (1952), Anna Freud (1965), Sigmund Freud (1938), Mahler (1972), Erickson (1950), and Developmental Therapy (Wood, Combs, Gunn, & Weller, 1986).

O'Connor (1994, 2000) believes that people are motivated by biological drives that move them to seek rewards and to maximize their own gratification at the same time they seek to avoid punishment. Initially, the behavior generated by these drives is extremely egocentric, but as the individual matures, his or her behavior is tempered by interaction with others and becomes more social and less egocentric. According to this theory, personality is a result of the interaction between the individual's experience and developmental progress (in social, emotional, and behavioral areas).

In ecosystemic play therapy, psychopathology can derive from three different sources (O'Connor, 1994, 2000). Pathology can have its origins in the following:

1. The individual. When this is the case, the origin of pathology may be genetic, biological, neurological, cognitive, or even constitutional in nature.
2. Interactions between individuals. When this is the case, neither the individuals involved nor the environment is specifically triggering the pathology. Instead, the psychopathology seems to be rooted in the interaction of those specific individuals in that particular environment.
3. A pathological or pathogenic system. When this is the case, the environment is triggering the pathology.

No matter what the origin, in this theory, psychopathology is viewed as the individual's best attempt to cope with his or her internal or external situation, rather than as a deviant response or an irretrievable flaw. O'Connor (1994) suggested that children and parents who come to play therapy are stuck in their negative behavior patterns and cannot engage in appropriate problem solving to consider alternative behaviors. The function of the play therapist is to help them see themselves and their world in a new light and to help them begin to engage in problem solving and consideration of new behaviors.

Phases of the Counseling Process

O'Connor (1994, 2000) borrowed the six stages proposed by Jernberg (1979) in Theraplay to describe the phases of ecosystemic play therapy. They are (a) introduction, (b) exploration, (c) tentative acceptance, (d) negative reaction, (e) growing and trusting, and (f) termination.

In the introduction stage, the therapist introduces himself or herself to children, explains the process of play therapy, and lays out the basic expectations for their interactions. Children explore the playroom and any available materials.

In the exploration stage, children start to use the play materials and interact with the play therapist. They begin to become more active and may gently test limits. During this time, they are mainly gathering information about what happens in the playroom and what the therapist does.

The stage of tentative acceptance is the time when children begin to feel a bit more relaxed in the playroom and in the company of the play therapist. They may temporarily yield to the therapist's control and tentatively believe that the playroom is a safe place.

In ecosystemic play therapy, the therapist maintains a great deal of control during sessions. Many of the children who come to play therapy use control to get their needs met. When these children experience the loss of control necessitated by the directive nature of ecosystemic play therapy, they frequently have negative reactions as they try to continue the behaviors they have used in the past to get their needs met. During the negative reaction phase, children may decide that they do not like the therapist, the playroom, or other aspects of the therapy.

As children realize that the ecosystemic play therapist uses his or her control only to ensure their welfare, they move on toward the growing and trusting phase of play therapy. Through the corrective experiences of the play therapy process, children begin to get less "stuck" in their way of looking at themselves and their world. By gaining a better understanding of their experiences, they can begin to experiment with new, more appropriate behaviors.

When the changes that evolve during the growing and trusting phase of therapy are consolidated and the learning transferred to other situations and relationships, children are ready to terminate play therapy. During the termination stage, many children reexperience the issues and problems that originally brought them to therapy. The therapist helps them once again gain an understanding of what is happening and works with them on meeting their own needs without infringing on the rights of others.

Role of the Therapist

The role of the therapist in ecosystemic play therapy is extremely active and directive (O'Connor, 1994, 1997, 2000; O'Connor & Ammen, 1997). The therapist chooses the toys to be used during a particular session and decides on the activities and their sequence. The primary function of the ecosystemic play therapist in a session is to maintain the child at "an optimal level of arousal so that learning and change can occur" (O'Connor, 1997, p. 264). The therapist does this through several intervention strategies pioneered by Jernberg (1979) in Theraplay. These intervention behaviors include the following:

1. Structuring—behaviors the therapist does to reduce the child's level of arousal and keep the child safe. Structuring would include the therapist choosing the appropriate toys for a session and setting limits.

2. Challenging—behaviors the therapist does to increase the child's level of arousal by pushing him or her to function slightly higher than the current developmental level. Challenging behaviors would include problem-solving interventions and therapist interpretations.
3. Intruding—behaviors designed to increase the child's level of arousal by pushing him or her to deal with issues or experiences that are not particularly comfortable. These behaviors may include entering the child's physical space or using language to focus the child on a specific behavior or problem.
4. Nurturing—behaviors that maintain the child at his or her current level of arousal. Nurturing behaviors would include verbally reinforcing a child, patting a child's head, and giving hugs and kisses.

Once the therapist has established the child's arousal level within the appropriate range for learning, the therapist engages the child in problem solving by (a) involving him or her in alternative/corrective experiences or (b) providing the child with new cognitive insight for specific problems or situations in which the child currently feels "stuck." The therapist may also serve as an advocate for the child in the various systems in the child's ecosystem.

Alternative/corrective experiences can occur in the context of the play session or in the child's interactions outside the play session. They may be symbolically experienced (e.g., through pretend play in which the child uses puppets or dolls to act out problem situations with new, more appropriate resolutions) or actually experienced (e.g., through effectively resolving real situations and conflicts in the relationship with the play therapist).

The therapist can bring about alternate cognitive understandings of specific problems through the problem-solving process or through the use of interpretations. O'Connor (1991) presented a five-stage model of interpretations used in ecosystemic play therapy: (a) reflection, (b) pattern, (c) simple dynamic, (d) generalized dynamic, and (e) genetic. A reflection is when the therapist interprets a thought, feeling, or motive that the child has not expressed directly. A pattern interpretation is when the therapist points out similarities or consistencies that have occurred over a period of time in the child's behavior. In a simple dynamic interpretation, the therapist identifies a relationship connecting the child's unexpressed thoughts, feelings, or motives with patterns in his or her behavior. A generalized dynamic interpretation involves the therapist pointing out how this pattern is transferred across various settings and interactions. In a genetic interpretation, the therapist attempts to identify the historical source for this pattern, stressing the differences between the source event and current situations that seem to trigger the behavior. The purpose in using interpretations is to help the child begin to see situations and relationships differently and to help him or her learn new behavioral responses to getting his or her needs met.

Goals of Therapy

The primary goal in ecosystemic play therapy is to "facilitate the child's resumption of normal development and to maximize the child's ability to get his or her needs met while interfering as little as possible with the gratification of others' needs" (O'Connor, 1994, p. 71). To accomplish this main goal, the ecosystemic therapist must achieve several intermediate individualized goals structured for the particular child, including (a) gathering information to facilitate an understanding of the origins of the child's psychopathology, (b) making a treatment plan based on this understanding, (c) executing the treatment plan, and (d) evaluating the effectiveness of the treatment plan.

For each child, the therapist develops specific treatment objectives based on an assessment that includes interviews with the child and his or her parents, standardized instruments, developmental assessment tools, behavior rating instruments, projective assessment tools, observation of play, and play interviews (O'Connor & Ammen, 1997). On the basis of all of the gathered data, the therapist summarizes the child's functioning in the areas of cognition, emotions, behavior, physical and motor development, family, and social interactions. Using this summary, the therapist develops hypotheses about the child's psychopathology—which of the child's needs are not being met, ineffective response repertoires, etiological factors in the development of pathology, ecosystemic factors related to the pathology, and so forth. From these hypotheses, the therapist decides on specific goals and plans treatment objectives and treatment modalities. The treatment plan includes stage goals (based on the stage of therapy), materials needed, experiential components, verbal components, and collaborative components (advocacy, consultation, education, and evaluation).

Approach to Working With Parents

O'Connor (2000) stressed the importance of working with parents as part of ecosystemic play therapy. Typical ecosystemic interactions with parents may include (a) information exchange so that the therapist can incorporate data about what is happening in the child's life into sessions, (b) consultation about behavior management strategies or general parenting skills, and (c) problem-solving sessions to devise ways parents can help support the changes their child might be making. In ecosystemic play therapy, the session is usually divided between the parents and the child, with parents meeting the therapist for about 20 minutes and the child playing for about 30 minutes.

In some cases, the therapist may wish to teach the parents play therapy techniques that they can use outside the sessions to facilitate the parent–child relationship. In other cases, it might be helpful to conduct conjoint parent–child sessions so as to be able to observe parent–child interactions and to model appropriate boundary setting and other important concepts. Sometimes a parent might need individual work on personal issues, or the parents might need couples counseling.

Distinctive Features

As should be evident from the descriptions of the therapeutic constructs, the role of the therapist, and the goals of the therapeutic process, there are many distinctive features of ecosystemic play therapy. The purposeful limitation of structural elements to the theory is unique. By requiring each therapist to supply the fill elements of the theory, including devising his or her own personal theory of psychotherapy, O'Connor has increased the flexibility of his approach and made each individual application of ecosystemic play therapy different from all others.

The role of the ecosystemic therapist is both more narrowly defined and more individual than in other approaches. The therapist has a certain framework within which to operate that sets strict parameters on the amount of control and structure that the therapist must provide in this approach. However, within that structure, each therapist has the freedom to choose how to work with children and their families. The therapist must adhere to the philosophical framework and focus on the ecosystem of each child and on helping the child get his or her needs met in more appropriate ways. As long as these conditions are met, the therapist can actuate the role of the therapist in any way that fits his or her personality or setting.

The complexity of the steps necessary for attaining the goals of therapy is also a unique feature of ecosystemic play therapy. The data gathering in this theory is extensive. This is partly due to the necessity of understanding the various elements of each child's ecosystem. It is also due to the underlying belief that, to be able to help a child, the therapist must understand the child's psychopathology as a basis for conceptualizing the child and formulating a treatment plan.

The treatment plans in ecosystemic play therapy are much more intricate and thorough than they are in any other approach to play therapy. Each session is planned out in detail—what the therapist wishes to accomplish, how those wishes fit into the overall conceptualization of the client, the particular materials and activities to be used, possible interpretations that might be helpful, and so forth. The level of detail and intention in the design of intervention strategies is different than that in other approaches to play therapy.

Gestalt Play Therapy

Gestalt play therapy is based on concepts from Gestalt therapy, a humanistic, process-oriented approach to therapy that is concerned with the healthy functioning of the total organism (including senses, body, emotions, and intellect) (Carroll & Oaklander, 1997; Oaklander, 1978/1992, 1993, 1994, 2000).

Important Theoretical Constructs

The important theoretical constructs of Gestalt play therapy are the I/Thou relationship, organismic self-regulation, contact–boundary disturbances, and awareness and experience (Oaklander, 1978/1992, 1993, 1994, 2000). All of these theoretical constructs originated in Gestalt therapy with adults but have special importance in work with children.

I/Thou relationship. Based on the work of Buber (1958), the I/Thou relationship involves a meeting of two individuals who are equal in power and entitlement. In Gestalt play therapy, the I/Thou relationship is characterized by both parties being willing to fully bring themselves into the interaction, with complete honesty and no walls or pretenses (Oaklander, 1993, 1994, 2000). The relationship is filled with mutual honor and respect, genuineness, and congruence. Although therapists may have more knowledge and status than the child client, it is essential that they never see themselves as more important or powerful than the child in this relationship. As part of the therapeutic process, therapists stay in touch with their own boundaries and limitations, not losing themselves in the child's circumstances but not being afraid of them either. Each session is an existential encounter in which therapists may have goals or plans but have no expectations of the child or the child's behaviors, and no need to push the child beyond a place where the child is capable or willing to go.

Organismic self-regulation. According the practitioners of Gestalt therapy, each organism seeks homeostasis as a way to maintain health (Carroll & Oaklander, 1997; Oaklander, 1993, 1994). As change occurs in the environment and the needs of the organism change because of development, the organism seeks ways to satisfy needs and achieve equilibrium. Human beings use the organismic self-regulation process to get their needs met and to integrate their experiences. This process results in "learning, growth, and fulfillment of the potentialities of the child" (Carroll & Oaklander, 1997, p. 184).

When children encounter difficulties, such as loss, family problems, or trauma, they react in different ways, trying to get their needs met and to maintain homeostasis (Oaklander, 1994). The coping strategies that they choose may not work to restore balance and equilibrium, but they will continue to seek out ways to do so.

Contact–boundary disturbances. People make contact with others and their environment at the boundary of the self (Oaklander, 1993, 1994, 2000). Many times, people are afraid to make contact. They feel a need to protect themselves from others and from the environment and are afraid that they will not be able to get their needs met if they make contact. In the process of trying to protect themselves, children may inhibit, block, repress, or restrict various aspects of their organism—the senses, the body, the emotions, and/or the intellect.

When children block any aspect of their organism, it causes contact–boundary disturbances, which can lead to the development of adversarial behaviors and/or psychological, emotional, or physical symptoms (Carroll & Oaklander, 1997). Contact–boundary disturbances can include (a) retroflection (pulling in energy that needs to be directed outward, doing to themselves what they would like to do to others), (b) deflection (turning away from feelings of grief or anger), (c) confluence (merging with others to the point of the denial of self and the need for individuation and separation), (d) projection (denying personal experiences and responsibility, projecting personal feelings onto others), or (e) introjection (incorporating negative or conditional messages from others about the self into the self-image).

Although all children tend to suffer from some form of contact–boundary disturbance, those who come to play therapy have such major disturbances in this area that their sense of self is weak and fragile (Oaklander, 1994). In the quest for homeostasis and equilibrium, children may desensitize themselves, restrict their bodily feelings and functions, block their emotions, and/or inhibit their intellect. The Gestalt play therapist seeks to restore the children to their original organismic self-regulation, improve the level of contact with others and their environment, and instill a sense of self that is strong and positive.

Awareness and experience. Children who suffer from a weak sense of self have limited awareness of their own experiences (Oaklander, 1994). Through experiences and experiments in the play therapy process, the Gestalt play therapist helps children become more aware of themselves in play sessions, which can lead to an increase in their general level of awareness of themselves, others, and the world around them.

Phases of the Counseling Process

The Gestalt play therapy process does not have a prescribed sequence of steps or stages. However, to work toward the therapeutic goals of Gestalt play therapy, most play therapists strive to (a) develop an I/Thou relationship, (b) evaluate and establish contact, (c) strengthen the child's sense of self and self-support, (d) encourage emotional expression, (e) help the child learn to provide self-nurturing, (f) focus on the child's process, and (g) finalize the therapy (Oaklander, 1993, 1994).

The first component in Gestalt play therapy is the development of an I/Thou relationship between the therapist and the client (Oaklander, 1993, 1994). The main vehicle for establishing this relationship is genuine respect and patience. The therapist lets go of all expectations about the relationship and the child, entering into the interaction with a sense of adventure and empathy for the child.

Contact involves making a connection with the environment and with other people (Oaklander, 1993, 1994). In play therapy, this contact means interacting with the play materials and the play therapist. There are many children who are uncomfortable sustaining contact with others, using contact–boundary disturbances to diminish the "danger" they perceive in contact. During the first several sessions with the child, the Gestalt play therapist evaluates the child's ability to make and maintain contact by observing the child's behavior. With children who have difficulty establishing and sustaining contact, the therapist will plan play and art experiences to encourage the child to begin to establish contact with the play therapy environment and the play therapist.

During the first sessions, the Gestalt play therapist is also evaluating the child's sense of self and ability to provide self-support (Oaklander, 1993, 1994). Most children who come to play therapy have a weak sense of self and limited ability to provide self-support. They may be blocking their own emotions, blaming themselves for traumatic experiences, and introjecting negative messages about themselves. To help them strengthen their own sense of self, the therapist designs activities to (a) stimulate the use of their senses; (b) increase their awareness of their own bodies; and (c) help them cognitively define who they are by talking about their attitudes, ideas, and opinions.

The process of encouraging emotional expression involves tapping into aggressive energy and learning to express feelings (Oaklander, 1993, 1994). In Gestalt terms, aggressive energy is the energy it takes to promote action. Most children who come to play therapy are confused about their own aggressive energy. They may use this energy too much, resulting in acting-out behavior, or they may suppress it altogether, resulting in passivity and fearfulness. By teaching children to tap into their own aggressive energy and use it appropriately, the Gestalt play therapist helps them to become comfortable expressing their own inner power. The therapist also wants to help children learn to express their feelings. By using different kinds of play, storytelling, music, art, body movement, photography, and sensory awareness activities, the therapist can help children become more aware of their own emotions and learn to express them.

Children need to learn to accept the parts of themselves that they do not like (Oaklander, 1993, 1994). Self-nurturing helps them to achieve this acceptance and teaches them skills for taking care of themselves and treating themselves well. Many children, as they increase their sense of self and their ability to provide self-nurturing, stop exhibiting negative behaviors and other symptoms. Other children continue to use negative behaviors and other symptoms to try to get their needs met (Oaklander, 1993, 1994). With these children, the Gestalt play therapist begins to focus on the negative process. Without making judgments or suggesting that they might want to change, the therapist asks children to pay attention to what they are doing and how they are feeling when they exhibit these behaviors.

Children are usually ready to terminate the current installment of therapy when they have worked through their issues as far as their developmental level will allow (Oaklander, 1994). Through several different sessions, children are invited to review progress, celebrate changes, and express mixed feelings about bringing this important relationship to closure.

Role of the Therapist

The role of the therapist in Gestalt play therapy is twofold—partly nondirective and partly directive (Oaklander, 1994). In the nondirective component of the therapeutic role, the play therapist works to establish the I/Thou relationship and to encourage the child to maintain contact with him or her in a session. This is done through conveying acceptance without expectations, simply being together in existential moment after existential moment. The Gestalt play therapist does not use many of the basic play therapy skills of tracking, restating content, reflecting feelings, and so forth (V. Oaklander, personal communication, October 1997). These skills are not necessary for establishing an I/Thou relationship and are not particularly helpful in the more directive component of Gestalt play therapy.

In the directive component of the therapeutic role, the Gestalt play therapist preselects play media and art materials and designs activities and experiments to provide children with experiences that are different from the experiences they have encountered in other settings and other relationships (V.

Oaklander, personal communication, October 1997). The therapist directs children to use the materials in the playroom to increase their contact with the environment, enhance their sense of self, express their emotions, and learn self-nurturing skills. When being more directive, the Gestalt play therapist uses many advanced play therapy skills, including creative dramatics, role-plays, video enactments, mutual storytelling, therapeutic metaphors, art projects, confrontation, guided imagery, and so forth (Oaklander, 1978/1992).

Goals of Therapy

"The disturbed child needs help to restore healthy organismic self-regulation, to reawaken an awareness of internal and external events, and to be able to use the resources available in her environment to get her needs met" (Carroll & Oaklander, 1997, p. 188). These are the general goals of Gestalt play therapy: (a) to restore a sense of self, (b) to accept previously unacceptable parts of the self, (c) to learn to support the self, and (d) to be able and willing to experience pain and discomfort. The therapist must also be willing to work with the various social systems in which the child interacts to enhance system support for the child and his or her emotional, physical, and intellectual functioning. Related to these general goals and to the components of the therapeutic process, the therapist has goals for each child in therapy. These goals reflect the need to form a therapeutic relationship, restore sensory and motor functioning, develop self-support, organize aggressive energy, express emotions, integrate organismic functioning, and decrease contact–boundary disturbances (Carroll & Oaklander, 1997).

Approach to Working With Parents

Parents are an integral part of the Gestalt play therapy process. V. Oaklander (personal communication, October 1997) works with them for at least part of every play therapy session. She believes in educating parents about the therapeutic process and engaging them to support changes the child is making through homework assignments. Oaklander views parents as an important source of information about what is happening with children at home and at school. She provides parenting suggestions for them so that they can avoid exacerbating children's contact–boundary disturbances. By encouraging parents to increase their own level of awareness and to express their emotions, the Gestalt play therapist can optimize parental functioning, which in turn can free children to set off on their own "rightful, healthy path of growth" (Oaklander, 1994, p. 156).

Distinctive Features

Gestalt play therapy is a unique combination of nondirective and direct elements. Establishing the relationship is extremely nondirective, using few if any play therapy skills to build rapport between the child and the therapist. In contrast, the therapist uses many advanced directive skills in later sessions to facilitate increased sensory awareness and expression of emotions.

Psychodynamic Play Therapy

Although there are several different schools of psychodynamic play therapy (Benedict & Narcavage, 1997; A. Freud, 1965, 1968; M. Klein, 1932), the work of Anna Freud seems to be the dominant influence in psychodynamic play therapy theory and practice. Therefore, the description in this section focuses on the ideas articulated in Anna Freud's approach to play therapy.

Important Theoretical Constructs

The origin of all psychodynamic theoretical constructs is in the writings of Sigmund Freud (1938). Because most students studying counseling and psychology have been exposed to a wide range of information related to Freudian theory, I do not go into depth about the theoretical constructs of this approach.

Sigmund Freud (1938) believed that human personalities develop from the striving of biological drives toward gratification. He viewed human development as following predictable psychosexual stages: oral, anal, phallic, and genital stages. Part of this developmental process is resolving Oedipal feelings and sexual attraction to the opposite-sex parent.

According to Lee (1997), Sigmund Freud described several different models of the functions of the mental apparatus. The models that have meaning for psychodynamic play therapy include the structural model (id, ego, and superego), the economic model (movement of instinctual energy toward discharge and attainment of homeostasis), and the dynamic model (movement of awareness from the unconscious, to the preconscious, to the conscious).

Although Anna Freud incorporated her father's structural model and the psychosexual stages into her own work with children, her emphasis was on the functioning of the ego (Cangelosi, 1993). Her particular interests were the working of defense mechanisms and the ego's striving toward mastery (A. Freud, 1965, 1968).

In working with children, Anna Freud (1968) suggested that they could benefit from analysis when they experienced the following:

1. Conflicts between and among the id, ego, and superego that limit the energy available for life tasks.
2. Unsuitable or inappropriate defenses that limit the efficiency of ego functioning.
3. Overwhelming levels of anxiety that limit functioning.
4. Fixations of large amounts of sexual energy that prevent appropriate developmental progress.
5. Strong repression or denial of aggression that limit ability to maintain productive levels of activity.

Phases of the Counseling Process

Lee (1997) described the treatment stages in psychodynamic play therapy as being (a) introduction/orientation, (b) negative reactions, (c) working through, and (d) termination. The introduction/orientation phase includes interactions with both the child and the parents. With parents, the therapist outlines the schedule of appointments, the need for attendance, and policies for missed sessions. With the child, the therapist gives an explanation of the reason for therapy, the rules for conduct in the playroom, and a description of the procedures of the therapist. The therapist may also introduce the child to the "language of therapy" (Lee, 1997, p. 71), including feeling vocabulary. During this phase, the therapist works to establish the therapeutic alliance with the child, using basic play therapy skills such as tracking and restating content.

In the negative-reaction phase, the child may exhibit hostility and resistance to the therapeutic process (Cangelosi, 1993; Lee, 1997). This hostility and resistance can occur in the context of the transference relationship, causing the child to (at least initially) reject the therapist and the play therapy process. The therapist must acknowledge the child's negative reactions and make interpretations about the underlying dynamics of the hostility and resistance. However, it is important to do this in a gentle, nonconfrontive manner so as to avoid exacerbating the negative reactions.

During the working-through phase of play therapy, the therapist elaborates and extends his or her interpretations to different contexts, situations, and directions so that the client "withdraws his investment in a particular pattern of mental activity or behavior in favor of a more ego-adaptive solution" (Lee, 1997, p. 73). The therapist may have to repeat interpretations over and over again to help the child let go of defenses and coping strategies that are not currently effective and move on to the next level of development.

Because the loss of love objects is a central issue in psychodynamic theory, termination is considered to be an essential stage in psychodynamic play therapy. The therapist must concentrate on helping the child resolve any transference ties and acknowledge the impending pain of another loss of an important object (the therapist).

Role of the Therapist

For most psychodynamic play therapists, the role of the therapist is relatively nondirective. The therapist follows the behavioral lead of the child, allowing the child to direct the play, choose the toys, and so forth (Cangelosi, 1993; Lee, 1997). At the same time, the psychodynamic therapist uses four interventions (confrontation, clarification, interpretation, and education) that are somewhat directive and interpretive (Cangelosi, 1993).

The therapist uses "confrontation" to point out behavior, play themes, and other important observable phenomena. The purpose of this intervention is to make issues explicit to the child so as to enhance ego mastery. The therapist may also use "clarification" in this process, asking detailed questions to clarify various behaviors, to increase the child's awareness of defenses, and to explore related affect.

Shifting away from the conscious processes highlighted with confrontation and clarification, the therapist moves toward "interpretation" of unconscious material (Cangelosi, 1993; Esman, 1983). Interpretations, from a psychodynamic play therapist, provide explanations of the source, history, and meaning of defenses and drives.

With many young children, the therapist may also take on educative functions to strengthen ego functioning and encourage ego mastery

(Cangelosi, 1993). The therapist may use therapeutic metaphors or engage in teaching, role-playing, or problem solving to help children replace non-adaptive defenses and behaviors with more appropriate and adaptive ones.

Goals of Therapy

"Psychoanalytic play therapy aims at resolving the fixations, regressions, and where possible, developmental deficiencies and deviations that derail the child's normal development" (Lee, 1997, p. 64). On the basis of Anna Freud's (1928, 1946) description of reasons for children entering analysis, the therapist would want to help children accomplish the following:

1. Resolve conflicts between and among the id, ego, and superego and increase the energy available for life tasks.
2. Eliminate unsuitable or inappropriate defenses that can limit the efficiency of ego functioning, replacing them with more functional defenses.
3. Reduce levels of anxiety that interfere with functioning.
4. Eliminate fixations of sexual energy, and free children to make appropriate developmental progress.
5. Acknowledge and appropriately channel aggression to optimize productive levels of activity.

Approach to Working With Parents

Although there seem to be no universal guidelines for working with parents, most psychodynamic play therapists seem to favor some collateral work with parents (Cangelosi, 1993; Lee, 1997). This work may include (a) parent consultation to discuss behavior management; (b) information-gathering sessions to solicit data about child development, current functioning, and so forth; and (c) individual therapy sessions to facilitate parents working on their own issues.

Distinctive Features

Although the description of the therapist's role in the initial stages of therapy sounds much like that in child-centered therapy, the psychodynamic therapist is constantly analyzing and storing impressions about the underlying issues present in the child's play. As the relationship progresses, the therapist shares his or her ideas about the unconscious dynamics of the child's behavior and motivations with the child. The use of this type of interpretation is unique to the psychodynamic approach to play therapy, as is the emphasis on the analysis of the transference and countertransference issues present in the therapeutic process.

Theraplay

Theraplay is an engaging, playful treatment method that is modeled on the healthy interaction between parents and their children (Jernberg, 1979; Jernberg & Booth, 1999; Munns, 2000). It is an intensive, short-term approach that actively involves parents—first as observers and later as cotherapists. The goal is to enhance attachment, self-esteem, trust, and joyful engagement and to empower parents to continue, on their own, the health-promoting interactions of the treatment sessions (Koller & Booth, 1997).

Important Theoretical Constructs

Theraplay is based on a model of healthy parent–child interactions because Jernberg (1979) believed that "the early interaction between parent and child is the crucible in which the self and personality develop" (Koller & Booth, 1997, p. 206). Jernberg's (1979) ideas about personality development stemmed from those of several interactional theories of human development, especially self psychology (Kohut, 1971, 1977) and object relations theory (Winnicott, 1958, 1971). Practitioners of Theraplay believe that playful, empathic, joyful responses from a child's caretakers result in the child developing a strong sense of self; feelings of self-worth; and strong, secure attachment (Jernberg & Booth, 1999; Koller & Booth, 1997). According to this theory, when a child does not have these elements in interactions with caretakers, the child can be vulnerable to the development of intrapersonal and interpersonal difficulties.

Jernberg (1979; Jernberg & Booth, 1999) believed that children learn to soothe and nurture themselves from being soothed and nurtured by their caretakers when they are very young. Children who do not receive this kind of comforting from caretakers grow up to deal poorly with separation and loss and other situations in which self-comforting would be appropriate.

Jernberg (1979; Jernberg & Booth, 1999) also felt that children who have strong, loving, and empathic relationships with their caretakers develop a view of themselves as being lovable, competent, and capable; a view of others as loving and trustworthy; and a view of the world as a safe and exciting place to explore. Children who do not have these experiences tend to view themselves as unworthy of love, others are untrustworthy and unresponsive, and the world as threatening and negative (Koller & Booth, 1997).

The elements of healthy parent–child interactions became the Theraplay dimensions that are used to remediate difficulties in the attachment process that result in problems for children (Jernberg & Booth, 1999; Jernberg & Jernberg, 1993). These dimensions are (a) structure, (b) challenge, (c) intrusion/engagement, and (d) nurture.

Structure in the parent–child relationship occurs when the parent provides rules and responses to ensure the safety and comfort of the child (Jernberg & Booth, 1999). In Theraplay, the dimension of structure is exhibited through clearly stated rules for safety; through experiences that have a beginning, a middle, and an end (e.g., singing games); and through activities designed to define body boundaries.

Challenge in the parent–child relationship occurs when the parent challenges the child to stretch beyond his or her usual comfort zone (Jernberg & Booth, 1999). These experiences help the child learn to deal with anxiety-provoking experiences and increase a sense of mastery and competence. In Theraplay, the dimension of challenge is exhibited when the therapist encourages the child to take small age-appropriate risks—to try behaviors that he or she would not ordinarily try—to build feelings of mastery and self-confidence.

Intrusion/engagement in the parent–child relationship occurs when the parent does things to draw the child into interaction with others (Jernberg & Booth, 1999). In Theraplay, the dimension of intrusion/engagement is exhibited when the therapist invites the child to interact in a playful, spontaneous manner. The therapeutic purpose of this dimension is to teach the child that the world is a fun, enjoyable, and exciting place and that others can be both stimulating and trustworthy.

Nurture in the parent–child relationship occurs when the parent does things to sooth, calm, quiet, and reassure the child (Jernberg & Booth, 1999). The parent engages in activities designed to meet the child's emotional needs. In Theraplay, this dimension is exhibited when the therapist engages in activities designed to sooth, calm, quiet, and reassure the child by meeting his or her early unsatisfied emotional needs. These experiences can include activities such as feeding, making lotion hand prints, or swinging the child in a blanket.

Phases of the Counseling Process

Theraplay is intensive and short term. With most children, the beginning interview and assessment with the parents and the initial contract of 8 to 12 Theraplay sessions are enough to make the necessary changes in the child, the parents, and their relationship so that the family can carry on the therapeutic process without outside intervention. These 8 to 12 Theraplay sessions follow a standard format of (a) introduction/orientation, (b) negative reaction, (c) working through, and (d) termination (Koller, 1994; Koller & Booth, 1997).

Before the work with the child begins, there is an initial interview with the parents and an assessment of the parent–child relationship using the Marschak Interaction Method (Marschak, 1960). The next session is a feedback session with the parents in which the therapists explain the Theraplay philosophy, begin to build rapport with the parents, give feedback from the initial assessment, and make a treatment plan. The therapists also explain the logistics of the Theraplay process (Koller & Booth, 1997). These logistics include the fact that there are usually two different therapists participating in each session—the Theraplay therapist, who works directly with the child, and the Interpreting therapist, who works directly with the parents. During the first 4 sessions and the first 15 minutes of the second 4 sessions, the Interpreting therapist and the parents watch the session from behind a one-way mirror with the therapist explaining the therapeutic interaction to the parents. During the second 4 sessions, in the last 15 minutes of each session, the Interpreting therapist and the parents join the child and the Theraplay therapist in the play.

In the first session with the child, the Theraplay therapist communicates (either by demonstration or by explanation) the rules of Theraplay (Koller, 1994). These rules are as follows:

1. The therapist is in charge of the session.
2. Sessions are fun.
3. Sessions are active.
4. Sessions are structured and predictable.
5. Sessions are free from physical hurting.

Part of the first session (and all subsequent sessions) is devoted to exploring the ways the therapist and the child are alike and different (e.g., height, favorite color, and eye color). All four Theraplay dimensions come into play in each session with the child.

Sometime during the first several sessions of Theraplay (either actually during a session or outside of the sessions), the child will express negative reactions to the therapy process (Koller & Booth, 1997). This negative reaction is considered to be normal and helpful in the Theraplay process—an opportunity for parents and the therapist to show the child that they will keep on working on the relationship and caring for the child even when he or she expresses hostility and anger.

In the working-through phase of Theraplay, the child begins to accept the therapist being in control and to enjoy being nurtured and soothed (Koller & Booth, 1997). This process frequently leads to regressive behaviors, in which the child acts much younger than his or her chronological age. These episodes of relaxed and regressive behavior may alternate with lapses into hostile, angry behavior and other forms of negative reaction until the child becomes comfortable trusting adults and feeling more confident and competent.

A major part of the working-through phase is helping the parents learn to interact appropriately with the child (Jernberg & Jernberg, 1993; Koller & Booth, 1997). This process involves the parents spending 15 minutes in every session participating in the interactions using the four Theraplay dimensions modeled by the Theraplay therapist and coached by the Interpreting therapist.

As parents gain competence and confidence in their ability to appropriately handle the child, the therapists set a date for termination (Jernberg & Jernberg, 1993; Koller & Booth, 1997). To make sure that parents will continue to incorporate the four Theraplay dimensions in the interactions with the child, the therapists schedule several follow-up sessions. During the follow-up sessions, the therapists provide support and suggestions for the continuation of the development of a healthy parent–child relationship.

Role of the Therapist

The role of the Theraplay therapist is active and directive. He or she does not spend very much time talking—the doing is the focus of all Theraplay sessions. Before each session begins, the therapist has a plan for how the session will go—with specific activities and materials chosen to facilitate the various dimensions. Each session is tailored to the needs of the individual child—with the percentage of time spent on each dimension based on the issues of that particular family. As the session unfolds, the therapist may change or adapt some of the activities, depending on the child's mood and/or the child's reactions to the interaction or activities.

The role of the Interpreting therapist is verbal and directive. The Interpreting therapist (a) explains the process unfolding between the child and the Theraplay therapist, (b) describes different activities that could help the child, (c) elaborates on the need for the various Theraplay dimensions in the parent–child relationship, (d) coaches parents as they enter the Theraplay process and participate in activities, and (e) provides support and encouragement for changes the parents make in their interactions with the child.

Goals of Therapy

"The goal of Theraplay is to enhance children's view of themselves and to increase their joy in the world" (Jernberg & Jernberg, 1993, p. 48). Theraplay therapists believe that the best way to promote children's positive views of themselves, others, and the world is through activities modeled on the healthy attachment-enhancing behaviors between parent and infant. By working toward an improvement in the attachment between parent and child, practitioners of Theraplay believe they can move children toward feeling more trusting, having a higher level of self-worth, and being more willing to let others have control in age-appropriate situations.

For each child and his or her parents, the Theraplay therapist devises specific goals for the therapy process. These goals usually include forming a more secure attachment, shifting the child's view of self and others from negative to positive, teaching the child self-soothing behaviors, and changing the patterns inherent in the parent–child interactions so that the parents can appropriately provide the four Theraplay dimensions in the relationship outside the therapy sessions. The therapist may also work on school issues, marital issues, sibling issues, and personal issues of one or both of the parents.

Approach to Working With Parents

As I have indicated in the previous sections, the approach to working with parents in Theraplay is intensive. The parent is actively involved in every half-hour session. He or she has a separate therapist (the Interpreting therapist) devoted to explaining the process and involving the parent.

Distinctive Features

There are many distinctive features in Theraplay that make it significantly different from other approaches to play therapy. The therapists seldom use any of the standard basic play therapy intervention strategies, such as tracking, restating content, and reflecting feelings, or the advanced play therapy intervention skills, such as role-playing or mutual storytelling. The Theraplay therapist engages the child in playful activities and games using limited materials in an empty room on a mat-covered floor. Theraplay sessions are very short—only a half hour—and intense, with two therapists being actively involved in the process, one with the child and one with the parents.

The extensive involvement of the parents is also unique to Theraplay. Although other play therapy approaches may include parents in the process, in Theraplay a primary objective is to teach the parents skills so that they can assume primary responsibility for providing the child with a nurturing relationship.

Eclectic Prescriptive Play Therapy

Because of the very nature of the eclectic prescriptive approach to play therapy, it is impossible to describe this orientation in the same kind of detail devoted to the other approaches to play therapy. Practitioners of eclectic prescriptive play therapy (Schaefer, 1993, 2000) individually tailor their interventions for each child. To do this in a theoretically consistent way, they must have a depth of knowledge—both conceptually and practically— about each of the various theoretical orientations to play therapy so that they can appropriately conceptualize the client and his or her problems. Eclectic prescriptive therapists must also have a great deal of experience working with children and their parents so that they can apply specific intervention strategies with skill.

Kaduson et al. (1997) advocated a model of eclectic prescriptive play therapy based on the following factors:

1. the psychological and emotional issues common to specific childhood disorders,
2. the biopsychological variables unique to each individual child,
3. the short- and long-term needs of each individual child related to his or her specific presenting problem,
4. treatment planning designed to integrate and implement the specific therapeutic factors of play related to the child's needs and situation, and
5. the skillful application of intervention strategies designed to address the therapeutic goals of the individual child and his or her parents.

Kaduson et al. (1997) advocated "synthetic eclecticism" (Norcross, 1987), which stresses applying various theories into "one interactive and coordinated modality of treatment" (Kaduson et al., 1997, p. xi). They cautioned play therapists to avoid "kitchen-sink eclecticism" (Norcross, 1987), an atheoretical approach in which practitioners haphazardly apply techniques without considering the theories underlying them.

According to Kaduson et al. (1997), the synthetically eclectic play therapist must

1. be familiar with virtually every approach to play therapy, including the theoretical constructs and the main treatment strategies;
2. be skilled in the application of this wide range of theoretical constructs and treatment strategies;
3. have integrated the numerous philosophical ideas about people, their motivation, the change process, the role of the therapist, and a myriad of other aspects of psychological theory formation into an internally consistent model of personality development and therapeutic process;
4. understand the various psychological and emotional issues related to common childhood disorders;
5. know enough about the short- and long-term needs of children with specific diagnoses and presenting problems to be able to formulate treatment plans based on those needs;
6. be skilled at discovering the specific biopsychosocial variables unique to individual children; and

7. know the research related to each common childhood disorder and presenting problem well enough to evaluate the efficacy of various intervention strategies with specific populations.

One essential element to developing an effective eclectic approach is to focus on the internal consistency of the underlying theoretical conceptualization of the client. This means that the clinician must have a clear understanding of each theory and the philosophical concepts on which the theory is based.

Questions to Ponder

1. What is your reaction to this quote? "Play therapy may be directive in form—that is, the therapist may assume responsibility for guidance and interpretation, or it may be nondirective; the therapist may leave responsibility and direction to the child" (Axline, 1947, p. 9).
2. What do you think about the Adlerian concept that the therapist's role should change depending on the phase of counseling?
3. What is your reaction to the child-centered principle that all people have an innate tendency to move in a positive direction, striving toward self-actualization and constructive growth?
4. Do you agree or disagree with the child-centered concept of organismic valuing? Explain your reasoning.
5. What do you think about Axline's principles of play therapy? With which ones do you agree? With which ones do you disagree? Explain your reasoning.
6. How does the cognitive–behavioral emphasis on developing more adaptive thoughts and behaviors fit into your view of play therapy?
7. How comfortable would you be with an assessment stage like the cognitive–behavioral assessment period in which the therapist uses formal and informal instruments to assess the current functioning of the child and his or her parents?
8. What would you want to include in the "fill" for your approach to play therapy (if you were following O'Connor's idea that each individual therapist should provide the bulk of the "fill" for his or her approach to play therapy)?
9. What is your reaction to the level of control the ecosystemic play therapist maintains in a session?

10. What would be the most difficult part for you of establishing an I/Thou relationship as required in Gestalt play therapy?
11. What kinds of contact–boundary disturbances do you have? What factors contribute to your own reluctance to make contact with other people and the environment?
12. What is your stance on sharing psychodynamic interpretations with the child? With the parents?
13. What is your reaction to Jernberg's contention that many problems experienced by children are due to problems in the early interaction between parent and child? If you agree with Jernberg's contention, how do you keep from blaming parents or sounding as if you blame parents when you explain these ideas to parents?
14. What would be the potential practical problems related to the Theraplay practice of working with two therapists for each child and his or her parents?
15. For each theoretical approach to play therapy described in this chapter, what do you feel are the positive aspects of the approach? Negative aspects?

Part 2
Basic Skills

Chapter 4

Logistical Aspects of Play Therapy

This chapter covers important logistical aspects of play therapy, including (a) setting up a space for therapy, (b) choosing and arranging toys, (c) explaining the play therapy process (including confidentiality) to parents and to children, (d) handling the initial session, (e) ending each session, (f) assessing patterns in children's behavior in the playroom, (g) writing session reports, and (h) terminating play therapy. Although every approach to play therapy and each individual play therapist will probably have unique methods of making decisions about how to deal with these logistical concerns, I have tried to raise important issues related to them to help inform your decision-making process.

Many of the descriptions contained in this chapter are based on the "ideal" situation, which, of course, does not really exist—a large, acoustically tight space in a beautiful child-proof building; all the money you need to buy whatever toys, materials, and furniture you want; intelligent, insightful children with only minor problems who quickly respond to therapy; parents who are optimally cooperative; colleagues who understand and support what you are doing; and insurance companies that provide unlimited reimbursement for your services. You must remember, however, that you may never have even one of these ideal conditions in the real world. Realistically, most of the decisions you make about logistical matters will be based on the practical considerations of your professional position, the clients you serve, and the setting of your work.

Setting Up a Space for Therapy

Landreth (1991) provided a description of an "ideal" playroom. His specifications included information about the playroom size, location, and accommodations.

1. The room should measure approximately 12 feet by 15 feet, with an area of between 150 and 200 square feet. This would provide children with room to navigate and move but would not be so much space that they would feel overwhelmed or would be able to evade the attention of the play therapist.
2. The room must have privacy so that children can feel safe revealing information and feelings without fear of others overhearing. If there is a window in the room, there should be curtains or blinds that children can close if they wish to do so.
3. Wall coverings should be washable so that children can make messes with impunity. Probably the best arrangement is to paint the walls with a neutral color of washable enamel.
4. If possible, the floors should be covered with vinyl tile, which is an easy surface to clean or replace if necessary.
5. There should be enough shelves to accommodate the toys and materials so they are not crowded. To assure that smaller children can reach the top shelf, it would be helpful if the shelves were no taller than 38 inches. Shelves for toys should be securely attached to walls so that they cannot be toppled—either accidentally or purposely.

6. A small sink should have cold running water, but not hot water, which could potentially be dangerous.

7. If possible, having some countertop space (either connected with the sink or separate) is helpful for providing a place for artwork or "school" work. A child-size desk with a storage area can also fill this purpose.

8. A cabinet for storing materials such as paint, clay, and extra paper is extremely helpful.

9. A marker board or chalkboard (attached to either a wall or an easel) can be a place for children to express themselves without verbalization.

10. By having a small bathroom attached to the main room, the therapist can avoid many problems with children who want to wander the halls looking for a bathroom.

11. The playroom should be located in an area of the building in which noise will not present a problem—either to other inhabitants of the building or to people passing.

12. If possible, the ceiling of the room should be fitted with acoustical tile to reduce noise. Because acoustical tile on the walls is a tempting target for children (painting or drawing on it, pulling pieces off, etc.), it is probably inadvisable to install it anywhere other than the ceiling.

13. Furniture (e.g., a small desk or table and several chairs) should be constructed of wood or molded plastic and designed to accommodate children. If the therapist will be working with parents in the playroom, it is important to have furniture available to accommodate them too.

14. The therapist will need a place to sit. This chair (or pillow) should meet the therapist's standards for being comfortable without being so relaxing that it would undermine the ability to focus on the child.

15. Installing a one-way mirror and equipment for listening to sessions and videotaping sessions can enhance the opportunity for supervision, training, and self-monitoring.

This description is meant for a room in which the therapist would do individual play therapy. If the therapist is working with groups or families, the space should be bigger, and there should be enough furniture to accommodate whoever participates in sessions. O'Connor (1991) suggested that a room for group play therapy should be approximately 15 feet by 25 feet.

Obviously, there is no prohibition about doing play therapy if you do not have a space that fits this description. I have done play therapy in a closet in an elementary school, and I now have my own custom-designed playroom in my house, which, because of the limitations of the available space, does not have all of the ideal features that I just described. I have not noticed that the quality of the therapy or the results of my interactions with children have been significantly different in either setting.

The most important factor in establishing a place to do play therapy is your own personal feeling of comfort, because if you feel safe, happy, and welcome in the space, so will children. Your play therapy setting should fit your style of interacting with children and their parents. You will need to think about how you work with children and about any personal preferences for the arrangement of space in designing your setting for play therapy. For instance, if you like to sit on the floor, it would make sense to have big, soft pillows scattered on the floor; if you feel uncomfortable with a lot of potential clutter, it would help to have many built-in shelves and bins for toys.

Choosing and Arranging Toys

Although most of the approaches to play therapy have differing classifications of the types of toys best used for attaining the therapeutic goals of that approach, there seem to be several common ideas about toy selection. Most play therapists would agree with Landreth's (1991) suggestion that toys and play materials used in play therapy should (a) facilitate a wide range of emotional and creative expression by children, (b) engage the interest of children in some way, (c) encourage verbal and nonverbal investigation and expression by children, (d) provide mastery experiences in which children can experience success without having to follow certain rules about how to use them, and (e) be sturdy and safe for children to use in play. Play therapists must also take into account different ethnic and cultural factors in selecting toys for the playroom, including baby dolls and doll families with a variety of racial identities.

Most play therapists try to make sure that the placement of toys and play materials is predictable and consistent. Toys should go back to approximately the same place after every session. The purpose of this strategy is to help establish the playroom as a place where the child can count on routine and structure, a place where things are predictable and consistent.

One way to facilitate the return of toys and play materials to their usual spots is to arrange them according to specific categories. In my playroom, for example, the snakes share a shelf, the dinosaurs share another shelf, the transportation toys share their own shelf, and all of the puppets go on a puppet tree. This arrangement makes it easier to put the toys back where they belong at the end of a session, and it makes it easier for children to remember where they are located. In my playroom, children sometimes say things like, "OK, this is where the snakes go, so that green snake must be somewhere on this shelf."

If the therapist does not have a stationary playroom but travels to different settings to work with children, he or she can still maintain the standard of consistent and predictable arrangement of the toys. This can be accomplished by placing the toys in a certain order on the floor or on a table in whatever space is currently the "playroom."

There seem to be two basic trends in the selection of toys and play materials—maximalist and minimalist. Playrooms in which maximalism is the guiding philosophy have a wide range and variety of all different kinds of toys. Minimalist playrooms, in contrast, contain only a few play materials selected especially for a certain child, for a specific intervention, or to attain a particular goal.

Those who would probably fit into the maximalist category include most play therapists who subscribe to the Adlerian, child-centered, cognitive–behavioral, eclectic prescriptive, Jungian psychoanalytic, and Thematic approaches. These playrooms contain extensive inventories of toys to maximize the possibility that they will have the "'right' object(s) available for each child, the right object being one that appeals to the child enough to encourage its use, carries some symbolic meaning, and can be used in resolving the particular issue the child is facing at the time" (O'Connor, 1991, p. 202). In these playrooms, children have the freedom and opportunity to choose the toys or play materials they want to use at that particular moment.

In contrast, the minimalists (usually therapists from the ecosystemic, Gestalt, and Theraplay schools of thought) believe that they have a better grasp than the child about which toys can be helpful at a particular juncture in therapy. Their playrooms are relatively empty, and they usually store their play materials in other rooms or in locked cabinets. At the beginning of each session or at times throughout the session, these therapists introduce certain preselected toys chosen to facilitate children working on specific issues.

In my playroom, I have toys that represent each of five distinct categories (Kottman, 1995). These categories are family/nurturing toys, scary toys, aggressive toys, expressive toys, and pretend/fantasy toys. Although there are a variety of toys and play materials listed for each category, it is not necessary to have every single toy listed. It is more important to have representative toys from each category.

The purpose of family/nurturing toys in the playroom is to provide opportunities for children to build a relationship with the therapist, explore family relationships, and represent situations that happen outside the playroom. These toys can include a dollhouse; baby dolls; a cradle; animal families; a warm, soft blanket; people puppets; baby clothes; baby bottles; stuffed toys; sand in a sandbox; several different families of dolls (with removable clothing and bendable bodies if possible); pots; pans; dishes; silverware; empty food containers; and play kitchen appliances (e.g., a sink and a stove). The dolls and people puppets should represent a broad spectrum of ethnic origins.

The purpose of scary toys is to provide opportunities for children to deal with their fears. These toys can include snakes, rats, plastic monsters, dinosaurs, sharks, insects, dragons, alligators, and "fierce" animal puppets (e.g., a wolf, a bear, or an alligator). With children who have experienced a traumatic event, toys that would not normally be considered particularly frightening (e.g., cars, trucks, or ambulances with children who have been injured in wrecks) may qualify as scary toys. If the therapist knows about events that might have been frightening for particular children, it can be helpful to include toys that could represent various aspects of the trauma in the playroom.

The purpose of aggressive toys is to provide opportunities for children to symbolically express anger and aggression, to protect themselves from their fears, and to explore control issues. These toys could include a bop bag, weapons (e.g., play guns, swords, and knives), toy soldiers and military vehicles, small pillows for pillow fights, a foam bat, plastic shields, and handcuffs.

The purpose of expressive toys is to provide opportunities for children to express feelings, enhance a sense of mastery, practice problem-solving skills, and express creativity. These materials could include an easel and paints, watercolors, crayons, markers, glue, newsprint, Play Doh or clay, finger paints, scissors, tape, egg cartons, feathers, material for making masks, and pipe cleaners.

The purpose of pretend/fantasy toys is to provide opportunities for children to express feelings, explore a variety of roles, experiment with different behaviors and attitudes, and act out situations and relationships from outside the playroom. These toys can include masks, costumes, magic wands, hats, jewelry, purses, a doctor kit, telephones, blocks and other building materials, people figures, zoo and farm animals, puppets and a puppet theater, a sandbox, trucks and construction equipment, kitchen appliances, pots, pans, dishes, silverware, and empty food containers.

Explaining the Play Therapy Process

Parents and their children come to play therapy with ideas about the process and what it entails. Some of these ideas are accurate, and some of them are inaccurate. To provide clarity and a sense of safety and to avoid misunderstandings, it is essential to have a plan for communicating important information about play therapy—what it is and what it is not—to parents and to children. Before you begin seeing play therapy clients, you will need to think about (a) what you want to discuss with parents and children about the play therapy process and (b) how you might go about explaining the concepts you want them to understand.

To Parents

Parents frequently come to the office of a play therapist with a distorted picture of what child therapy is. They may bring in a child who is dressed in his or her best clothes—clothes that it would be a tragedy to wear while painting or playing in the sandbox. Parents might expect a report (either from the child or from the therapist) about exactly what happened in the session—what the child played, what the child said, what the therapist said, and so forth. Parents also tend to expect to have the therapist use a single session to "examine" the child and then present them with a "diagnosis" (an explanation of what is "wrong" with the child) and a plan for "fixing" the child. Many of these ideas are based on trips to physicians' offices—where the model is "decide what is wrong and fix it as expediently as possible."

This model does not work well when applied to the process of play therapy, and it will be your job to explain that to the parents. To counteract many of these erroneous preconceptions, you will need to describe how play therapy works and why you have chosen to use play as a modality to help children. You should describe your generic goals for children in play therapy and your philosophy about working with parents and children.

What play therapy is. You will need to tell parents that play therapy is usually a relatively slow process of gradual unfolding. It will take time for you to understand what is going on with their child. Changes in a child's attitudes, perceptions, feelings, and behaviors brought about by play therapy generally evolve over time. It is essential to explain that the child will probably not be coming to the playroom and verbally spewing information about what is happening in his or her life. The child will be coming in and *playing!* You will need to do your best to communicate to parents that this playing is exactly what needs to be happening—that it will help you learn the important things about their child and help the child grow and change in positive ways.

The following is an example of how you might explain what play therapy is to parents:

"Little kids don't know how to tell us about their problems with words like grown-ups do. They can show us what is happening in their lives in their play. In play therapy, my job is to watch what Claire does and try to figure out how she is feeling and what she is thinking about what is happening in her life. We usually won't do very much talking—the main thing that happens in play therapy is playing."

What children should wear. On a practical note, there will be less confusion later if you explain that you generally ask that children not wear good or expensive clothes to play therapy. They should wear "play" clothes that they can get messy and dirty and not worry about damaging.

Reports about the session. Because you will not want parents demanding a verbatim report about the content of the session from their child, you will need some strategies for explaining this to parents. It is sometimes helpful to suggest that children may not act naturally or play in ways that will be optimally helpful if they think that they must remember what they have done in the playroom and make a report about it. With some parents, it can also be helpful to discuss the years of training it has taken for you to learn how to gain meaning from children's behavior in the playroom.

The following is an example of how you might suggest to parents that they avoid asking children about the specifics of a session:

"I usually ask parents to avoid asking kids a lot of questions about a session after the session is over. I have found that kids don't usually remember a lot of specific details about what happened. Kids who are trying to concentrate on remembering exactly what happened so they can tell their parents don't really play the way they would otherwise, which can slow the process down."

Notice that I have phrased these requests in general terms—describing what I usually say to "parents." This practice tends to defuse potentially negative reactions from parents in response to this suggestion. It is difficult for parents to feel defensive when you are simply explaining your usual procedures (which, of course, also apply to them).

Confidentiality. Sometime during this discussion, it is essential that the therapist explain to the parents the child's right to confidentiality. This is a difficult concept to present on two different fronts. First of all, it may be hard to explain why it is important for a child to have privacy if all he or she is doing is playing. It sometimes helps to repeat the explanation that play is equivalent to adult conversation and to equate the child's desire for privacy about the specific details of play with the parents' desire for privacy about their conversations.

The other difficulty in explaining confidentiality in play therapy is the conflict between ethical guidelines and legal issues. Although professional codes of ethics clearly state that the therapist's first duty is to the client and that the client has the right to confidentiality (except in cases of clear and eminent danger to self or others, child abuse, or a court order), the legal system in the United States does not recognize children as having the right to privacy. The therapist must balance the parents' legal right to know what is happening in their child's life so as to make appropriate decisions with the child's ethical right to preserve his or her confidentiality.

I believe that it is important for children to feel that they can trust me not to tell their parents everything that transpires in the playroom so that they can play out what they need to play out. However, I also believe that parents need to understand what is going on with their children to be able to help them.

The following is an example of one method of explaining confidentiality to parents:

"I won't be reporting everything that Nancy does or says in the playroom to you, but I will talk to you about themes and patterns I see in the playroom. I will also try to use my understanding of Nancy and the situation to help you learn new ways of thinking about her and her behaviors, attitudes, and motivation. I will use the information I gather in the playroom from the play and from my interaction with Nancy to make suggestions about ways you can help and support her. I may also think up some ideas for helping solve problems more smoothly in the family."

On the basis of observations in the playroom, the therapist can ask questions about how the child behaves in specific situations at home. Because a child's behavior is usually relatively consistent across situations and settings, parents' reports about behavior at home can serve as a basis for making suggestions or revealing information about the child without going into detail about interactions in the playroom.

The following is an example of how to use information gathered in the playroom to ask questions about how the child behaves at home:

Jadzia is a child who seems to thrive on power struggles. She often gets into power struggles with the therapist in the playroom and frequently acts out power struggles with the animal families and the dolls. Instead of describing this playroom behavior to her mother, the therapist could ask, "How do things go at home when Jadzia does not get her way?" As Jadzia's mother describes her behavior, the therapist can make guesses about what is going on and suggestions for different ways of handling the power struggles on the basis of observations of and interactions with Jadzia in the playroom without revealing anything that happened in a therapy session.

Explanation handout/introductory book. Even when the therapist explains all of these aspects of play therapy to parents (sometimes on the telephone before the first session and then again in the first session), some misconceptions may still persist. To help eliminate as many of these misconceptions as possible, it can be useful to have a brief handout explaining the play therapy process and any requests you have about how you would like parents to handle the practical aspects of the play therapy process. There is an example of such a handout in Appendix B.

I also loan parents *A Child's First Book About Play Therapy* (Nemiroff & Annunziata, 1990) and ask them to read it to their child before the child's first session. This book gives a clear and concrete explanation of what play therapy is, and reading it seems to help clarify the play therapy process for both children and adults.

Therapeutic goals. Depending on your approach to play therapy, you may also want to come to a consensus with the parents about therapeutic goals for the child. As you do this, you will need to clarify what exactly play therapy can and cannot do for the child. It is important to try to work with parents on generating realistic, concrete, and appropriate goals for change. One helpful method to facilitate this discussion is to ask parents, "How will we know when we are done? What will need to happen (with the child, with the family, at school, and so forth) before we can begin to terminate the sessions?"

Roles and responsibilities. You may also want to define the roles and responsibilities of the various people involved in the change process. It is helpful to discuss your role and the role of the child. If you expect parents to participate in the process, it is appropriate to discuss the specifics of their participation during your first session with them. You will need to tell them how often you will want them to come to sessions, what you will discuss in your sessions with them, and what you will expect of them in terms of making specific changes in their own behaviors and interactions with the child. If you want other people in the family (siblings, grandparents, stepparents, etc.) to be involved in the process, you should explain the details of their involvement as well.

Information about insurance and managed health care. If you are working with managed health care companies or insurance companies, parents should understand the procedures and risks involved with this process. It is important for you to explain that their child will have to have a mental health diagnosis to qualify for services. You might also wish to explain to them any potential risks you see in having such a diagnosis on record.

Once the parents have given permission to the therapist to release information to the insurance company or managed health care organization, employees of these companies can ask any number of probing questions about what happened in sessions and the backgrounds of various family members with impunity. You must explain all of this to the parents—that when they file a claim and sign a release they have waived their rights and the rights of their child to privacy.

Other important information. I find it helpful to explain my theoretical orientation and the way I work with children. I talk to parents about my basic beliefs about people, and I describe how I conceptualize problems. I give them a "tour" of my playroom, and I briefly discuss a "typical" play therapy session—what a child might do and say and what I might do and say.

I also tell parents that many children in play therapy get worse before they get better. Because things are changing and change is frightening, quite frequently children escalate whatever negative behavior they were manifesting before they started in therapy, or they invent new ways to maintain the status quo. In alerting parents to this possibility, I make some suggestions for how to handle potential problems, and I try to normalize any negative reactions in their child. With children who do get worse, I have helped the parents acquire tools for dealing with problems, and I have established some credibility as being a person who knows what she is doing. With children who do not get worse, this warning makes me look like a wonderful therapist and the child look like a miracle child who responds positively to the therapy process much more quickly than other children. Neither of these perceptions will hurt your relationship with parents.

Professional disclosure statement. You might want to consider providing parents or guardians with a professional disclosure statement during the first session. According to James (1997), such a statement should contain information about (a) the orientation of the therapist related to theory and techniques, (b) the therapist's credentials and training, (c) personal bias on the part of the therapist that might have an impact on the course of the relationship with the child or any other family member (e.g., if the therapist is a "Christian therapist" or a "feminist therapist"), (d) the fee schedule and policies for missed sessions, (e) the abrogation of confidentiality when a third-party payer (e.g., an insurance company) is involved, (f) procedures for after-hours contact, (g) the limits of the client–therapist relationship, and (h) procedures for reporting violations of clients' rights.

To Children

Explaining the play therapy process to children is more dependent on the theoretical orientation of the therapist than explaining the process to parents. In most nondirective approaches to play therapy, the therapist keeps the explanation of the play therapy process and confidentiality to a minimum. The play therapy process is usually described in a short statement at the beginning of the initial session (e.g., "This is the playroom, and in here, you can play in many of the ways you want to play."). In explaining confidentiality, most nondirective play therapists make a comment like, "I will not tell your parents what you do or say in the playroom unless you tell me that someone is hurting you or that you might hurt yourself or someone else."

In some of the more directive approaches, the therapist may give a detailed description of the play therapy process to the child. For instance, I concretely describe my role and the process (e.g., "I work with a lot of different children. Sometimes I will get to decide what we are going to do, and sometimes you will get to decide what we are going to do. Some days we will play, some days we will draw and do artwork, some days we will talk, and some days we do a couple of these things."). I also explain logistical details to the child (when sessions are scheduled, how often the child will come, how long each session lasts, parent consultation, and confidentiality).

However, in other directive approaches to play therapy, the therapist does not give any explanation of the process at all. For instance, in Theraplay, the therapist just begins the session and immediately involves the child without describing what is going to happen or why (Jernberg, 1979). The initial session would begin with the therapist making an announcement such as, "I am Barbara. I am really excited because you and I are going to hop down the hall together. Let's go."

Your Personal Application

As you decide what you believe is important to discuss with parents and with children, it might help you clarify your thoughts if you make two separate lists—one for parents and one for children. Once you have made the two lists, you will need to plan strategies for conveying this information in a way that is clear and developmentally appropriate. If you can make the process of play therapy sound useful, interesting, nonthreatening, and fun, parents and children will be more likely to want to be involved. It is also important to strike a balance between giving your clients so much information that they feel overwhelmed and giving them so little information that they feel lost.

The Initial Session

It is important to remember that very few children wake up one day and think to themselves, "I need to go see a therapist!" Your first meeting with the child and the initial session of play therapy set the tone for all the other sessions. From the very second you meet the child, you will want to communicate that (even though he or she may not have wanted to come and may not really understand what is going to happen) this is going to be a fun and exciting process. I find it helpful to do this in a way that reveals some of my personality and the way I do therapy.

When I introduce myself to the child, I greet the child by name, making sure to get down on his or her eye level; establish eye contact; and smile. I tell the child my name and describe very briefly the nature of play therapy. When I sense the child is ready to go, I suggest we go into the playroom. For example, I might say, "Hi, Zack. My name is Terry, and I am glad you're here. I am the one who is going to be with you in the playroom. We will have a lot of fun. Let's go in and see the playroom. Your grandmother will be waiting for you right here when we are done." If the child is unwilling to go with me, I usually request that the parent or guardian accompany us to the playroom by saying something like, "Grandma, would you like to come to the playroom with us to scope it out so that Zack can show you all the neat things in there?"

With children who are still reluctant, you may choose to ask the parent to stay and watch part of the session until the child feels safe and secure enough to stay in the playroom without the parent. However, you will eventually want to have the parent leave the room—either to go back to the waiting room or to sit in the hall outside the door.

It is essential to avoid stating the invitation to the playroom as a question (e.g., "Are you ready to do to the playroom?" or "Do you want to go back to my office now?"), because this is a trap for both you and the child. If you use a question instead of a statement, you imply that the child has a choice. With a child who answers that he or she does not want to go to the playroom, you will be forced to either honor that choice or communicate (by insisting on going to the playroom) that you do not really care about what the child wants.

To avoid getting into a power struggle or exacerbating a child's anxiety, I have found that it is helpful to observe the child and his or her reactions to my greeting and adjust the timing and phrasing of my invitation to the playroom accordingly. With children who avoid eye contact and move closer to their parents as I greet them, I may remain sitting on the floor beside them and initiate some play activities in the waiting room rather than prematurely suggesting that we venture to the playroom. Some children just need time to get used to me before they are willing to walk into some unknown territory with me, so I may sit down and draw pictures for them or tell them a funny story, show them the rainbow shoelaces on my sneakers or a pair of mismatched funny earrings I am wearing, or make a comment about something they are wearing. The whole purpose of this interaction is to build rapport with the child so that he or she can feel comfortable enough with me and who I am to take a risk and come with me to visit "our" playroom.

After entering the playroom, sometime during that first session, the therapist will give an explanation of the play therapy process and continue to establish a relationship with the child. In most approaches to play therapy, the therapist uses tracking, restatement of content, and reflection of feelings (see chapters 5, 6, and 7, respectively) during that initial session to gently begin building rapport and conveying the idea that the playroom is a safe place for the child. The therapist may want to describe the layout of the playroom and provide any information the child will need to know about the session or the office (the location of the bathroom, how to close blinds for more privacy, etc.).

There are many different ways the first session can unfold. Usually, however, the child will want to explore the toys and the therapist. This exploration may involve touching, picking up, and putting down the various contents of the playroom; giving very brief puppet shows; standing still and looking around the room; interrogating the therapist about his or her life; or using assorted other strategies for making contact with a place and a person.

In most approaches to play therapy, your primary job during this time is to convey acceptance and warmth, without trying too hard to "bond" with the child. Patience is a real key in the first session, even with a child who is eager, willing, and excited to be in the playroom. Most play therapists (except those who are very directive) try avoid communicating, even unintentionally, that the child "should" play or talk to them. To ensure that you do not do this, avoid making comments like, "There are a lot of things to do in here," "You might want to check out the sandbox," or "Most kids really like playing with the dart guns." If you cannot think of anything particularly helpful to say, it is better to smile warmly, make lots of eye contact, and say nothing at all.

Ending a Session

The primary decision for the therapist to make concerning the procedure for ending play therapy sessions is whether to have the child participate in picking up the toys. There are two distinct positions on this, which can be represented by the client-centered perspective (Axline, 1969) and the Adlerian perspective (Kottman, 1995). Axline believed that it is detrimental to the child to have to help clean up the room because this would be the equivalent of asking an adult to "clean up" his or her words. Kottman suggested that, when the therapist and the child collaborate in putting away the toys, it can be potentially helpful to the therapeutic relationship. For each of these two approaches, there is a standard procedure for the end of a session.

Therapist Cleans the Room

If you decide that you do not wish to engage the child in the picking-up process, 5 minutes before the time for the session expires, you can make an announcement that sounds something like this: "In 5 minutes, our time together will be over, and it will be time for us to leave the playroom." When the time is over, you will say, "All right. Our time is up for today."

Therapist and Child Clean the Room Together

If you decide to work collaboratively with the child to pick up the toys, 10 minutes before the end of the session, you will announce to the child, "In 5 minutes, it will time for us to pick up the room together." When there are 5 minutes left in the session, you will stand up and say something like, "It is time for us to pick up the room together. What do you want me to pick up, and what are you going to pick up?" The child is then in charge of delegating the clean-up process.

Most children are perfectly willing to work with the therapist to clean up the room. Some children are a little resistant, and the therapist may need to make the procedure more fun by making the picking-up time into a cooperative game (e.g., a race against the clock) or a competitive game (e.g., a race against one another). When this happens, it is important for the therapist to consider the reason for the child's reluctant behavior.

In the rare event that children choose not to participate in the picking-up process, I follow several steps for setting up logical consequences (Kottman, 1995).

1. I tell the child in a friendly, neutral voice, "If you choose not to help pick up, you choose not to be in this playroom (or have all of these toys) next session."
2. If the child continues to choose not to collaborate, I say in a friendly, neutral voice, "Okay, since you choose not to participate in picking up the toys, next time we will have only a couple of toys that I will choose for us." At this point, even the most resistant children usually decide to participate in the clean-up process.
3. However, for those who do decide not to collaborate on picking up, I follow through in the next session by either moving the location of the therapy and bringing several toys chosen from the playroom or getting rid of most of the toys in the playroom. Again, this is done in a friendly, affective tone to avoid the appearance of setting up a punishment for noncompliance.

There are some children and some situations for which this strategy is contraindicated (Kottman, 1995). With children who are overanxious or overresponsible, the opportunity to participate in making a mess they do not have to help clean up can be very freeing. With children who have power and control issues, asking them to collaborate on any task could be counterproductive to the therapeutic relationship. If the presenting problem is related to messiness or room cleaning, sometimes it is wiser not to replicate an already established power struggle in the playroom. Children with ADHD may feel overwhelmed in a playroom filled with toys, and they sometimes opt out of that setting by choosing not to help clean up. In my clinical practice, children with ADHD are the only ones who have repeatedly chosen to avoid participating in cleaning up. Children such as these should be moved to a more spartan location before they need to resort to this strategy.

Handling Children Who Do Not Wish to Leave the Room

Most children will follow the standard procedure for leaving the room. However, there are some who are reluctant to leave the session, and a strategy for moving them out of the room is essential. Most of the time, simply reflecting their feelings about wanting to stay in the playroom or making a guess about the purpose of their behavior is enough to get them moving. Sometimes, you may have to take more drastic measures, such as turning off the light, asking their parents to remove them, taking their arm and escorting them out, and so forth. You should consider your stance on using physical measures to help children exit the playroom and your stance on involving parents in this process before you work directly with children in a play therapy situation. It would also be helpful to have a plan for how you want to handle such a situation if it occurs.

Assessing Patterns in the Child's Play

During the first session and in all subsequent sessions, the therapist observes the child's play behavior, attitudes, and verbalizations to help understand the child's personality and assess difficulties related to the presenting problem and any other factors involved in the child's coming to play therapy. Although the interpretation of the meaning of the child's behavior, attitudes, and verbalizations will depend, to an extent, on the therapist's theoretical orientation, play therapists should consider the following factors in their work with children.

Differences Between the Child's Behavior With the Therapist and With the Parents

If the child has more appropriate behavior and attitudes with the therapist than with his or her parents, it may indicate that there are problems in the relationship between the child and the parents. The therapist should consider whether family therapy, parent training, or filial therapy training should be recommended in addition to play therapy.

Differences Between the Child in the Playroom and the Parent Description of the Child

Some parents tend to exaggerate the child's difficulties, whereas other parents downplay any problems the child may be experiencing. Parents often seem to be so focused on the problem that they may not be able to acknowledge the child's positive qualities. If there is a wide gap between the parents' description of the child and the therapist's observation of the child, it is important to also explore the underlying dynamics of the parent–child interaction. In some instances, the discrepancy may be due to the fact that the child's difficulty is manifested only in a particular setting—such as at home, on the playground, or in the classroom. When this is the case, the therapist will want to learn more about the interactions and relationships in that setting.

How the Child Plays Out the Presenting Problem and Other Significant Concerns

By the time the child enters the playroom, the therapist will have already heard at least one version of the presenting problem—usually from the adult who has decided that the child needs counseling. The therapist can get insight into the child's concerns by observing the play and the child's interaction with the therapist.

You could learn about how Arturo views his parents' impending divorce by watching how he plays with the dollhouse and the doll family. He may set up two separate houses and have the doll children running back and forth between the two, crying. He might set up two houses and have the doll children refuse to enter one of them. He might have the doll children freely move between the houses, expressing relief that their parents are not fighting any-

more. All three of these possible scenarios would indicate differences in the way Arturo is reacting to the divorce.

Many times, the child does not view the presenting problem as an impediment. He or she may be struggling more with some other difficulty that the parents do not view as significant. When this is the case, these themes frequently get played out in the play.

Tito's mother brings him to counseling because she thinks that he is depressed and feeling displaced because of the birth of his baby brother. However, if Tito plays happily with the baby doll in a very nurturing way, the therapist might decide his problems lie elsewhere, especially if he also plays with a small puppet who is "being picked on by a gang of other puppets who live close by in the forest. They don't like him because he has to use crutches to walk."

How the Child Talks About the Presenting Problem and Other Significant Concerns

By listening carefully to the child's tone of voice and what the child says, the therapist can frequently discern how the child feels about specific relationships, situations, or issues. It is important to notice if the child has an overly vehement reaction to discussions about specific topics or if the child tends to discount the severity of a problem or a situation. When a child brings up the presenting problem in a rather stilted manner, without having an obvious reason for initiating the discussion, it may mean that his or her parents suggested that he or she should discuss the topic with the play therapist.

At times, the child may also bring up a topic and then change the subject or refuse to discuss it further. Although there are a myriad of possible explanations for this behavior, the therapist must consider that the topic is too painful or embarrassing for the child to discuss directly or that someone has told the child not to discuss the topic.

A child will often repeatedly bring up a topic unrelated to the presenting problem that seems to be causing him or her distress. The play therapist must be aware of this and try to facilitate a discussion about that topic. If the child initiates a discussion only once and does not demonstrate much negative affect associated with the topic, it is probably not essential to pursue it. When a problem situation or relationship is truly bothering a child, he or she will almost always find a way to bring it up repeatedly over a period of time.

Repetitive Play That Seems to Upset, Rather Than Sooth, the Child

Children frequently repeat play sequences in therapy, and this is not usually a problem. By repeating a scenario, a child can often resolve negative feelings connected to a traumatic experience. Repetitive play can also be useful in generating and practicing different responses to troublesome situations or relationships and in helping a child gain a sense of mastery over specific experiences. When repetitive play is serving a therapeutic function for the child, he or she will seem comforted or satisfied at the end of the play.

There are times, however, when a child seems to be agitated or retraumatized by repetitive play. This type of repetitive play is called posttraumatic play (Terr, 1983, 1990) and is not therapeutic for the child. It is important for the play therapist to take note of specific scenarios that a child repeats in a single session or over a series of sessions and to pay close attention to the child's reaction at the end of the play (Gil, 1991). When this happens, it is important for the play therapist to help the child break out of the posttraumatic play and replace it with play that is self-nurturing. Gil (1991) provided many valuable suggestions for helping children with this process.

Level of Aggression and Challenge to the Authority of the Play Therapist

Behaviors in this category would include (a) repeated defiant responses to limiting, (b) attempts at physical or verbal aggression toward the therapist, (c) violent use of toys (e.g., punching, kicking, or slamming), and (d) violent themes in the play (e.g., murder, mayhem, or torture). To determine if the level of aggression and challenge to authority is within the "normal" range, it is helpful to compare each child's pattern of aggression with that of other children who come to play therapy. It is also helpful to consider the purpose of the behavior for this particular child. Some children have witnessed and/or experienced a great deal of violence and may not have learned other ways to interact with the environment. Other children are simply testing limits to see how the therapist will respond. Other children feel that this is a setting in which they can safely express their true feelings, including rage, which may not be accepted in other settings. If the therapist believes that this behavior is therapeutic in some way for the child, even if it is out-

side the normal range, it is probably appropriate to let the behavior continue as long as there is no danger to the child, the therapist, or the playroom.

However, there are many times when this behavior seems to be exacerbating the child's problems by sanctioning behavior that would be deemed
unacceptable in most settings. This frequently seems to be the case with
children diagnosed as having conduct disorder or oppositional defiant disorder. Their "venting" may just increase their hostility and aggression, rather
than serving an abreactive or cathartic function. If the therapist feels consistently that he or she, the child, or the playroom is at risk or that the
behavior is not therapeutic and cannot be redirected, it may be appropriate
to terminate play therapy sessions and try some other form of intervention.

Desire for Secrecy or Privacy

There are children who manifest behavior in the playroom that suggests a
strong need for secrecy or privacy. This behavior may involve a pattern of
hiding themselves or building barriers between themselves and the therapist.
It may also involve hiding or burying toys. Some children tell the therapist
that they have a secret or that there are things they cannot discuss. There are
several common interpretations of this behavior. Some children manifest
this behavior because they believe they have something to hide or something
they think is too shameful to share with others (e.g., children who experience abuse or encopresis). For other children, this behavior suggests that
they live in an environment in which they do not feel that they have access
to privacy (e.g., children who live in crowded quarters or whose parents are
enmeshed or intrusive). Some children use these behaviors as a way of assert-
ing control over the course of the play therapy session (e.g., children who
want to hide and have the therapist find them).

Overtly Sexual Play, Artwork, or Verbalizations

These behaviors would include sexually explicit (a) acts by the child (e.g.,
"humping" the therapist's leg); (b) acts by the toys (e.g., the child places a
boy doll on top of a girl doll and moves their pelvic regions together in a
rhythmic manner); (c) drawings, paintings, or clay sculptures (e.g., drawings
with exaggerated genitals); or (d) suggestions or comments by the child
(e.g., asking whether the therapist wants to "get sexed"). Blatantly sexual
behavior may indicate that the child has experienced sexual abuse or wit-

nessed sexually explicit material or activities. However, this is not always the case. Some children are simply exploring sexuality or newly acquired information about sex through their play. It is essential to further explore the origins of this behavior and the possibility that the child has been abused, but it is also imperative to consider the child's developmental level and to watch for patterns or repeated occurrences of this kind of behavior to accurately interpret the meaning of this play.

Level of Anxiety

The therapist must assess children's anxiety over time to determine if anxiety is chronic and part of the overall problem or just a temporary reaction. Most children manifest at least some nervousness during the first session or two of play therapy. Anxiety is frequently demonstrated in opposite extremes of behavior. Anxious children may not make eye contact with the therapist, or they may stare constantly at the therapist; they may stand very close to the therapist and not venture into other parts of the room, or they may wander aimlessly; or they may constantly chatter or not utter a word. These are all normal reactions to being in a new situation in which the rules and requirements are not immediately clear. By the third or fourth session, most children seem to relax and enter into the play with enthusiasm. With children who continue to express high levels of nervousness and inhibition after the initial adjustment, the therapist may wish to assess the level of anxiety they manifest in other situations to determine whether chronic anxiety is contributing to their difficulties.

Willingness to Take Risks

The therapist must also assess children's willingness to take risks. I find it easiest to think about this factor on a continuum ranging from children who take too few risks to children who take too many risks. Children who take too few risks are afraid of making a mistake or of being a failure. Their unwillingness to take risks inhibits their acquisition of new skills and development of self-confidence. In the playroom, these children are reluctant to try new behaviors and may refuse to engage in any kind of play that could result in them experiencing less than perfect performance (which they would classify as failure). They typically play with blocks, sand, or other easy play materials, refusing to explore more dangerous materials. These children ask for direction and reassurance to an unusual degree—they are unwilling to make any decision for themselves. Behavior that fits into this extreme of the continuum may be an indicator of high levels of anxiety or tendencies toward maladaptive perfectionism.

Some children take too many risks because they are not afraid of anything. These children can be a danger to self and others because they do not consider the consequences of their actions. In the playroom, they may climb on top of shelves or precariously stack a pile of toys. They tend not to anticipate potential negative consequences and may be extremely impulsive. Behavior that fits into this extreme of the continuum may be an indicator of ADHD.

Level of Activity

The therapist should also be noticing children's activity level over time. Although it is not unusual for children's energy level to ebb and flow during a session and across sessions, it is important to note extremes. Children with consistently elevated levels of activity are those who cannot stop moving about the playroom. They may chatter at the same time they are moving. Some of these children seem to feel overwhelmed in playrooms with a lot of toys. There is a good chance that these children either are highly anxious or are manifesting symptoms of ADHD.

Children with consistently depressed levels of anxiety are those who move very little. They may not talk at all during entire sessions. These children may be so anxious about making a mistake that they would rather not do anything at all. They may also be manifesting symptoms of depression or thyroid problems, both of which warrant a referral to a physician.

Desire for Order and Structure

Children who have a strong desire for order and structure usually do a lot of sorting and tidying up in the playroom. They may also ask the therapist for more guidance than other children usually do. With nondirective therapists, these children may purposely violate rules to get the therapist to provide more structure for them. There are two rather contradictory basic interpretations of this behavior. Many of these children live chaotic lives in which they frequently feel out of control. Sorting toys into categories and putting play materials into the "correct" location on the shelves in the playroom provides them with a sense of orderliness and consistency that is missing from their lives. Other children who manifest this kind of behavior live in families in which age-inappropriate order and structure are demanded of them. With these children, the sorting and tidying is usually accompanied by a certain level of worry about the consequences of disorder—they are afraid that they will get into trouble if they do not impose order on the relative chaos of the playroom.

Desire for Power and Control

A large percentage of children referred for play therapy have a strong desire for power and control—either over themselves or over others. By watching children interact with other family members, watching the scenes they act out with puppets and dolls, and watching children's reactions to limits, the therapist can assess their desire for power and control. Children who have an elevated need for control strive mightily to avoid compliance with anyone else's rules. They like to boss other family members, classmates, teachers, and the therapist, and when they play out scenes in the playroom, there is always one puppet or doll who is clearly "in charge" of everything and everyone. I believe that this behavior is manifested in children who have (a) too much power in their interactions with others; (b) too little power in their interactions with others; or (c) chaotic, out-of-control families (Kottman, 1995).

Metaphors That Express the Child's View of Self, Others, and the World

In play therapy, the communication is frequently couched in metaphor. It is important to notice patterns in the metaphors that the child uses consistently to represent himself or herself, other people (allies and foes) in his or her life, situations that may be troublesome, and his or her worldview. If the therapist can use the child's own metaphors to communicate, the child will be more accepting of the messages that the therapist wishes to convey.

Developmental Issues

When working with children, it is always imperative for the therapist to consider the child's developmental level. There are many behaviors that would be perfectly acceptable at one age but inappropriate at another age. The therapist must consider whether there is a gap between the child's chronological age and developmental age. Some possible explanations for an overall developmental delay could involve (a) child neglect, which can prevent the child from getting the stimulation necessary for proper development; (b) trauma, resulting in the child being "stuck" at a certain age; or (c) neurological problems that prevent age-appropriate levels of maturity. For instance, if Hillary is 3 or 4 years old and talks "baby talk," this is not particularly unusual. However, if she is 10 years old, this could present social problems and might be an indicator of other difficulties, such as a developmental delay or regression. Sometimes the child's overall development is within the normal range, but there are certain areas that seem to be delayed. An example of this would be Howard, a 10-year-old who is age appropriate in every way in the playroom, except that he grabs a baby bottle and starts sucking on it every time the therapist mentions his grandfather. When this is the case, the therapist needs to explore the child's history and current circumstances to determine the cause of the delay in that particular area.

I have listed many of the elements that I assess as I work with a child. I try to communicate to parents my understanding of these factors and what they mean in that particular child's life, along with a formal diagnosis in situations in which it is necessary. I base my therapeutic goals on my assessment of the child's personality, presenting problem, other situations or relationships that might be troubling to the child, and the child's strengths. I also use my assessment of these facets of the child to plan my interventions. These are certainly not the only factors to consider in assessing children and their behavior. Other play therapists may consider these and a wide variety of diverse factors in their assessment of children and their issues.

Writing Session Reports

Depending on the work setting, most play therapists keep a record of each play therapy session. There are multiple purposes for writing reports of therapy sessions. The therapist can use this record (a) to document what happened between the therapist and the client and between the client and the toys; (b) to facilitate recognition of patterns or themes across sessions; (c) to refresh his or her memory of what went on in the previous session or sessions with a particular client before the beginning of a session; (d) to track changes in behavior, feelings, thoughts, and attitudes; or (e) to provide documentation for insurance companies or court cases.

It is generally helpful to include demographic data such as the date of the session, the therapist's name, the child's name, the parents' names, the child's date of birth and age, the number of the session, the child's physician's name, a list of who was present during the session, and a list of medications the child is taking. Other information that might be helpful is the therapist's assessment (usually using a numerical scale or several word descriptors) of any situational stressor the child is experiencing and a subjective assessment of the child's mood during the session. The therapist may also want to make note of the sequence of toys the child used during a session, what the child did with the toys, verbalizations the child made during the session, limits that were set, and the child's reaction to the limits. It can be helpful to record any themes or patterns in play or verbalizations observed during the session or across several sessions. If there is a change in the child's behavior—which might include the child doing something he or she has never done, a shift in intensity of the child's play or verbalizations, or the discontinuation of play that had occurred several times—the therapist should note this change. Depending on the play therapist's theoretical approach, both short-term and long-term goals for the child and a concrete plan for how to meet those goals should also be incorporated in the record. If the therapist works with parents on a regular basis, it is important to have a space on the form to record parent interactions.

There are some play therapists who restrict their notes to objective information—who, what, when, where, and how, recording as little as possible in the way of personal opinion or professional speculation. Other therapists include much more detailed information and may range into theories about the underlying causes and factors in the child's problem. This practice is more risky because it is not data-based. If you have to testify in court or make a case for your treatment with a third-party payer, you will need to explain and justify your thoughts and speculations in a court of law or to third-party payers (Mitchell, 2001).

Termination

There are many issues related to termination in play therapy. These include consideration of (a) when to terminate, (b) who makes the termination decision, (c) how to handle the termination process, and (d) how the child will react to the termination.

When to Terminate

In deciding when to terminate therapy, the therapist should consider factors related to the presenting problem and to the child's behavior in the play therapy sessions. The therapist is looking for positive changes in both of these areas.

The primary question related to the presenting problem is "Have the child's attitudes, relationships, and/or behaviors at home or school that were creating difficulties changed in a positive direction?" This question can be answered through reports from family members or teachers. The therapist can also solicit self-reports from the child about the presenting problem. Frequently, the child may volunteer comments like, "I don't need to come here anymore. I get along a lot better with my family now." Another helpful informal assessment involves observation of the child's behavior with family members in the waiting room or in family sessions in the playroom and/or with teachers and classmates in the school.

To determine whether it is time to terminate, it is helpful to compare the child's current functioning with the child's initial functioning. The therapist would be looking for general changes in the playroom in the following areas: (a) dependence on the therapist; (b) confusion; (c) ability to directly express needs; (d) ability to focus on self; (e) acceptance of responsibility for personal actions and feelings; (f) self-monitoring and self-control; (g) flexibility; (h) tolerance of situations, self, and others; (i) initiation of activities; (j) manifestation of cooperation, but not conformity; (k) appropriate expression of anger; (l) movement away from negative–sad affect toward positive–happy affect; (m) level of self-acceptance; and (n) shift in play so that play has direction (Landreth, 1991).

Other therapists look for indications of a change in the intensity of sessions and the willingness of children to productively use the sessions. Children may ask to have fewer sessions, they may skip several sessions without valid excuses, or they may express an interest in being someplace else. They may also act bored, complain that the playroom does not interest them anymore, or ask to bring in friends or siblings to play.

Who Makes the Termination Decision

There seems to be no consensus among the approaches to therapy about who makes the decision to terminate therapy. Obviously, the therapist should be a key person in the decision, but sometimes the therapist is excluded from the decision making (e.g., when parents decide to pull a child out of therapy or when the managed health care company will not grant additional sessions). Ideally, the therapist should always collaborate with the child and the parents in making the decision to terminate, with additional input (when appropriate) from teachers, siblings, grandparents, and other interested parties.

How to Handle the Termination Process

Most therapists start the procedure by bringing up the idea with the parents and the child at least several weeks before they actually wish to terminate. This allows time for a discussion about whether all parties agree that the child is ready and allows time to prepare the child in advance for the eventuality of the final session. After coming to a consensus that the child is ready for termination, most therapists begin a kind of countdown toward termination, reminding the child each week that there are *X* number of sessions left. It is important to include a time for processing the child's feelings about terminating in those last few sessions. It is also frequently helpful to let the child know how to go about contacting the play therapist if he or she feels a need to resume sessions or to communicate about a specific situation.

Many play therapists develop rituals as a way of handling the termination process. Some therapists have a session in which they sit down with the child and look through all of the artwork that the child has created during their relationship. Other therapists use the last session as an opportunity for a party or some other celebration of the child's progress. Many therapists give the child a small gift or work on a final project with the child so that the child will have a tangible reminder of the therapy process.

It may also be important to prepare the family to take on some of the functions performed by the therapist. For example, filial therapists (B. Guerney, 1964; L. Guerney, 1997) may train parents to use nondirective play therapy techniques with their children at home.

Child Reactions to the Termination Decision

If the decision to terminate is appropriately made, the child's reaction should be predominantly positive. However, because there will undoubtedly be a certain amount of anxiety and sadness about the ending of a relationship that has been very important to the child, he or she may also express some negative feelings. The therapist must be alert to the whole gamut of feelings and convey empathy and acceptance to all of the emotions expressed by the child.

If the decision to terminate is made prematurely, the child will probably express anger and hostility in addition to anxiety and sadness. One way to tell if this is the case is to watch for the ambivalence that is usually expressed by children who are ready for termination. If the ambivalence is absent and the child expresses only negative feelings about the termination, it may be appropriate to reopen the discussion about whether to end therapy.

Most children use the last several sessions of therapy to recapitulate many of the play therapy themes from earlier sessions. If, after the decision to terminate, children go back to old patterns (both at home or school and in the playroom), they may seem to be regressing. This behavior is perfectly normal as long as it does not last for a prolonged period of time. Recapitulation becomes regression, however, if it is pervasive and lasts for more than 4 to 6 weeks. It is important to warn parents and teachers of the tendency for children to go back to earlier patterns in behavior and interactional patterns so that they do not overreact. By helping parents and teachers generate a plan for dealing with such an eventuality, the therapist can help them feel prepared to cope effectively.

Questions to Ponder

1. What do you think will be your top three priorities among all of the specifications for designing a playroom listed by Landreth?
2. What are some factors (either from the list by Landreth or other elements you think are important) you might want to adjust in your play

therapy setting so that the space will fit your style of interacting with children and their families?

3. Do you think you will prefer a large, empty, open space for your play therapy setting or a room with shelves and furniture? Explain.

4. What is your reaction to the suggestion that toys should go back to approximately the same place at the end of every session? Explain your reasoning.

5. Do you think you will probably tend toward letting children choose toys from a wide selection or toward bringing in toys and materials selected for that particular child on that particular day? Explain your reasoning.

6. Are there certain categories of toys you think will be essential in play therapy? If not, why? If yes, what are they, and why do you think they will be essential?

7. Are there certain categories of toys you will not want to have in your playroom? If so, explain your reasoning.

8. What information do you think is essential to communicate with parents about the process of play therapy? Why is that information essential?

9. What information do you think is essential to communicate with children about the process of play therapy? Why is that information essential?

10. How do you think you will deal with the potential conflict between parents' legal right to know exactly what goes on in the play therapy session and children's ethical right to confidentiality?

11. How will you explain confidentiality to parents? To children?

12. How do you plan to introduce children to the playroom and the play therapy process?

13. How do you plan to deal with children who are reluctant to go to your play therapy setting?

14. What is your stance on cleaning up the playroom together at the end of a session? Explain your reasoning.

15. How do you plan to deal with children who are reluctant to leave the playroom?

16. In making decisions about termination, which of the two main factors do you think is most important: progress on the presenting problem or behavior in the playroom? Explain.

17. Who do you think should be involved in the termination decision? Explain your reasoning.

18. How do you think you will handle the situation if everyone (including you) but the child believes the child is ready for termination?

19. What thoughts do you have about the way you would like to handle termination? (For instance, will you have some kind of special interaction, or will you just have a standard countdown?) If you are going to have a special interaction, what are your ideas about that process?

20. How can you prepare yourself for termination with a child?

Chapter 5

Tracking

Tracking is one of the basic skills used in most approaches to play therapy (Kottman, 1995, 1997a; Landreth & Sweeney, 1997). When the therapist tracks, he or she describes, in a literal, noninterpretive way, what is happening in the playroom (either what the child is doing or what the play objects are "doing").

The purpose of tracking is to let the child know that the therapist is paying attention to what he or she is doing and that the communication in the play is important to the therapist (Kottman, 1995, 1997a; Landreth & Sweeney, 1997). This skill is one method of building a relationship with the child. Although there is no direct parallel in adult therapy to tracking, it serves the same purpose as paraphrasing in adult therapy.

How to Track

There are two different approaches to tracking—the therapist can track what the client is doing or what the play objects are doing. By tracking the client, the therapist concretely describes what he or she is doing. An example of this type of tracking would be, "You picked that up." By tracking what the play objects are doing, the therapist concretely describes what they are doing. An example of this type of tracking would be, "It is moving up and down."

There is no general rule governing which method of tracking to use. In some cases, this decision stems from issues related to the therapist, and in other cases, it stems from issues related to the client. Some therapists arbitrarily mix both methods of tracking in play therapy sessions. Some therapists purposely use more tracking of play objects in early sessions and then move toward using more tracking of the child's behavior in later sessions. Others decide which method of tracking to use depending on the individual child's reaction to the intervention. Some children seem to be more resistant or defensive when the therapist tracks their behavior and more open and accepting when the tracking is focused on the play objects. These children seem to be relatively indirect in their communication with others. Other children are more responsive to tracking that involves their behavior and seem rather uninterested in tracking that focuses on play objects. These children are frequently those whose communication is direct and those who like to be the center of the therapist's attention.

You will have to decide which method best fits your style. This may be determined by your theoretical approach, your usual mode of communication, your understanding of the child, or some combination of all of these factors. You will need to think about whether you wish to have a standard method of tracking or whether you wish to vary the focus of your tracking on the basis of the reactions of individual children.

Because play therapy is a projective method of therapy, it is essential for the child to impose his or her own meaning on the objects in the playroom. To facilitate this process, when the therapist tracks, it is helpful to avoid labeling—both nouns and verbs when possible. For example, instead of saying, "The horse is running around the house," the therapist would say, "That thing is moving around." By avoiding labeling, the therapist allows the child to decide what the "horse" is, what the "house" is, what they are doing, and what their relationship is. By not labeling the nouns, the therapist encourages the child to project his or her "vision" of what these objects are. By not labeling the verbs, the therapist encourages the child to project his or her "vision" of the relationship between the objects and to decide what each of them is doing. This process may be grammatically awkward at times, but it is potentially very liberating for the client.

At times (depending on how nondirective you wish to be), you may decide to ask the child what the objects are and what they are doing. Be sure that you do this in an effort to advance the play therapy process or to increase your understanding of what the child is doing or your ability to accurately reflect the meaning of the play, rather than just to satisfy your own curiosity or to avoid grammatical awkwardness.

If the child has supplied a label for either objects or actions, it is fine for the therapist to use the child's label. However, the therapist must monitor the child's nonverbal reactions and verbal feedback to make sure that he or she is consistent with the child's current interpretation of the noun or verb. What was a bean stalk for a giant last week or even 5 minutes ago may now be a dart gun used to shoot pygmies, so the therapist must be ready to be flexible and follow the child's "vision."

Monitoring Children's Reactions to Tracking

When tracking, the therapist must watch for the child's reaction to tracking statements. Reactions from the child can take the form of direct or indirect feedback and the form of verbal or nonverbal communication. The style of reaction from the client can guide the therapist in deciding on future directions for tracking and which method of tracking will work with this particular child.

Many times, children will directly correct the therapist if the tracking response does not fit with their image of what is happening. They will make comments like, "That's not right," "Of course that carrot can't jump," or "Why would you think that was a cow?"

They may also directly correct the therapist if the tracking response is aimed in the wrong direction. When this happens—when they want the tracking to focus more on their own behaviors—they will make comments like, "Why do you always tell me what the toys are doing? I don't care what they do since I make them move anyway." When they want the tracking to focus more on the play objects and not on their own behaviors, they will make comments like, "Don't always talk about what I am doing. It's not me that makes stuff happen in here; it's the toys."

Sometimes children will let the therapist know that the tracking response is aimed in the wrong direction in more subtle, indirect ways by verbally correcting the therapist's behavior without being direct about why and what they would prefer in the way of tracking. Those children who would be more comfortable with tracking of themselves might tell the therapist to switch the focus away from the play objects with comments like, "Don't you know anything? Of course that dog didn't save the girl. I did that." or "The puppet did not pick that up. I did it." Those who would be more comfortable with tracking of play objects might tell the therapist to switch the focus away from them with comments like, "I didn't cry when that happened. The baby did." or "It wasn't me who knocked all the sand out. It was that truck over there."

Other reactions that might help the therapist gain insight into the child's response to tracking comments are nonverbal. Sometimes these reactions seem to be deliberate, thought-out responses to the therapist's comments—the child makes eye contact with the therapist and nods, stares defiantly, or throws down a toy and goes to the other side of the room to play. This feedback is a direct form of nonverbal communication. In other cases, the feedback may take an indirect form—gradually moving away from the therapist, slowly changing the focus of the play, and so forth. Indirect nonverbal feedback may also involve an involuntary nonverbal reaction, such as a shrug, a nod, or a twitch.

With some children, combined patterns of indirect verbal and nonverbal reactions can be a helpful tool for the therapist. For instance, if Jeannette, who tends to be anxious to please you, suddenly starts using the same phrases you did in describing an object or action and continually visually checks on your reaction, you may be getting too concrete in your statements, causing her to change her vision to correspond with your interpretations. If Lucille, a child who tends to be openly defiant and hostile, constantly corrects everything that you say when you track, you may want to move toward even more nonspecific and vague descriptions if possible.

You will need to pay close attention to these reactions and notice themes and patterns. The feedback you get from tracking can help you gain insight into children's thoughts and feelings and their usual mode of communication. Children who respond in a more direct fashion will usually use that style in communicating with others, whereas children who respond in a more indirect fashion will usually use that style in communicating with others.

If you plan on adjusting the focus of your tracking on the basis of children's preferences (when they have them), you will need to watch for patterns in the way they respond to tracking. That way, you can decide whether to use tracking of the child or tracking of the play objects according to the preference of the individual. Also, with children who tend to communicate directly, you may wish to tailor your interactions with them to use a more open and concrete communication style yourself, and with children who tend to communicate indirectly or nonverbally, you may wish to tailor your interactions with them to use a more subtle, metaphoric style.

Applications in Different Theoretical Orientations

Tracking is such a basic skill that it is appropriate in most approaches to play therapy. Of the contemporary experts in play therapy theory whom I surveyed about their application of play therapy techniques, only two of them (Kevin O'Connor [ecosystemic] and Violet Oaklander [Gestalt]) reported that they do not use tracking in their approach to play therapy.

There seem to be several trends in the use of tracking. With the more nondirective approaches (e.g., client-centered and Jungian), tracking is usually used throughout the play therapy process as one of the primary tools for interacting with children. Nondirective play therapists usually use tracking extensively in the initial sessions of therapy. In the middle and later sessions, they continue to use tracking as an interactional skill but with some reduction in the frequency of use. With the more directive approaches (e.g., Adlerian, cognitive–behavioral, eclectic prescriptive, and Thematic play therapy), tracking is usually used more during early sessions when the therapist is establishing a relationship with the client. As time passes, most directive therapists seem to limit tracking responses and use other skills in interacting with the client.

Eighty percent of the play therapy experts surveyed made a distinction between tracking a child's behavior and tracking the play materials or objects in the playroom. The majority of those who made this distinction tracked the child's behavior more frequently than they tracked the play materials' "behavior." The experts variously attributed their decision about the focus of tracking interventions to (a) their perceptions of the content and process of the play, (b) their perceptions of individual children, and (c) the timing of the session. There were several different elements of the child and his or her dynamics that were listed as factors in this decision: the child's style of communication, the child's level of intensity, the child's self-esteem, and the degree to which the child seemed to be in charge.

The use of tracking varied from individual to individual even among those who adhere to the same theoretical orientation. This variance may be due to a combination of individual therapeutic styles and comfort with tracking as an intervention, the individual personalities of each of the experts, differing interpretations of theory, or personal philosophies about modifying the theoretical approach to individual clients.

Examples of Tracking

After each of the following scenarios, there are several examples of possible tracking responses.

* *Heidi picks up a dog puppet, approaches the play therapist, and puts the puppet into the therapist's hand.*

1. "You're bringing that over to me."
2. "You put that on me."
3. "He came over to me."
4. "That thing is on top."

* *Jorge throws the father and mother dolls on the ground and stomps on them.*

1. "You are moving up and down on them."
2. "You put them down there and now you're moving up and down on them."
3. "Looks like they are getting squished."
4. "They are down there, and someone is moving up and down on them."

* *Sophia picks up the bigger turtle figure and puts it on the smaller turtle figure.*

1. "You put that one on top of the other."
2. "You placed that one just where you wanted it."
3. "You moved it so it is over (or under) the other one."
4. "The bigger one is on top of the little one."

5. "The smaller one is under the bigger one."

6. "One of them is over (or under) the other one."

* *Jasper points a gun at the therapist and smiles broadly at her.*

1. "You are pointing that at me."

2. "You decided where you want to point that."

3. "The gun is pointing toward me."

4. "The gun is turned in my direction."

* *Yuki lies down on the floor and piles pillows on herself.*

1. "You are under there."

2. "You put those on top of yourself."

3. "You decided to be under those things."

4. "Those things are all piled on top."

5. "They are up there."

Practice Exercises

For each of the following scenarios, write four possible tracking responses. When possible, generate two responses that track what the child is doing and two responses that track what the play objects are doing. Label which ones are directed toward the child and which ones are directed toward the play objects. [Note: Not all of the examples provide opportunities to do both types of tracking.]

1. Nazir (5) picks up a grasshopper and has it jump up and down all over the room.

2. Kathy (8) gets the mother doll and uses it to hit the baby doll.

3. Griff (4) pushes a chair around the room as if it is a wheelchair.

4. Chwan (9) puts a hat on her head and makes faces in the mirror.

5. Sam (8) throws a ball in the air for several minutes and then drops it on the floor.

6. Nancy (5) uses the wolf puppet to bite her own hand.

7. Then Nancy brings it over and starts to bite your hands and feet with it.

8. Star (6) drapes snakes all over her head, torso, arms, and legs.

9. Keshawn (7) paints stripes all over a piece of paper.

10. Esther (4) puts food in the pots and pans, cooks the food, and brings it over to you and wants to feed it to you.

11. Gunthur (8) purposely knocks over the trash can, spilling out all the trash and staring defiantly at you.

12. Sally (7) draws a picture of you, brings it over, and asks if you like it.

13. Emilio (4) picks up a book (and even though you know he doesn't know how to read) pretends to read it.

14. Candy (7) arranges the tiger family with the parents at one end of the sandbox and the children at the other end, with a wall of blocks in between them.

15. Liam (3) sits and smiles at you.

16. Deepa (6) arranges the animal figures from the largest to the smallest.

17. Rick (8) puts on a cape, grabs a sword, comes over, and brandishes it at you—far enough away from you so that you know he does not intend to actually threaten or hit you.

18. Jessie (5) turns the dollhouse upside down, spilling its contents onto the floor.

19. Abdullah (7) carefully constructs a very tall tower out of blocks and then knocks them all down.

20. Using the biggest dinosaur, Filomena (4) bites all of the smaller dinosaurs and then throws the smaller dinosaurs on the floor and throws the bigger dinosaur across the room.

Questions to Ponder

1. What was the easiest part of tracking for you in doing the practice exercises?

2. What was the most difficult part of tracking for you in doing the practice exercises?

3. Explain your view of the advantages and disadvantages of using tracking in play therapy.

4. Do you think you will use tracking in your play therapy? Why would you use it? Why would you not use it?

5. What do you think about this distinction between tracking the child and tracking the play objects or materials? Do you think you will use this distinction in your work? Why or why not?

6. If you decide to make this distinction, how do you think you will decide when to track the child and when to track the play materials? Why?

7. As you practice tracking with children in sample play sessions, notice whether it is more difficult than you expected it to be, easier than you expected it to be, or about what you expected it to be. Explain.

Chapter 6

Restating Content

A nother basic skill used in most approaches to play
therapy is restating content (Kottman, 1995). When
the play therapist restates content, he or she paraphrases
what the child has just said. When the therapist uses restatement of content, the intent is to provide the child with a
mirror of his or her remark, so the therapist's response
should be interchangeable with the child's remark, without
any added meaning or interpretation.

The purpose of restating content is to let the child know
that the therapist is listening to what he or she is saying and
hearing his or her message (Kottman, 1995). Paraphrasing
what the child says is another method of building a relationship with him or her.

How to Restate Content

Although it sounds relatively simple, it actually takes skill and practice to effectively use restatement of content in play therapy. Children tend to expect adults not to listen to them and may initially feel suspicious about an adult who spends a great deal of time and energy conveying the essence of what they said back to them. Many children are sensitive to the possibility that other people, especially those whom they perceive to be more powerful than they are, might be "mocking" them. Other children think that an adult who tells them what they just said is "stupid" or "talks funny," and they may reject anything the adult says in restating content.

One way to prevent children from reacting negatively to restatement of content is to convey respect and genuine interest in what they are saying. The play therapist can contribute to the children feeling cared for and respected by making eye contact, getting down at the children's level as they speak, and presenting a "listening" body posture. This attentive body posture is usually taught as leaning forward, with open arms and legs. However, I believe that the most important element of a listening posture is for the listener to be relaxed and comfortable, with a stance that faces toward the speaker.

Another important factor in effective restatement of content in play therapy is creating a balance between using vocabulary that is age-appropriate and avoiding parroting the child's exact words and exact intonation. By using your own words and not the child's words, you will show the child that you have heard the message and have thought about it enough to be able to translate it into a paraphrase, rather than repeat like a parrot. You must also use your own natural intonation, rather than mimicking the child's. Otherwise, the restatement of content sounds artificial, which can lead the child to distrust that you really care about what he or she is saying.

While trying to use your own words to paraphrase what the child said, it is also important to remember to use words that the child can understand. If you use vocabulary that is beyond the child's developmental and intellectual grasp, even with the best intention, he or she will feel unheard and unrespected. When you are in doubt, it is better to use words that the child will probably understand, rather than risk having the child feel confused. However, if you choose to use a word that the child might not comprehend, you should watch the child's nonverbal reaction and provide a more clear explanation if he or she is struggling with a vocabulary mismatch.

Focus of Restatements

There are three different ways that children talk in play therapy sessions about emotions, situations, interactions, and the other aspects of their world: (a) directly, (b) about the play media, and (c) through the play media. Sometimes children talk directly to the therapist about events, feelings, relationships, and so forth in their lives (e.g., "My father didn't pick me up this weekend, even though he promised that he would."). Sometimes they talk about the play media (e.g., "This little boy's daddy didn't pick him up last weekend, even though he said he would."). Sometimes they talk through the play media (e.g., having a doll say to another doll or to the therapist, "My daddy didn't pick me up this weekend, even though he said he would.").

It is important to try to match the child's method of expression. If the child talks in a direct fashion, the restatement of content should also be direct (e.g., "Your dad promised to pick you up this weekend, but he didn't."). If the child talks about the play media, the restatement should be about the play media (e.g., "That little boy's dad said he would pick him up this weekend, but he didn't do it."). If the child talks through the play media, the restatement should also be through the play media (e.g., the therapist could use the other doll to do the restatement by saying to the little boy doll something like, "Your dad didn't pick you up this weekend, even though he said that he would.").

Influencing Children by Using Restatement of Content

Although most nondirective play therapists would not purposely do so, there is a subtle possibility for influencing children's thinking and the direction of a session in the skill of restatement. By choosing to focus on specific words or concepts in children's statements or by the arrangement of the order of the words in his or her response, the therapist may guide children to explore different aspects of their comments.

For example, suppose Samantha says, "My mother has started dating a new boyfriend. He isn't anything like my father, and I hate him." This statement has many disparate elements in it, and the therapist will usually choose to respond to one or more of them but probably not all of them at the same time. If the therapist wanted to be relatively neutral and guide the child in giving more details about the mother's new beau, a response like, "Your mom has a new boyfriend," might be most appropriate. If the therapist wants to explore the child's feelings about her relationship with her father, the therapist might begin the response with an emphasis on Samantha's father by saying something like, "Your father isn't anything like your mother's new boyfriend." If the therapist wants to explore the child's feelings about her mother's new boyfriend, it might be appropriate to say something like, "You really don't like this new man your mom's dating."

Monitoring Children's Reactions to Restating Content

Just as in tracking, the therapist must observe the child's reaction to restatements of content. Again, feedback from the child can be either direct or indirect, verbal or nonverbal. The child's reaction can help the therapist more clearly understand the child and the child's view of his or her life situation. If the therapist is purposely guiding the conversation in a certain direction, the child's reaction may also help with decisions about what to explore further.

Direct verbal feedback is usually typified by the child telling the therapist that the restatement of content was inaccurate or accurate. The child will make a comment such as, "You don't know what you are talking about" or "That's right." In indirect verbal feedback, the child corrects the content of the restatement without actually overtly challenging the therapist's grasp of the meaning of his or her verbalization. The following dialogue illustrates indirect verbal feedback:

Allison: "I have had my new heart for 10 weeks now."
Therapist: "You have had that heart for a long time."
Allison: "I have had it for only 10 weeks."

Nonverbal feedback is usually more subtle than verbal feedback. Direct nonverbal feedback consists of behavior that the child exhibits that is an obvious and conscious reaction to something the therapist has said. In the child's response to restatement of content, direct nonverbal feedback usually consists of the child nodding, shrugging, shaking his or her head, or making a face—some kind of action that clearly indicates the child's conscious thoughts and feelings about what the therapist has said. Indirect nonverbal feedback consists of behavior that the child exhibits that is a more subtle reaction to the therapist's comments, such as a slight movement of the body, switching of play patterns, and so forth. This form of feedback is usually involuntary or out of the child's awareness. It may, however, just be a safe communication vehicle for a child who does not wish to "own" his or her reaction to the therapist's comments.

It will be important for you to practice observing children's reactions to your interventions, because many times these reactions will contain the most important information conveyed in a session. By noticing patterns in reactions, you will be able to begin to understand how the child perceives his or her place in the world and how the child generally communicates with the other people in his or her life.

Applications in Different Theoretical Orientations

Restating content is another basic skill that is used in most approaches to play therapy. Of the contemporary experts whom I surveyed about their use of play therapy skills, only Kevin O'Connor (ecosystemic) and Violet Oaklander (Gestalt) reported that they do not use restatement of content in their sessions. The other therapists surveyed stated that they use restatement of content less often than they use tracking.

Like tracking, restating content is generally used more in the nondirective approaches (e.g., client-centered or Jungian) than in the more directive approaches (e.g., Adlerian, cognitive–behavioral, prescriptive eclectic, or Thematic). The trend across theories was a tendency to use restatement of content more in the beginning stages of therapy when the therapist was working to establish rapport and less in the middle and ending stages of therapy when the therapist was working on client issues.

Examples of Restating Content

After each of the following scenarios, there are several possible restatements of content appropriate for that situation. For every example, I have tried to provide several that are simple restatements with no intention of leading or influencing the child's thinking, feelings, attitudes, or behaviors and several that do try to lead or influence. For the responses designed to lead the child, I have given one possible explanation of the direction and the rationale for leading in that particular case.

As Heidi picks up the dog puppet, she says, "This dog is going to bite your hand."

1. "The dog is going to chew on me." (not leading)
2. "He's going to bite me." (not leading)
3. "He is moving over to bite my hand." (not leading)
4. "The dog is planning on biting me on the hand." (By using the word *planning*, the therapist might lead the child to think about the purposeful or planful action of the dog.)

As Jorge throws the father and mother dolls on the ground and stomps on them, he shouts, "That's what happens to people who try to tell me what to do. They get hurt."

1. "So, people who tell you what to do get hurt." (not leading)
2. "Folks who try to boss you around get injured." (not leading)
3. "Bad things happen to people who try to tell you what to do." (By generalizing from *they get hurt* to *bad things happen*, the therapist might influence the child to think about whether more than just physical injuries can happen to people who cross him.)
4. "You want to punish people who try to tell you what to do." (By emphasizing the child's desire for revenge rather than the actual act of revenge, the therapist may be able to help him to learn to use symbolic means to punish others.)

Sophia, as she picks up the smaller turtle figure and puts it on top of the bigger turtle figure, says in a high voice, "I'm the baby turtle and my mother is giving me a ride. I like to get taken places on my mother's back."

1. "Baby Turtle, you think it is neat to ride on the back of your mother?" (not leading)
2. "Your mother is taking you for a ride, and you like that." (not leading)
3. "You like going for rides on top of your mother." (not leading)
4. "Your mother is taking you places, which pleases you." (not leading)
5. Using the mother turtle, say to the baby turtle, "You like to go for rides on my back." (not leading)

6. "You think it is neat to be with your mother." (By emphasizing a desire for closeness with the mother, this response could influence the child to explore or reveal more about her relationship with her mother.)

7. Using the mother turtle, say to the baby turtle, "You like it when I take care of you." (By emphasizing the positive aspect of being nurtured, this response could influence the child to explore her own need for nurturing and how that need is being met; it could also lead her to explore or reveal more about her relationship with her mother.)

* Yacob points a gun at the therapist and says, "This is what happened in my village in Israel. Don't move. I will put a bullet in your head if you don't do exactly what I tell you to do."

1. "You don't want me to move." (not leading)

2. "If I move, you will shoot me in the head." (not leading)

3. "You intend to shoot me if I don't follow your orders." (The emphasis on intentionality with *intend* could lead the child to explore his own control over the situation.)

4. "You want me to do exactly what you tell me to do." (This restatement generalizes from the specific situation to the general, possibly inviting the child to explore his need to control others.)

5. "You want me to do just what you tell me, and if I don't, you will shoot me." (Same as Number 4, but it also incorporates the idea that the child is willing to threaten others to get what he wants.)

* Jongyeun lies down on the floor, piling pillows on herself, and says, "Now no one can find me."

1. "Not one single person can find out where you are." (not leading)

2. "No one can see you." (not leading)

3. "You are so well hidden that you can't be found." (The emphasis on hiding might suggest to the child that hiding is a viable coping skill for dealing with problem situations.)

4. "You know how to hide so that no one can see where you are." (By stressing her ability to take care of herself, the therapist could influence the child to consider this as a possible personal asset.)

Practice Exercises

For each of the following scenarios, write four possible restatements of content. When possible, generate two responses (a and b) that simply restate what the child is saying without trying to influence the child's thoughts, feelings, or behavior. Then generate two restatements (c and d) that could lead the child in a specific direction. For the two influencing restatements, give an explanation of how you believe your restatement might influence the child's thoughts, feelings, attitudes, or behaviors. (Even if you are leaning toward a nondirective approach that would not condone purposely leading the child, this can be helpful practice in learning how easy it is to weight your restatement and in being intentional in your avoidance of this tendency.)

1. Mustafa (5) picks up the grasshopper and says, "He really knows how to jump, but he isn't as good at jumping as I am."
2. Dimitri (5) picks up the grasshopper and says, "He is a good jumper. I don't know how to jump like that. People from my country are supposed to be good at sports, but I am not."
3. Kathy (8) has the mother doll hitting the baby doll and says in a "mother" voice, "Take that you brat. That will teach you not to talk back to me."
4. Griff (4) pours sand from one container to another, saying, "This one has more than that one. That one doesn't have as much as this other one."
5. Katrinka (9) puts on a hat, looks in the mirror, and says, "I am ugly. I hate my face."
6. Sam (8) throws a ball in the air for several minutes, drops it on the floor, and says, "That ball is stupid. I hate it in here. There is nothing fun to do."
7. Brigitte (5) uses the wolf puppet to bite her own hand, saying in a gruff voice, "I am a wolf. I can bite you any time I want and you don't even know how to stop me."
8. Then she brings it over and starts to bite your hands and feet with it, saying in that same gruff voice, "You can't stop me either. No one can stop me. I can't even stop myself."
9. Bright Star (6) drapes snakes all over her head, torso, arms, and legs. She laughs and says, "There are snakes everywhere all over me. They are my friends."

10. Zack (7) paints stripes all over a piece of paper. Then he says, "This is a jail like the one where my auntie lives. We go visit her there."

11. Yasmin (4) cooks food for you and says in a "nurturing" voice, "Now you need to eat this food baby. I know that you don't like it, but it is good for you, and you always need to eat food that is good for you."

12. Walter (8) purposely spills all the trash from the trash can saying, "This place is a dump. Can't you keep it clean?"

13. Antonia (7) draws a picture of you, gives it to you, and says, "Do you like it? My mother never likes the pictures I draw. She says I am not a good artist."

14. Deepak (4) has a bunny puppet "read" to an owl puppet, and then the owl puppet says to the bunny, "You didn't read those words right. I don't think you really know how to read. You are just pretending."

15. Olga (7) arranges the tiger family with the parents at one end of the sandbox and the children at the other end, with a wall of blocks in between them. The mother tiger turns to the father tiger and says, "Well, we got rid of those children. They were more trouble than they were worth anyway. They were just more mouths to feed, and I am so tired."

16. Kali (6) arranges the animal figures from the largest to the smallest and says to you, "The biggest ones are the boys, and they are the most important. The little ones are the girls, and they are not important at all."

17. Rick (8) puts on a cape, grabs a sword, and says, "Let's have a sword fight. I think I can beat you. I am pretty good with a sword."

18. Jessie (5) turns the dollhouse upside down, yelling, "Everybody out. Nobody can stay in there. It just isn't safe."

19. Akihito (7) makes a tower and knocks it down, saying, "That wasn't the way it was supposed to be. I have to get it perfect."

20. Emer (4) uses the biggest dinosaur to bite the heads off of the smaller dinosaurs and says in a loud, mean voice, "No one can mess with me. I can get every single one of those little ones and bite their heads off."

Questions to Ponder

1. In the practice exercises, what was the most difficult aspect of restating content for you?
2. How will you ensure that you convey respect to the child when you restate content?
3. What do you think/how do you feel about using the emphasis in restating content to influence or lead a child in a certain direction?
4. Do you think you will choose to use restatements to influence or lead children? Why or why not?
5. How could mirroring what the child is doing or saying help to build a relationship with the child?
6. In your sample sessions with a child, what has been the easiest aspect of restating content? The most difficult aspect? Explain.
7. In your sample sessions with a child, have you used the emphasis in restating content to influence or lead the child? How has this worked for you? What is your reaction/feeling to doing this?

Chapter 7

Reflecting Feelings

One of the reasons for using play as the medium for communication in therapy is that children do not have the abstract verbal-reasoning skills to adequately describe their feelings (James, 1997; Kottman, 1995; Landreth, 1991). This does not mean that children do not have feelings—they do! It does mean that children may not be able to clearly articulate their feelings. Most children can (and do) express their feelings both verbally and nonverbally—in their voices, in their facial expressions, in their posture, in their behavior, in their play, and in their stories.

There are several purposes for reflecting feelings in the playroom. Because of children's incomplete understanding of affective concepts, they often have truncated awareness and understanding of their own emotions. By making guesses about children's feelings in the process of play therapy, the therapist can help children begin to understand the emotions they experience. This assistance in enhancing their awareness and understanding of feelings can be invaluable to children.

The therapist can also expand children's feeling vocabulary. Young children tend to know the concepts of sad, mad, glad, and scared. They may know several words to express each of these concepts, but they are usually rather unsophisticated in their expression of the nuances of various feelings. The playroom can serve as a setting in which children can experiment with their understanding and use of new feeling vocabulary.

How to Reflect Feelings

The skill of reflecting feelings involves making guesses or statements about what the therapist thinks the client is feeling. The therapist can point out one or more specific feelings that the child is experiencing at that moment (e.g., "You seem really sad right now.") or a pattern of feelings that the child consistently expresses (e.g., "I have noticed that whenever you talk about your grandmother, you smile and act really happy.").

Reflections should be clear and to the point. Although the therapist may want to include a brief attribution or connection of the feeling to an antecedent event or to the child's reasoning, it is inappropriate to give the child complex explanations or interpretations about why he or she is experiencing that particular feeling (Kottman, 1995).

It is also essential for the therapist to refrain from trying to convince children that certain feelings are inappropriate. People have the right to whatever feelings they experience, and it is the ultimate exhibition of disrespect to tell them that they should not feel a certain way. Even if I do not understand why a child feels a particular feeling (happy to see his father who beats him, sad and tearful because a cartoon show was canceled, etc.), I do not have the right to tell the child that his or her feeling is misplaced or disproportionate.

I abstain from asking children how they feel or why they are feeling certain emotions. Most of the time, they are not able to answer these questions and may get frustrated with my insisting that they supply me with descriptions of their emotions or the causes of their emotions.

I also try to avoid the phrase "makes you feel" in my reflections (Kottman, 1995). This is due to my belief that nothing can "make" a person feel a certain way and that every individual has a certain level of control over what he or she chooses to feel and to express in the way of feelings. Although some children express themselves using the "makes me" configuration, (e.g., "My brother always makes me mad, so I hit him." or "This really makes me very sad."), it is usually best not to get into a power struggle with them trying to teach them not to use this formula. Modeling that there are other ways to express these feelings (e.g., "You feel mad at your brother, and you decided to punch him." or "You seem very sad about that.") is probably a better way of handling these situations.

What to Reflect

In deciding what to reflect, the therapist must consider the manner in which children express their feelings and the depth of feelings expressed by children. The therapist must also make choices regarding what to reflect when children simultaneously express more than one feeling.

Manner of Expression

In addition to reflecting the feelings verbally expressed in a direct manner by the child, it is also important for the therapist to reflect the emotions inherent in the play. This would include reflecting (a) the feelings expressed nonverbally through the child's facial expressions, body language, and so forth; (b) the feelings expressed in the general affective tone of the play; and (c) the feelings expressed in an implicit way in the child's comments. It is also essential to reflect feelings communicated (both verbally and nonverbally) by various play media, such as the dolls, puppets, and animal figures.

Direct verbal expression. Sometimes it is easy to recognize the feeling expressed by a child because he or she clearly verbalizes the feeling in a way that shows he or she "owns" the feeling (e.g., "I am really angry at my mom today."). This is the simplest type of feeling expression, and the reflection should be equally simple. The therapist just mirrors the feeling back to the child (e.g., "You are very mad at your mother.").

Indirect expression. The indirect types of feeling expression are frequently more difficult to recognize than the direct acknowledgment of emotions. With some children, nonverbal expression of feelings is obvious, and the therapist can begin to make guesses in the first session about the emotions expressed in this manner. However, because nonverbal expression of emotions is both individually and culturally based, many times the therapist will need to observe an individual child's facial expressions, voice tone, voice inflection, speed of speech production, body posture, and proximics for several sessions to get an idea about how that particular child expresses feelings. It is also essential to understand the cultural influences on ways the child and his or her family nonverbally express themselves (Coleman, Parmer, & Barker, 1993; Gopaul-McNicol & Thomas-Presswood, 1998; Johnson-Powell & Yamamoto, 1997; Locke, 1998; Martinez & Valdez, 1992).

The same is true for the affective tone of the session, which is expressed by the patterns in what the child says and does during the session and how the child emotes throughout the session. For instance, both Jacquee and Sam could play in the dollhouse the entire session, saying things like, "This mother really likes the little boy." If Jacquee plays with no animation, speaks in a sad or listless voice, and does not make any eye contact, the affective tone of her session would be significantly different than that of Sam's session, in which he plays and speaks in a lively manner, smiling, laughing, and making eye contact with the therapist.

The affective tone may also relate to the play themes that the therapist observes during the course of a session. By watching what the child plays and noticing consistent patterns in what the play is about, the therapist can draw some conclusions about the affective tone of the session. For instance, if Georgine consistently plays with the dolls or animal figures by having them hit one another and make negative, disparaging comments to one another, the affective tone of her session would probably seem rather angry.

At times, children verbally express feelings but in subtle, indirect ways because the emotions are implicit in what they say. When they do this, they may not openly acknowledge feeling a certain way, but what they say implies an emotional content. For instance, Garry could say, "Do I have to go in there?" Depending on the nonverbals, the implicit feeling in this question could be anxiety, timidity, or another similar emotion, or it could be defiance or hostility.

With all three of these types of indirect communication of feelings (nonverbal expression, the affective tone of the session, and implicit feelings), the therapist should usually be relatively tentative in his or her reflection of the feelings. This is due to the fact that the child may be less willing to acknowledge feelings indirectly expressed and that the therapist will probably be less sure of his or her recognition of the feelings expressed. By using tentative hypotheses or guesses in the reflection rather than definitive statements, the therapist can convey the idea that he or she believes this is what is happening with the child on an emotional level but that corrective input from the child would be welcome and helpful.

Because play therapy depends on the child's play for communication, the therapist must never neglect to pay attention to the emotions expressed by the child through the surrogates—the toys—present in the playroom. The dolls, puppets, animal figures, and even the less obvious toys such as the guns, cars, blocks and so forth can all "speak"—both verbally and nonverbally—for the child about feelings.

When the child chooses to express emotions through a "spokestoy," the therapist can direct the reflection of feelings either toward the toy (e.g., "So, Mr. Wolf, you are feeling really angry right now.") or toward the child about the toy (e.g., "Mr. Wolf seems to be really angry right now."). Some children are more comfortable with the therapist directly addressing the toy, some are more comfortable with the therapist addressing them and discussing the toy's feelings, and others do not seem to have a preference. You should experiment with both ways of handling this type of feeling expression with individual children. You will usually make a decision about how to reflect the toy's feelings on the basis of the specific child's reactions to your reflections.

Delivery of the reflection in situations in which toys express the child's feelings should parallel the delivery in which there is no play intermediary. When a toy directly expresses a feeling, the therapist should directly and simply reflect the feeling. For instance, when Siri picks up the ant, bounces it up and down, and says in a squeaky voice, "Hooray. I am excited!" the therapist would say something like, "The ant is really excited." When a toy nonverbally expresses a feeling, the therapist would make a guess about the emotion the toy might be expressing. For instance, when Sly picks up two puppets and has the wolf puppet beat up the lamb puppet, and then the lamb puppet curls up in a ball and cries, the therapist might say, "Lamb, it seems like you are really sad because you got hurt by the wolf." When there is an affective tone typically attributed to a certain toy, the therapist would use a tentative hypothesis about what is going on with that toy. For instance, if Pilar has one doll that always picks on all the other dolls and consistently seems angry, the therapist could reflect the pattern of feelings associated with that doll by saying, "Yolanda, the doll, seems to get mad at the other dolls a lot."

Reflecting Deeper Feelings

The therapist should always acknowledge the obvious surface feelings but must also remember to look for deeper feelings that may be less blatant. Children tend to exhibit feelings with which they are relatively comfortable, but they may hide other feelings that are unacceptable to them—because of a sense of vulnerability, personal values, or family rules. For instance, James may think that it is perfectly acceptable to express anger and hostility, but if he has learned that "boys do not cry," he may feel unable or unwilling to express sadness, disappointment, or loneliness.

If, after getting to know the child and his or her behavior patterns, you believe that there are underlying feelings present, it can be very helpful for you to make some guesses about those feelings. It is important to do this in a tentative fashion and to closely watch the child's reaction to gauge the impact of the tentative reflection.

In other situations, the therapist knows that there are underlying feelings present on that basis of his or her knowledge of the child's life circumstances or culture (Johnson-Powell & Yamamoto, 1997). For instance, 9-year-old Lixue's little brother died from a rare disease the previous year. In her culture, grief is considered to be private, not to be openly discussed. For several sessions, she comes into the playroom and has the larger giraffe hovering over the baby giraffe. Then she has the larger giraffe scolding the baby giraffe, making comments like, "You should not have done that." The therapist, knowing that sadness is probably one of the emotions Lixue is feeling, might choose to acknowledge both the surface feeling and the underlying feeling by saying something like, "That bigger one seems kind of mad at the baby. I am guessing that she may also be worried or sad about something that could happen to the baby." Although the therapist can reflect a variety of feelings in the play session, he or she must also remember that it is important not to push the child to acknowledge a feeling that would not be acceptable or appropriate to express in his or her culture.

Feelings in the Here and Now Versus Patterns of Feelings

Some play therapists focus strictly on feelings in the here and now. Others may also look for affective patterns within a session or across sessions. The decision to focus on here-and-now feelings, affective patterns, or some combination of the two may depend on (a) the particular client and his or her specific issues and therapeutic goals, (b) the therapist's theoretical orientation, or (c) the therapist's personal style.

The client. Sometimes the choice of whether to focus on the here and now, to look for affective patterns, or to integrate elements of both is related to the particular issues or play of certain children and the goals in their therapy. In this case, the therapist bases his or her decision regarding where to focus feeling reflections on an assessment of the child's current needs. Many times, the therapist will choose to primarily concentrate on reflecting present feelings but will occasionally use a reflection of an affective pattern with certain children.

With some children, the affective themes are so obvious and so deep that it would almost seem a waste not to point them out. For example, Chereese talks a lot about various people in her life. She is usually a lively, cheerful child who always has a kind word to say about others. However, when she refers to her paternal grandfather, her animation dies, and she seems angry and sad. This pattern occurs over a period of 10 sessions. The therapist would probably be remiss in not bringing up this pattern in a therapy session.

With other children, the here and now is so intense and potentially overwhelming that it is all they can handle. It is more important with these children to simply stay in the present and not ask them to think about affective patterns. For instance, Henry's adored grandfather has died. Every time he brings up a topic or activity even tangentially related to his grandfather or death, Henry begins to cry. Although this is a pattern, it would probably not be helpful for the therapist to point this out to Henry. He already knows that he is hurting and sad and that this is a theme for him right now. It would most likely be much more useful for the therapist to simply stay in the here and now with him and support him by providing empathy and warmth.

Theoretical orientation. Theory may also affect the therapist's thinking about where to focus reflections. Many nondirective play therapists believe that the currently experienced feelings should be the sole focal point for reflection of feelings (Axline, 1969; Landreth, 1991; Perry, 1993). Even when therapists observe affective themes in a session or across sessions, they may not share those observations with the child because they believe that it would detract from the child's being in the present. Most more directive play therapists think that it is helpful to notice patterns in affective expression and to reflect those to children as well as to reflect feelings from the present moment (Benedict & Narcavage, 1997; Kottman, 1995; O'Connor, 1991).

Therapist's personal style. The therapist's personal style of observation and communication may also influence his or her decision about the focus of feeling reflections. For instance, if the therapist tends to be a person who looks for connections between disparate thoughts, feelings, behaviors, attitudes, perceptions, and so forth, he or she might be uncomfortable with not pointing out patterns to children. In contrast, if the therapist tends to be a person who lives primarily in the present moment, he or she might be most comfortable focusing only on the here and now with children.

Multiple Feelings

There may be several feelings present in the child's communication. The therapist will need to decide whether to try to reflect all of the feelings present or to focus on only one or two feelings. This decision will partly depend on the child's developmental age. With children who are verbally and intellectually advanced, it can be productive to reflect several feelings, especially if the feelings tend to be mixed or have different levels of intensity. With children who are developmentally or chronologically young, it is frequently better to focus on only one feeling at a time. That way, they will be more likely to be able to process the therapist's feedback in a productive manner.

If there are several emotions expressed by the child at the same time and the therapist wishes to narrow the focus, he or she will have to choose which of the feelings to reflect. Although this decision may depend somewhat on the therapist's theoretical orientation, it will most likely be determined by the therapist's intuitive judgment about which of the feelings is most important at that particular moment. This may be related to a pattern of emotions expressed by the child or to the relative intensity of the various feelings. It may also stem from the therapist's sense of which of the emotions the child is ready to accept at that point in the therapeutic process.

Monitoring Children's Responses to Reflection of Feelings

When the therapist reflects a feeling, he or she must not expect the child to verbally acknowledge the reflection. Many times, the child will react in a nonverbal mode—either through body language or through the play. The child may frown, smile, shrug, shudder, turn away from the therapist, or use any number of other nonverbal responses.

The child may also do something in the play (either overt or covert) in reaction to the therapist's comments. Overt reactions would include behaviors such as turning and shooting the therapist, having the father doll hit the mother doll, throwing the puppet down and stomping on it, having one animal figure make a comment about the reflection, and so forth. Covert reactions would usually involve a "play disruption" (Perry & Landreth, 1991), which is abruptly dropping the current play and switching to a different type of play, different toys, or a different locale in the playroom.

The child may react with a combination of verbal and nonverbal responses. The therapist must watch the intensity of these reactions for an idea of how the child is truly feeling about the reflection. For instance, if MaryBeth mildly says, "No, I am really not feeling angry right now," the therapist was probably wrong in the guess about the feeling she expressed. In this case, it is appropriate for the therapist to convey an apology or an acknowledgment of the error by saying something like, " Oh, I missed that one." If MaryBeth has a rather violent reaction like screaming loudly, "NO!!!! You are so stupid. Of course I am not angry," the therapist was probably correct in the guess about the feeling. In such cases, the therapist will have to consider various options for responding to the child's reaction. Some of these would be to (a) metacommunicate about the child's reaction (e.g., "You seem really upset that I said you might be mad about that"; see chapter 13, "Advanced Play Therapy Skills"), (b) ignore the child's reaction, or (c) make some comment that would invite the child to consider the therapist's hypothesis at a later time (e.g., "Well, it is something to think about.").

Even when the therapist thinks that his or her guess about the child's feeling was correct, it is essential not to argue with the child about this. The child must be the expert on his or her own feelings, and the therapist should be respectful of the child's right to decide which feelings to acknowledge at that particular moment. Sometimes the child is not ready to acknowledge a specific feeling, and it is important that he or she has control over this.

To a certain extent, the method of dealing with the child's reaction stems from the therapist's theoretical orientation. Many nondirective play therapists notice the reaction but may not verbally acknowledge it, preferring to integrate the response into their mental image of the process of the interaction rather than risk leading the child in a direction in which the child does not choose to go.

More directive therapists tend to make interpretations of the reaction to the child (e.g., "It looked like I reminded you about your father when I said that about you being angry.") or to metacommunicate about the reaction by making a comment about the nonverbal communication (e.g., "You frowned when I said you were mad. I am thinking that maybe you don't like it when I think you are angry."). When the therapist verbally acknowledges the child's reaction, it is necessary to be cautious. By presenting these thoughts in a tentative form, the therapist can usually avoid evoking a defensive reaction from the child and refrain from imposing his or her own interpretation of the child's reaction onto the child.

Expanding Feeling Concepts and Vocabulary

Many play therapists believe that it is part of their job to expand the number of feeling concepts and feeling vocabulary words to which the child is exposed. By making guesses about feelings other than sad, mad, glad, and scared and by using words that express the subtle distinctions between different ways of feeling sad, mad, glad, and scared, therapists can help children learn about their own feelings. Although this process will not change children's abstract verbal-reasoning skills, it may increase the possibility that children can more frequently express their feelings to others in a verbal form that others can comprehend.

The following list contains feeling words that might be useful in play therapy sessions:

mad	irritated	frustrated	annoyed
enraged	outraged	angry	pissed off
glad	happy	joyful	excited
sad	bummed out	sorrowful	teary
scared	afraid	nervous	worried
anxious	terrified	horrified	concerned
disappointed	ashamed	embarrassed	antsy
proud	jealous	confused	lonely
powerful	shy	timid	bored
satisfied	gleeful	relieved	guilty
depressed	discouraged	distressed	peaceful
satisfied	dissatisfied	encouraged	distracted

The therapist will have to use his or her professional judgment and knowledge about child development in choosing words appropriate for the specific child.

Applications in Different Theoretical Orientations

Most play therapists use the skill of reflecting feelings, regardless of their theoretical orientation. Of the experts surveyed, only Violet Oaklander (Gestalt) reported that she does not reflect feelings in her work with children. The rest of the experts reported that they do reflect feelings, although the emphasis on this skill varied widely. Several of the nondirective therapists reported a great emphasis on feelings, whereas others reported limited emphasis on feelings. An even greater range occurred in the more directive therapists, with some of them reporting as much as 80% of their therapeutic interventions being focused on feeling reflections and others reporting as little as 5% of their therapeutic interventions being focused on feeling reflections.

This lack of a pattern seems to indicate that there are not clear theoretical guidelines about how much of an emphasis in play therapy should be on emotions. This seems to be a matter of personal preference and style.

However, there are definite theoretical guidelines about what feelings to reflect (here and now versus patterns) and how to react to children's responses to reflections. I have tried to explain these guidelines in the course of the chapter, but students of play therapy would be advised to do more reading in texts devoted to specific theories to further explore these issues (see Appendix A for selected references).

Examples of Reflecting Feelings

Following each of the scenarios below are several possible reflections of feelings:

Juana (6) comes into the playroom with shoulders drooping and a sorrowful expression on her face. She says, "My mom said we have to go to my grandmother's house again this weekend instead of going to the swimming pool with my friends."

1. "You seem disappointed that you aren't going to get to go to the swimming pool with your friends."
2. "You are bummed out that the family is going to your grandmother's instead of the swimming pool."
3. "You wish you could go swimming with your friends instead of going to your grandmother's house, and you're feeling kind of sad that your mother made that decision."

Guy (8) bounces into the playroom, smiles, and says, "I beat up my brother, and my mom thought it was his fault, so he got into trouble and I didn't."

1. "You are kind of excited about hitting your brother."
2. "It sounds like you feel relieved that your mother blamed your brother and not you."
3. "You seem very happy that you got away with beating your brother up and didn't get in trouble for it."

Lilly (5) is looking for a particular toy that she likes and cannot find it in the playroom. She stomps her foot and says, "I hate you. I hate this room. I want my dinosaur."

1. "You are really angry because you can't find the dinosaur."
2. "It seems like you're kind of disappointed that the dinosaur isn't where you think it should be."
3. "You seem very disappointed and angry that the dinosaur isn't here."

4. "You want me to know that you feel angry because the dinosaur isn't here."

Ed Blue Sky (6) comes into the playroom, looks down at the ground, and says, "I wish I could always stay here in this room."

1. "You seem sad that you can't stay in the playroom all the time."
2. "It sounds like you really feel happy and safe while you are here."
3. "I am thinking that you're kind of disappointed that you don't get to spend more time in the playroom."

Sally Rae (7) takes the baby turtle and buries it. In a high voice, Sally Rae (as the baby turtle) starts crying, and she moves the mother turtle over and has her dig up the baby turtle. Then the daddy turtle starts yelling at the baby turtle for crying.

1. "Baby Turtle, you seemed really sad and scared when the sand was on top of you."
2. "I am guessing that the baby turtle was scared that no one was going to come and save her when she was buried."
3. "Daddy Turtle, you sound very angry at Baby Turtle for crying."
4. "I bet the mommy turtle was worried about the baby turtle and she felt relieved when she got her out from under that sand."

Demetrio (7) has a wolf that he uses to communicate many of his feelings. He comes in, picks up the wolf, sits down, and hides the wolf's head under a pillow. Then he has the wolf peek out from underneath the pillow at the therapist and growl.

1. "Wolf, I can't tell if you are feeling shy or kind of mad at me today."
2. "Mr. Wolf, you seem kind of upset about something this afternoon."
3. "I am thinking that the wolf might be trying to tell me something— maybe that he is feeling shy right now or maybe that growling means that he is mad."
4. "Demetrio, can you help me out? I can't tell if the wolf is annoyed about something or he is just feeling a little shy today or something else is going on with him."

Geraldine's (9) father is in jail. While she talks about him a lot in sessions, her affect is always flat. She never acknowledges any feelings about him or his incarceration. In a session in which she is playing in the dollhouse, she has the little girl yell at the father for "not being where you are supposed to be."

1. "Sounds like that little girl is mad at her daddy."
2. "Seems like she is mad at the daddy, but I am thinking maybe she is also disappointed at him for not being where she thinks he should be."
3. To Geraldine, "Do you think maybe she is sad because her daddy isn't where she wants him?"
4. To the doll, "You sound really angry at your dad."
5. To the doll, "I am guessing that you are mad at him because you are feeling sad about him not being around when you want him to be."

Practice Exercises

For each of the following scenarios, generate three possible ways to reflect feelings:

1. In his second session, Guido (7) comes into the playroom, picks up a stuffed animal, and starts pounding on the punching bag—he looks very angry and shouts, "I hate you, you slimy jerk."
2. Guido picks up a stuffed animal and starts pounding on the punching bag—he smiles and giggles every time the punching bag falls to the ground.
3. In his third session, Guido comes into the playroom, picks up a stuffed animal, and starts pounding on the punching bag—he smiles and giggles every time the punching bag falls to the ground. You know he has had a bad day at school—got sent to the principal three times and did not want to come to his play therapy session.
4. In the fifth session, Guido comes into the playroom, picks up a stuffed animal, and starts pounding on the punching bag—he has no facial expression at all, which is not unusual for him. You know that he just won his class spelling bee.
5. Bobbie Sue (8) has the mother doll say to the baby doll, "I wish you had never been born."
6. After using the dinosaur puppet to devour all the smaller animals for six session in a row, Sly (6) comes in, throws it on the floor, smiles, and says, "I am done with that."

7. After her parents bring her to the playroom, Iolanthe (9) throws herself on the floor and wails, "I hate my mother for making me come here. I hate my father for letting her make me."

8. Griffith (4) buries all of the bugs under the sand while they scream, "Help. Help. Somebody save us."

9. Next, Griffith turns to you, smiles, and says, "Nobody is going to save them."

10. Lexi (8) is about to move to her third foster family in 3 years. She has really done well with the current foster family, but the wife is being transferred to another state, and they cannot take Lexi with them. Lexi sets up six or seven piles of furniture in various spots in the playroom and moves one little boy doll from pile to pile. She shows no affect and does not say anything while she is doing this.

11. Kenji (9) came to therapy because he was expressing suicidal thoughts. He has come to eight sessions and has played out various themes related to feeling as though he cannot live up to his parents' high standards. His parents and the school report that he is doing better, and he tells you that he has no more thoughts about hurting himself. His insurance coverage has run out, and this is his last session. He refuses to look at you or talk for the first 15 minutes of the session.

12. Jillian (3) looks around the playroom and asks, "Why don't you have any dolls in wheelchairs like mine?"

13. Hussein (5) cradles the baby doll, feeding it. When he notices you watching him, he puts it down and walks away, not making eye contact.

14. Clarice (6) uses the gorilla father to hit the gorilla mother, yelling, "You b****." The mother cries and tries to hide the children behind her.

15. Edgar (8) comes into the playroom, smiles, and says, "I think I am going to have fun here."

16. Rebekah (4) picks up the gun and frowns. From having talked to her mother, you know that the family does not let their children use weapons of any kind and disapproves of you having guns in your playroom.

17. Garvey (7) takes the baby doll, puts it under the pillows, turns to you, and says with a huge grin on his face, "I smothered him."
18. Hiroko (5) paints a picture, turns to you, smiles, and says, "My mother will like this. She will think this is a good picture. I am going to give it to her."
19. Lorali (5) paints a picture, turns to you, smiles, and says, "My mother will like this. I am going to give it to her." You know that her mother left the family several months before and has not contacted either of the children.
20. Santiago (3), in his last session, with tears in his eyes, hugs you and heads to the door without saying anything.

Questions to Ponder

1. What is your reaction to the suggestion that you should refrain from asking children how they feel?
2. How do you feel/what do you think about the suggestion to avoid asking children why they feel a certain way?
3. Explain your thoughts on the phrase "makes you feel."
4. Discuss your perspective on the issue of focusing solely on feelings in the here and now as opposed to focusing on both present feelings and affective patterns.
5. Do you believe there is a time when you would choose to ignore feelings expressed in the here and now? Explain your answer.
6. Do you think it is appropriate to use play therapy skills to increase children's affective vocabulary and concept development? Explain.
7. Consider your own issues and the rules in your family of origin about feelings and expression of emotion. How do you think these factors will affect your ability to reflect feelings in your play therapy sessions?
8. Are there certain feelings that you think you will be uncomfortable with children expressing in your sessions? What are they? Why are they a problem for you? What is your plan for preventing the expression of these specific feelings from being a problem?

Chapter 8

Setting Limits

Historically, some experts working with children (Rosenthal, 1956; Schiffer, 1952; Slavson, 1943) felt that setting limits was a "dangerous technique that undermines the very foundation of the therapeutic relationship" (Ginott, 1959, p. 160). These therapists advocated complete and unconditional permissiveness in therapy sessions so that children could act out whatever behavior they wanted or needed to act out so as to optimize effectiveness of therapy. They believed that the imposition of predetermined limits would seriously hamper therapeutic progress because these limits would not be specifically tailored to individual children and their needs and problems.

Beginning with Axline (1947), Bixler (1949), Moustakas (1953), and Ginott (1959), this trend shifted. Axline (1947) stated that limits "are set up as a prerequisite to satisfactory therapy" (p. 131). Moustakas (1953) said, "Without limits there would be no therapy" (p. 15). Bixler (1949) stated this proposition even more emphatically when he wrote an article titled "Limits Are Therapy" (p. 1).

In most contemporary approaches to play therapy, therapists set limits on certain specific behaviors that are not acceptable in the playroom. They do not usually limit children's verbalizations or symbolic expressions of aggression or hostility. As Ginott (1959) explained,

> Feelings, fantasies, thoughts, wishes, passions, dreams and desires, regardless of their content, are accepted, respected, and allowed expression through words and play. Direct acting out of destructive behavior is not permitted; when it occurs, the therapist intervenes and redirects it into symbolic outlets. (p. 161)

Limit setting usually involves some structured method of letting children know that certain specific behaviors are not permissible in the playroom. Although the majority of therapists seem to agree on the types of behaviors that should be limited in play therapy, there are differences of opinion on the purpose of limiting, when to limit, and how to limit.

There are myriad explanations of the rationale for limit setting in play therapy. Bixler (1949) suggested that limits (a) allow the therapist to be more accepting of children because they are not allowed to destroy property or hurt the therapist and (b) teach children the skills of conforming to the specific rules of different environments and relationships.

Ginott (1959) described six different reasons for the use of limits in play therapy.

1. Limits help children use symbolic means for catharsis.
2. Limits allow the therapist to be accepting, caring, and empathic toward clients.
3. Limits protect children and the therapist from physical harm.
4. Limits help children increase ego controls by giving them practice in curbing socially inappropriate impulses.
5. Limits can keep playroom behavior from violating legal, ethical, and social rules.

6. Limits can prevent excessive outlay of money for repair of the physical plant and replacement of broken toys and play materials.

Landreth (1991) described the following reasons for setting limits:

1. Limits help children feel physically and emotionally secure in the playroom, which maximizes their potential for growth.
2. Limits help protect the physical safety of the therapist, which increases his or her ability to fully accept children.
3. Limits help children develop skills in decision making, self-control, and self-responsibility.
4. Limits can anchor play therapy sessions to reality and help children focus on situations in the here and now.
5. Limits establish a sense of predictability and consistency in the play therapy relationship and environment.
6. Limits help maintain the parameters of the play therapy relationship within professional, ethical, and socially responsible guidelines.
7. Limits can reduce potential damage to toys, play therapy materials, and the playroom.

According to Kottman (1995), from an Adlerian position, the purpose of setting limits is (a) to build an egalitarian relationship with children in which power and responsibility are shared between the therapist and the client, (b) to enhance children's self-control, (c) to help children learn that they have the capacity for generating alternative appropriate behaviors and for redirecting their own socially unacceptable behaviors, (d) to encourage children to develop a sense of responsibility for complying with limits and consequences, and (e) to minimize power struggles in the play therapy process.

The different reasons for setting limits listed for each theoretical approach to play therapy reflect the basic goals of each approach. However, there seem to be several trends among the various rationales described. Most of the experts suggested that limits can help (a) to keep both the child and the therapist safe in the playroom; (b) to increase the child's awareness of and capacity for self-regulation and self-responsibility; (c) to keep the relationship within legal, ethical, and socially acceptable boundaries; and (d) to limit damage to property and play materials.

What to Limit

There is a consensus among most play therapists about the main targets of limit setting. Children are not supposed to do anything that might result in them hurting themselves, other children, their parents, or the therapist in the play therapy session. They are not supposed to be allowed to damage (on purpose) the toys or other play materials in the playroom, nor are they to harm the walls, floors, windows, furniture, or other physical property within the playroom. Other relatively universal rules are that children will stay in the session until the therapist has indicated the time for therapy has ended and will leave when the therapist has indicated the time has ended. Many therapists also have a rule that children should not leave the therapy room (without permission) to go to the bathroom, get a drink, and so forth. Most therapists also limit children from taking toys from the playroom, and some therapists limit children from bringing toys from other settings into the playroom.

These limits are usually considered to be absolute and nonnegotiable—especially the rules that prohibit harm to people and property—and practically all play therapists enforce them. Whether play therapists enforce other limits can depend on (a) the theoretical perspective of the therapist, (b) the setting of the therapist's practice, (c) the personality of the therapist, or (d) the individual situation and personality of the child.

Influence of Theoretical Perspective

Most nondirective therapists (e.g., child-centered, Jungian, and psychodynamic play therapists) attempt to keep limits to a minimum so as to create an atmosphere of optimal permissiveness. These therapists usually only limit behaviors that fall into the absolute category. Ginott (1959) suggested avoiding conditional limits because they have a tendency to be disruptive:

> Limits should be delineated in a manner that leaves no doubt in the child's mind as to what constitutes unacceptable conduct in the playroom. . . . A limit that states "you may splash me as long as you don't wet me too much" is inviting a deluge of trouble. (p. 162)

Play therapists who integrate both nondirective and directive elements (e.g., Adlerian, cognitive–behavioral, eclectic prescriptive, Gestalt, psychodynamic, and Thematic play therapists) may decide to evoke some rules that are negotiable in nature. These rules would usually revolve around behavior that could potentially be a minor nuisance or messy but probably not dangerous (e.g., how much water is added to the sandbox or whether the child is allowed to turn off the light in the playroom).

The therapist and the child work together to establish negotiable limits by engaging in a discussion about what would be reasonable in the situation. For instance, if the child wanted to pour six cups of water into the sandbox and the therapist felt that only one cup of water was needed, they could enter into a dialogue designed to generate a compromise position—perhaps three cups.

It is important to note that the negotiated limit should be defined in a way that is clear and measurable, thereby avoiding Ginott's (1959) description of conditional limits. The therapist should never use a vaguely stated limit (e.g., "It's against the rules to kick the ball hard."), but rather should work with the child until they arrive at a concretely stated limit (e.g., "It's against the rules to kick the ball so that it hits the lights, the window, or me.").

Play therapists who are on the directive side of the continuum (e.g., ecosystemic and Theraplay) tend to use structuring as a way of limiting. They tell children which toys they will use and what they will do in the session. Because they present their suggestions by acting as if children will do what they suggest, they frequently do not have to set up limits in a formal process. When children do not comply with the structure the therapists provide, these therapists may decide to intervene physically to ensure compliance. This is a controversial option, however. Play therapists who choose to intervene physically must be trained to do so safely, and they must consider possible legal or ethical ramifications should they decide to physically restrain a child or compel compliance from a child.

As you are thinking about which approach to play therapy might be the most comfortable for you, it is important to consider how you feel about the different types of limit setting. You should think about whether you would be more comfortable with (a) few limits that are nonnegotiable and clearly defined or (b) a moderate number of limits, some of which you would have to work out in conjunction with your clients. It would also be helpful to consider whether you would be comfortable with structuring as a limit-setting device in your sessions, being directive and in charge of what play materials children use and what they do with them. You must also decide whether you would feel nervous about physically intervening to ensure compliance with your directives.

Influence of the Therapist's Setting

Practically speaking, the setting of a play therapist's practice also influences the types of behaviors the therapist limits. The location of the therapist's office and the kind of job the therapist has may determine how strictly he or she enforces various rules. The following instances illustrate the influence of the therapist's setting on limit setting:

1. *George is a school counselor who uses play therapy as an intervention modality. He would be more likely than play therapists who work in mental health settings to limit wild behavior and inappropriate language simply because these behaviors are contrary to school rules. He believes that allowing children to flaunt school rules in the counselor's office can encourage them to flaunt rules in other areas in the school, which could result in negative consequences for the children. George has just moved offices. Last year, George's office was close to the principal's office, so he limited loud noises in his session. This year, his office is by the gym and the cafeteria, so George allows children to be rather noisy in their sessions with him. No matter what the location of George's office though, he provides time and some sort of activity for helping children make the transition from the relatively free and relaxed atmosphere in his office, which does not have a great many rules, to the classroom, which frequently does have many rules. George assumes that children will need help getting their behavior back into classroom-acceptable mode.*

2. *Huang is in private practice and has an office in an expensive building, with fine furniture and fancy toys. She sees both adults and children in her office. She is strict about enforcing rules with regard to damage to the property. Because she is personally responsible for expenses incurred by damage children inflict on the physical plant or the toys, she does not allow them to violate the rules regarding property damage.*

3. *When Terry was an intern at a university clinic, she was rather lax about enforcing the rule about getting paint on the walls. However, after she graduated and became the director of the clinic, she was much more vigilant about making sure her clients did not get paint on the walls because*

she realized how much it would cost to paint them and how inconvenient it would be to have this task done.

These examples are meant to illustrate that the number and kind of limits set will be related to the physical setting of the therapist's practice. This is a rather commonsense consideration, but it is important nevertheless. You will need to think about how the location of your office and the nature of your job can influence the way you limit. Hopefully, you will be proactive and intentional in making decisions about limits, while at the same time you acknowledge the practical realities of your situation.

Influence of the Therapist's Personality

The therapist's personality also influences what gets limited in play therapy. The therapist must feel comfortable with the behaviors that children are allowed to exhibit in the playroom. It is also important for the therapist to feel secure about his or her own safety and the safety of clients. The following instances illustrate the influence of the therapist's level of comfort with particular situations:

1. *Anna has a high need to maintain control over herself and over life situations. She equates being out of control with being in danger. This limits her ability to feel comfortable when she perceives children as wild or out of control. She may feel a need to impose limits on children's behaviors whenever she believes that their behavior is getting out of control.*
2. *Jean-Francoise has a high tolerance level for activities that some might consider to be dangerous or out of control. He is comfortable when children are acting out, loud, and aggressive, never feeling personally challenged or endangered. Jean-Francoise will probably not impose many limits on children.*
3. *Henrietta is personally timid. She does not like to take risks and does not understand why anyone would desire to do so. Henrietta believes that most things children do can constitute a threat to self or others. She will probably impose more limits on behavior than therapists who personally enjoy taking physical or emotional risks.*

Therapists' personalities can also influence their abilities to be accepting of children on the basis of their behaviors. There are some behaviors that are simply intolerable or uncomfortable to certain people. If the therapist does not limit these behaviors, he or she may have a reduced capacity to accept or be empathic to a child who is demonstrating those behaviors.

The following instances illustrate the influence of the therapist's ability to tolerate specific behaviors:

1. *Hank hates snakes. He gets extremely tense and breaks out into a sweat any time a child gets near him with a snake. He should probably limit having snakes placed on his body because he might not be able to keep his focus on the child and his or her issues while being draped with snakes.*

2. *Jamal's religious beliefs preclude using profanity. She would be extremely uncomfortable with a child swearing in her playroom. If she believes that her discomfort would prohibit her from being able to maintain an acceptable level of positive regard for the child, she should probably limit this behavior.*

3. *Dirk is an extremely laid-back person. He has been a hospital nurse for 10 years. He is comfortable with every aspect of the human body, and his theoretical orientation is psychodynamic, which allows for client regression. If a child wanted to "make poop," with some sand and water, and smear it on the floor of the playroom, Dirk would be quite comfortable with this behavior and would probably choose not to limit it.*

4. *Natalie has a need for structure and order. She works in a psychiatric hospital and frequently conducts play therapy sessions with children who are extremely chaotic and messy. When children come into the playroom, they often empty all of the contents of the shelves onto the floor. Although she is uncomfortable with this behavior, she chooses not to limit it. Instead, she reminds them that they will have to start picking up the room earlier than usual when they do this.*

Personal application. It is essential for prospective play therapists to examine themselves, their own personalities, and their own issues to learn about the behaviors they can and cannot accept in a playroom. If you are unaware of possible behaviors that may create difficulties in your ability to accept a child, you may inadvertently harm the relationship with the child and potentially harm the child. You will need to explore your own history and current situation—examining your thoughts, attitudes, feelings, and prejudices to determine whether there are behaviors you find intolerable. Then you will need to decide whether you can work through these issues so as to be able to maintain a level of acceptance if children act out those behaviors. If you cannot do this, you may need to automatically limit those behaviors in order to be accepting. With a child who continually exhibits behaviors that are intolerable to you, you may choose to refer that child to another counselor who does not share these issues.

Influence of the Individual Child

Developmental age, the personalities, and the life situations of individual children can sometimes be factors in deciding what to limit. Younger children usually need more rules and structure than older children. It is frequently helpful with developmentally very young children (developmentally 2–5 years of age) to provide quite a few limits, especially those related to physical safety and property damage. Many times, children in this age range do not have the experience base necessary to guide them in making decisions about what behaviors can be damaging to themselves, others, or the playroom. By setting limits and explaining the practical rationale behind each one, the therapist can begin to teach younger children how to judge whether an activity might be harmful.

In terms of personality factors, some children seem to need more structure than other children. One method of conceptualizing children that can provide insight into the influence of children's personalities related to limit setting in the play therapy process was developed by Kissel (1990), who suggested that children having problems can fit into two distinct categories— too loose or too tight.

Children who are too loose need more structure and limits than children who are too tight, because children who are too loose have difficulty with self-regulation and rule-governed behavior. Because they struggle with self-control, they may need for the therapist, at least in the initial stages of the play therapy relationship, to provide assistance to them so that they can stay in control of themselves. This means that the therapist would limit more behaviors with children who are too loose than with children who are too tight. He or she would probably avoid using too many negotiable limits because the negotiation procedure might be hampered by the thought processes and behaviors of children who are too loose.

Children who are too tight, in contrast, are too rigidly controlled and would probably benefit from being encouraged to be more free and spontaneous. With children who are too tight, the therapist could contribute significantly to their growth by imposing few limits and by allowing them to experiment with behavior that cannot be "perfect," such as shooting a dart gun at lights or throwing sand on the floor, as long as the results of these activities do not result in any permanent damage to the therapist or the property.

Life situations that can have an impact on what the therapist limits are usually related to children's sense of being out of control. For instance, children who are terminally ill, who have recently experienced a serious loss, or who have been sexually or physically abused may frequently feel that they have no power in their own lives—that they are powerless to stop harmful things. Depending on how this sense of futility is manifested in the playroom, the therapist may wish to make shifts in what gets limited. Some children in these circumstances act recklessly in the playroom, necessitating many limits on their behavior. Other children may withdraw and refuse to try any new behaviors in the playroom. With these children, the therapist would want to set very few limits so as to try to encourage them to take more risks.

When to Limit

Most play therapists believe that it is more helpful to set limits when the child is about to break a rule, rather than reciting a list of limits in the initial session. This helps to avoid power struggles with children who tend to be aggressive, for whom a list of limits would simply be a laundry list for future transgression. It also helps to encourage more timid children to try activities that they might normally avoid if given a formidable list of things they are not allowed to do in the playroom.

The best time to limit is immediately before a child actually violates a rule. To be able to anticipate potential problems, the therapist must be alert to the child's nonverbal behaviors. Most children physically telegraph their intentions before they actually do something that would be deemed inappropriate in the playroom. For example, Gloria may be about to shoot the therapist with a dart gun. She will pick up the gun, load it with darts, and aim it at the therapist. This would be the moment to set the limit—after she aims but before she pulls the trigger.

It is important to avoid setting a limit either too early or too late. If you set a limit too early, children frequently get into an argument about their intentions—taking offense because you have accused them of making plans for carrying out inappropriate behaviors. If you set a limit too late, you will miss the opportunity to prevent the targeted behavior. This can potentially result in children feeling guilty for doing something unacceptable or in them feeling triumphant for getting away with something inappropriate.

Some children become extremely anxious about not having a list of rules to govern their behavior (either by compliance or by defiance). These children would actually prefer a list of limits rather than having the rules of the playroom be nebulous or undefined. To help these children, L. Guerney (personal communication, October 1990) tells children, "If you are about to do something that is against the playroom rules, I will let you know." By doing this, she avoids the pitfalls of providing a list of limits, while at the same time she lets children who have a need for structure know that there are rules and that she will not let them blunder into transgressions.

Practical Considerations in Limiting

Before I discuss specific steps of the various approaches to limit setting, it might be helpful to discuss several practical considerations in delivering limits. The therapist must monitor his or her personal reactions, attitudes, and feelings regarding interactions with the child; moderate his or her tone of voice and body language; and avoid lecturing the child and unnecessarily repeating the child's name.

One of the key components in successful limiting is conveying acceptance and respect for the child even when he or she is doing something that is inappropriate or unacceptable in the playroom. To be able to do this, you must have a clear understanding of your own issues, reactions, attitudes, and emotions so that you do not inadvertently convey disapproval to the child. By understanding your own trigger points and monitoring your own physical and emotional responses to the child, you will be much more likely to be in control of the feedback you are sending via verbal and nonverbal channels. If there are behaviors that you cannot accept, you can refer children who manifest them to some other therapist, or you can work out your own issues outside the play therapy relationship, either with a personal therapist or a supervisor.

When you limit, the nonverbal aspect of the communication is usually even more important than the verbal component—both in the area of voice (tone, pitch, volume, and speed) and in the area of physical reactions (body posture, body movement, and facial expressions). It is essential to use your usual tone of voice, without changing the tonal pattern from the way you normally speak to the child. If, for example, you usually talk in a calm, level tone, without many tonal variations, this is the way you should limit. In contrast, if you normally talk in a lively, animated way, you should limit using that same varied tonality.

Do not use a sarcastic or singsong tonal pattern in the way you talk with children, because both of these tones will sabotage the limiting process. When the therapist limits in a sarcastic, facetious, or condescending tone of voice, children tend to take this as a challenge or an insult. When limits are delivered in this way, children frequently do not abide by them to show the therapist that he or she cannot tell them what to do. When the therapist limits in a baby or singsong tone of voice, children tend to ignore the limit. Children do not take these limits seriously because they infer from the tone of voice that the limits are not being set seriously.

It is important to have the same pitch you usually use. If your voice is usually relatively high, in most cases you would want to limit in that pitch. Otherwise, you might communicate to the child that you are panicking or that you are trying to control the child's behavior by overpowering him or her. If your voice is usually relatively low, in most cases you would want to limit in that pitch. Otherwise, you might communicate your own anxiety about the limiting process to the child. There are exceptions to this injunction, however. With some children, lowering your pitch makes the limit more effective, because they may be more likely to comply with a limit delivered in a deeper voice. With other children, raising the pitch of your voice may convey urgency, which might influence compliance.

It is very helpful to remember that your body posture, body movement, and facial expressions all convey your thoughts and feelings to the child. Again, the best strategy for delivering limits is to avoid changing these nonverbals from the way you usually do things. If you change any of the various physical means of communication, you should do it intentionally, having thought out what you wish for your body language to convey.

Whatever procedure you opt to use for setting limits, remember to keep it brief and concise. You will be much more successful in limiting if you can avoid lecturing or otherwise drawing out the procedure. The most effective limit does not involve a great deal of explanation or pontificating on the part of the therapist. Keep it simple, and keep it quick.

Many times, the therapist uses the child's name an inordinate number of times when limiting. This repetition seems to be related to the therapist's level of anxiety and his or her need to get the child's attention. The therapist may believe that saying the child's name a number of times will increase the likelihood of compliance. This is faulty reasoning. In limiting, the therapist should use the child's name a minimal number of times to avoid telegraphing trepidation about compliance.

It is also important to consider a child's culture and the methods used for discipline in that culture. For instance, in most Native American families, parents set few limits and expect children to discipline themselves, whereas in many old-order Amish families, a switch may be used as a consequence for disobedience, defiance, or stubbornness (Locke, 1998). Although the play therapist does not have to adhere strictly to the discipline patterns of each child's culture, he or she must learn what these patterns are and convey a sense of respect for that culture in relationship to setting limits.

Styles of Limiting

There are many different strategies for setting limits in play therapy. Some of them are related to various theories, and some are determined by the preferences of individual therapists. The list of limiting strategies presented in this section is not definitive or exhaustive. I have chosen to include techniques outlined by Ginott (1959), Landreth (1991), L. Guerney (personal communication, October 1997), Kottman (1995), and Benedict and Narcavage (1997) on the basis of the clarity and specificity of available descriptions of the technique and the ease with which practitioners could apply the technique in their practice. Several of these authors also described how to proceed when children do not comply with limits, whereas others leave this to the ingenuity of the therapist.

One of the limiting strategies described in this chapter sometimes involves physical intervention to ensure compliance with limits. As I noted earlier in this chapter, there are legal and ethical issues involved in using physical interventions with clients. The therapist must be sure to consider the consequences of such an intervention before making a decision to use this means to induce compliance with limits. Any therapist who is considering the use of this strategy must acquire training in violence management and appropriate therapeutic holding techniques. If physical intervention is an option, it is important to clearly communicate with parents about this possibility before such a strategy is used. It is also essential to document the circumstances that evoked this option and to explain the circumstances to parents when such an intervention has occurred. The therapist must keep in mind that this procedure can be extremely frightening for children, especially if the therapist does not seem to be calm and in control. Before embarking on such an intervention, the therapist should examine his or her own issues related to feeling out of control and his or her reactions to the situation. A decision to physically intervene should be based on the child's behavior, not on the therapist's thoughts, feelings, attitudes, or history. Many therapists believe that physical intervention is appropriate only with children who pose a danger to self or others or a major threat to property. If a therapist is challenged from a legal or ethical standpoint, it is clearly easier to defend the decision to use physical intervention in situations in which the therapist believes danger or damage is imminent.

Ginott

Ginott (1959) described a four-step procedure for limiting.

1. Acknowledge the child's feelings and/or desires and help him or her express them verbally (e.g., "You are mad at me and would like to shoot me.").
2. Clearly state the limit, in passive voice if possible (e.g., "The rule of the playroom is that I am not for shooting.").
3. Redirect the behavior of the child so that feelings and/or desires can be expressed through acceptable behaviors (e.g., "You could pretend the doll is me and shoot at her if you want.").
4. Acknowledge the child's feelings about the limit (e.g., "You are kind of disappointed about the rule that you can't shoot at me.").

Ginott (1959) suggested that the therapist always state the limit in a way that does not constitute a challenge to children's self-respect. He believed that children are much more likely to abide by limits that are stated impersonally (instead of saying, "You cannot shoot at me," the therapist would say, "No shooting the gun at people.") and in passive voice (instead of saying, "You must not shoot at me," the therapist would say, "People are not for shooting."). In this formulation, the therapist does not verbally target the child as being the one who is violating a limit.

According to Ginott (1959), in many cases the therapist can also set the limit nonverbally. For instance, if Josey begins to drip paint on the floor, the therapist could hand her several newspapers to put down under the easel. This action would effectively limit Josey's behavior without a word uttered by the therapist.

Ginott (1959) freely acknowledged that there are times when children do not abide by the limits placed on them in play therapy. Although he objected to removing children from the playroom, he did not provide concrete suggestions about how to deal with them when they are noncompliant. He stated that "no blanket recommendation can be made on how to deal with the child's aggression, since the therapeutic reaction will depend on the meaning of the child's specific action" (Ginott, 1959, p. 164).

Landreth

Landreth (1991) used the acronym ACT to represent his three-step limiting procedure, which is an adaptation of the process originated by Ginott (1959).

1. A—Acknowledge the feelings, wishes, and wants of the child (e.g., "You seem really angry at me, and you want to shoot the gun at me.").
2. C—Communicate the limit to the child, using passive voice formulation (e.g., "I am not for shooting.").
3. T—Target appropriate alternative behaviors (e.g., "Elizabeth, you can choose to shoot the doll or the bop bag instead.").

Landreth (1991) emphasized that the therapist must clearly define what is acceptable and what is unacceptable. For the third step, he also suggested using the child's name to get his or her attention and using nonverbal cues to divert the child's focus from the original target of the behavior. He acknowledged that there are times when the therapist cannot follow these procedures in order—in certain situations, it might be more important to limit quickly and then acknowledge the child's behavior.

With children who persist in a lack of cooperation in response to the ACT procedure, Landreth (1991) outlined a fourth step, which is to state a final choice or "ultimate" limit. This involves a consequence for continued noncompliance (e.g., "If you choose to shoot me one more time, you choose not to play with the gun anymore today."). An important feature of this style of setting consequences is the inclusion of the child in making choices about how the interaction will proceed. Leaving the playroom is one potential consequence, but if possible, the therapist should try to think of a consequence that is not so final so that the child will have a chance to continue the session with appropriate behavior.

Landreth (1991) emphasized that the therapist must exercise patience in this process and avoid using the fourth step whenever possible. He also stressed that the therapist's tone of voice and nonverbal behavior must continue to convey warmth, empathy, respect, and acceptance to the child even when he or she does not comply with limits. When the child continues to avoid compliance, G. Landreth (personal communication, April 1986) asks parents to intervene rather than risk damaging the therapeutic relationship between the child and the therapist by having the therapist physically intervene.

Guerney

L. Guerney (personal communication, October 1997) also adheres to a nondirective, client-centered orientation, but she uses three steps that differ from those described by Ginott (1959) and Landreth (1991).

1. The therapist states the rule (e.g., "You may not throw anything at me.").
2. If the child exhibits the behavior again, the therapist reminds the child of the rule (e.g., "Remember that I told you that you may not throw things at me?") and warns him or her of consequences of continued transgressions (e.g., "If that happens again, you will have to put the ball away.").
3. If the child exhibits the behavior a third time, the therapist follows through with the consequence (e.g., "Since you decided to throw the ball at me again, it will have to be put away on the shelf for the rest of the session.").

L. Guerney (personal communication, October 1997) stressed that, rather than naming the effect a child's behavior could have, the therapist should simply describe the prohibition in very operational terms (e.g., "You may not rip that doll with the hammer claw."). Although she sometimes uses a consequence related to the transgression, she is also willing to impose a consequence of leaving the playroom if the unacceptable behavior continues.

Kottman

Kottman (1995) described four steps for setting limits in Adlerian play therapy, which involves a collaborative process between the therapist and the child.

1. The therapist states the limit in a nonjudgmental way, emphasizing that the limit is a rule specific to the setting (e.g., "It is against the playroom rules to shoot at people.").
2. The therapist reflects the child's feeling or makes a guess about the purpose of the child's behavior (e.g., "I can tell you are really angry right now." or "You want to show me that I can't control your behavior.").
3. The therapist engages the child in generating alternative appropriate behaviors (e.g., "I bet you can think of something in the playroom you could shoot that would not be against the rules."). This statement opens the door for a negotiation process between the therapist and the child in which they devise a concrete, measurable contract for acceptable behavior (e.g., "Okay, remember that you can shoot anything but me, you, and the mirror.").

With most children, the third step is the end of the procedure. Kottman (1995) speculated that involving children in generating behaviors that are acceptable in the playroom gives them a sense of ownership and power that precludes further pursuit of the limited behavior. However, with children who persist in noncompliance, there is a fourth step, which involves a renewed reflection of feelings and/or a guess about the purpose of the behavior and then setting up logical consequences for further transgressions (e.g., "We will need to decide what the consequences will be if you choose to shoot me again."). The consequences should be related to the proscribed behavior and should be respectful to the child—not harsh or punitive. It is usually helpful if the consequence does not last the remainder of the session so that the child has a chance to behave appropriately within the same time interval in which the transgression occurred. A timer set for 5 or 10 minutes can assist the therapist in giving the child a chance to recover and play with that toy or handle that situation more appropriately. This technique is meant to prevent the child from leaving the playroom with the idea that he or she cannot handle a specific toy or situation.

There is a decision about timing that must be made about the fourth step. The therapist can (a) wait to see if the child adheres to the agreement made in the third step without outlining consequences of noncompliance or (b) combine the third and fourth steps and define the consequences at the same time the contract is set. Kottman (1995) suggested that deferring the generation of consequences communicates a belief that the child will comply. However, this is a matter of personal preference—each therapist will have to decide this on a case-by-case basis.

There are some behaviors that the therapist will probably not be willing to let happen more than once, like hitting someone or breaking a toy deliberately. With these situations, the therapist could link the third and fourth steps or present the consequence as a choice before the child actually breaks the limit (e.g., "If you choose to try to hit me with the sword, you choose to lose the sword for the rest of the session."). One difficulty with using this preemptive strike type of consequence setting is that it does not involve the child in generating the consequence. However, in some situations and with some children, it may be necessary to do this to prevent mayhem.

Benedict and Narcavage

Benedict and Narcavage (1997), proponents of Thematic play therapy, have a five-step limiting procedure that combines elements of several other methods of setting limits.

1. The therapist gives the child limited choices as a way of structuring his or her behavior (e.g., "Would you rather shoot at the bop bag or make a target on the paper attached to the easel?").
2. The therapist reminds the child of the rules and describes alternatives (e.g., "It is not OK to shoot people with the dart gun. You can shoot the bop bag or draw a target on the paper attached to the easel.").

3. The therapist warns the child of potential consequences of dangerous or inappropriate behaviors (e.g., "I will have to take the gun away from you if you keep on trying to shoot me.").

4. The therapist encourages the child to restrain his or her behavior before the therapist externally enforces the limit (e.g., "You are going to have to stop yourself from shooting at me with the gun.").

5. If necessary, the therapist provides external enforcement of the limit by removing any object used in an unacceptable manner by the child or holding the child until the child is able to restrain his or her own behavior and comply with the limits. Before taking this action, the therapist tells the child what is about to happen, the rationale for his or her action, and the time limit of the consequence (e.g., "I have asked you not to shoot me with the dart gun, and you haven't been about to stop yourself from doing this, so I am going to take the gun away from you until you can promise me that you will not shoot it at me anymore. As soon as you promise me that you will not shoot it at me anymore, you can have the gun back.").

Benedict and Narcavage (1997) suggested that the therapist consider whether external physical restraint of the child is possible and avoid using this consequence with children who are too large or too strong for effective application of external physical restraint. They also noted that it is essential for the therapist to use this consequence only when he or she is able to appear calm and feel relatively accepting of the child. If the decision to intervene physically with the child is based on the therapist's anger or aggravated feelings, this is an inappropriate intervention.

Examples of Limit Setting

To demonstrate each of the limit-setting methods described in this chapter, I provide several different scenarios and then give examples of how the therapist would limit using each of the methods. I have generated each of the applications of these methods, so if some aspect of my description of each process is inaccurate, it is due to a flaw in my understanding of that approach rather than a problem perpetrated by the originators of the approach.

  * *Omar's (9) parents describe him as "the apple of our eyes," but his school principal describes him as a defiant child who routinely responds to requests and*

limits with aggression and destruction of other people's property. He has been sent home from school several times during the year for damaging school property and hurting other children. His parents do not believe that he deserves these punishments but follow the school's request that he receive play therapy. In the third session, Omar comes into the playroom, picks up a plastic gun, and starts pounding the plastic dolls in the dollhouse. Several of them break before the therapist can intervene.

Ginott method—"You are very mad and would like to destroy all the dolls in the dollhouse. However, the dolls are not for breaking. You can hit the pillows or those stuffed animals with the hammer. I can tell that you would rather smash the dolls, but the rule is that the toys are not for breaking in here."

Landreth method—"You seem mad today, and you want to pound on those dolls with the gun. The dolls are not for smashing, though. Omar, you can decide to hit the pillows or the stuffed animals with the gun." If he continues, "If you choose to continue to pound the dolls with the gun, you choose not to play with the guns for this session."

Guerney method—"You may not smash the dolls with the gun." If he continues to squish the dolls, "Remember that I told you that you may not pound on the dolls? If that continues to happen, you will have to put the gun on the shelf." If Omar does not heed this warning, "Since you chose to continue to hammer on the dolls, the gun will have to be put on the shelf for the rest of the time we have."

Kottman method—"It is against the rules in the playroom to smash the toys. I can tell you are really angry about something, but it is not okay to destroy the dolls. Let's think of something that you can hit that would not violate the playroom rules." The therapist negotiates an agreement that Omar can smash egg cartons or rip paper to express his rage, rather than hitting dolls. If he goes back to hitting dolls or refuses to come to an agreement, "I see that you have decided to keep on breaking the rule about smashing toys. We will need to think of a consequence just in case you continue breaking toys." The therapist negotiates logical consequences that he will put the gun away for 15 minutes and then he can try to use the toy in an appropriate way for the rest of the session.

Benedict and Narcavage method—"Would you rather use the gun to pound on the pounding pegs or on the egg cartons that you can smash?" If the child does not respond appropriately, "It is not okay to smash the dolls. You can use the gun to pound on the pounding pegs or on the egg cartons. I will have to take the gun away from you if you keep on pounding on the dolls. You are going to have to stop yourself from smashing the dolls." If Omar continues, "I have asked you not to use the gun to smash the dolls, and you haven't been able to stop yourself from doing this, so I am going to take the gun away from you until you can promise me that you will not smash the dolls with it anymore. As soon as you promise me that you will not use the gun to pound the dolls, you can have the gun back." Therapist follows through.

* *Lottie (4) goes to the sink and pours water into a big bucket. She takes the bucket and gets ready to pour it in the sandbox.*

Ginott method—There is a good chance that a therapist using Ginott's philosophy would not limit this behavior, because the water probably would not hurt the property. If the therapist decides to limit, "You want to pour water in the sand, but the rule in here is that water is not for pouring in the sand. You can pour water in the sink. It seems like you are kind of sad that the water is not for pouring in the sand."

Landreth method—The therapist might limit this behavior because it has potential for making a mess that might prevent other children from having access to the sand. If the therapist limited, "I can tell that you would like to pour water in the sand, but the water is not for pouring into the sand. Lottie, you can choose to pour water in the sink instead." If she continues, "If you choose to begin pouring water in the sandbox, you choose not to play with either the water or the sand for the rest of today's play time."

Guerney method—"You may not pour water into the sand." If Lottie persists, "Remember that I said you may not pour water in the sandbox? If you keep pouring, you will have to put the water away and put the lid on the sandbox." If Lottie does not comply, "Since you decided to pour water in the sandbox, the water will have to be put into the sink and the lid will have to be put on the sandbox."

Kottman method—"It is against the playroom rules to dump that much water in the sandbox. It looks like you think it would be fun to dump all that water in the sand, but it would make it too soggy in there. How many cups of water (handing her the measuring cup) do you think would be enough to get things wet, but not enough to make things too soggy?" The therapist would negotiate with Lottie and come to an agreement on a reasonable amount of water. If she refuses to negotiate or does not abide by the agreement, "You would like to show me that I can't tell you what to do. But if you choose to pour more water into the sand than we decided was okay, you choose not to play with the water or the sand for 10 minutes."

Benedict and Narcavage method—"Would you rather pour water from the bucket in the sink or use the bucket to hold sand that you can pour in the sandbox?" If Lottie does not change her behavior, "It is not okay to pour water in the sandbox. You can pour water from the bucket in the sink or use the bucket to hold sand that you can pour in the sandbox. I will have to take the bucket of water away from you if you don't stop trying to pour it in the sandbox. You are going to have to stop yourself from pouring the water in the sandbox." If necessary, the therapist provides external enforcement of the limit following a warning, "I have asked you not to pour water in the sand, and you haven't been able to stop yourself from pouring the water into the sand. So, I am going to take the bucket of water away from you until you can tell me that you will not pour any more of the water into the sand. As soon as you promise me that you will not pour the water into the sand, you can have the water back." Therapist follows through with consequences.

*   Gabriella (5) is angry because the therapist has set a limit. She throws herself on the floor and starts banging her head against a concrete wall, screaming, "You bitch. You can't tell me what to do."*

Regardless of the method of limiting, the therapist must intervene to prevent the child from hurting herself. This intervention may involve a therapeutic restraint, calling for a parent to restrain the child, or doing something like putting a pillow between the child's head and the wall.

Ginott method—The therapist moves to stop the child from hitting her head and says, "You are not for hurting. You can hit the bop bag to let me know how you feel. You are really mad at me."

Landreth method—The therapist moves to stop the child from hitting her head and says, "Your head is not for hitting. You are very angry because

I told you the mirror is not for shooting. Gabriella, you can choose to stop hitting your head, or you can choose for your mother to come and carry you out of the playroom."

Guerney method—The therapist moves to stop the child from hitting her head and says, "You may not hit your head on the wall." If she continues to hit her head, "Remember that I told you that you may not hit your head on the wall. If you keep on doing this, I will have to hold you in my lap." If she does not stop, "Since you decided not to stop hitting your head, I will have to pick you up and hold you in my lap."

Kottman method—The therapist moves to stop the child from hitting her head and says, "It's against the rules to hit your head on the wall. You are angry, and you want to show me that I cannot tell you what to do. I bet you can choose something to hit for 2 minutes to show me how mad you are at me." The therapist negotiates with the child, and they decide that she is going to hit a pillow for 2 minutes.

Benedict and Narcavage method—The therapist moves to stop the child from hitting her head and says, "It is not okay to hit your head on the wall. Either you can stop pounding your head, you can pound your head on the pillows, or I will have to hold you to make sure that you don't hurt yourself. You are going to have to stop yourself from banging your head." If Gabriella persists, "I have asked you to stop banging your head, and you haven't been able to stop yourself from banging your head, so I am going to hold you to make sure that you don't keep on banging your head. As soon as you promise me that you will stop banging your head, I will be able to let you sit on your own. " Then the therapist follows through with this action.

Practice Exercises

Experiment with the steps of two different methods of limiting for each of the following situations. Identify the style of both limits and explain why you chose to use those styles to limit in that particular situation with that child. Also explain what you would do if the child does not abide by the limit.

1. Tami (8) is an adopted child who is struggling with issues about identity and feeling that she doesn't belong in her adoptive family. Her

adopted parents are White, and she is African American. She was adopted when she was 4, after the courts terminated her mother's parental rights because of physical and verbal abuse. She seems agitated that you have mentioned that perhaps the little girl doll (who is being beaten by the mother doll) wishes that she didn't have to keep on living with her mother. Tami stops playing with the dolls, gets the sword, lifts it over your head, and (in a very angry voice) says, "I am going to cut off your head."

2. Jerome is 4 years old. His parents are in the middle of a messy divorce and acrimonious custody battle. Jerome's presenting problems include night terrors, separation anxiety (from both his mother and his father), and excessive crying and clinging to adults. In his fourth session, he takes all of the figures from the dollhouse and tries to stick them into the furnace duct in the playroom.

3. Moneek (6) was referred to play therapy because she is disobedient and defiant at home and school. She is rude and disrespectful to both of her parents and bullies her two younger sisters. In her first session, staring straight at you, she starts to put coins from the cash register in her mouth, apparently getting ready to swallow them. She says, "I bet you can't stop me from eating these."

4. Simon (10) has been diagnosed as being developmentally delayed but having normal intelligence. The school psychologist thinks that he might have Asberger's syndrome. He does not have any friends and frequently ignores his teacher. He seldom makes eye contact and seems to avoid touching other people. His parents and teacher asked you to work with him on social skills and self-esteem issues. In his sixth session, he is using a spoon to bury soldiers in the sandbox when he accidentally knocks some sand out of the sandbox. He smiles and does it again. He begins to make a game of seeing how far out of the sandbox he can jettison sand with the spoon.

5. Four-year-old Juana's parents are divorced and have joint custody of Juana and her older brother. Her mother has brought her to play therapy because she thinks that her behavior is "getting out of hand." Juana tends to ignore directions from her mother, who reports that Juana "gets away with too many naughty behaviors when she is with her father." In her third session, Juana gets the finger paints out of the

cabinet and starts to smear them on her face and her dress, humming and smiling. When you ask her to stop, she ignores you.

6. Same scenario as Number 5, except that Juana starts putting the paint on you.

7. According to reports from his father, Itzak (5) has always tended to be very timid. His parents have no theories about why this is the case, although they report that this behavior seemed to originate when his grandfather, a survivor of the Holocaust, died. At the time he started therapy, in new situations he cried, and his entire body shook. Since the beginning of therapy, he has made significant progress on this issue. In the middle of the 14th session, he smiles at you and says, "I am going to go outside and play on that playground next door. See you later!"

8. Columbine (8) is the oldest of five children. Her parents report that she has always "marched to a different drummer." She tends to do whatever she wants to do, regardless of the consequences imposed. As a matter of fact, her parents tell you that they are at their wits' end because "nothing seems to phase her." In the fifth session, she comes into the playroom and begins to empty all of the shelves of their toys and then deliberately starts breaking toys.

9. Ivan (6) is the most "grown-up" child you have ever counseled. Every week, he comes into the playroom, sits down, and describes his week to you. He does not like to play with messy materials such as finger paints or sand. He does not seem to be making very much progress on his issues of being rigid and lacking spontaneity. You only have three more sessions with him, and so in your seventh session, you decide to be a little more directive than you have been in the past. You ask Ivan to squirt shaving cream onto a table and spread it with his hands. He tells you that he "absolutely won't do that." You insist, and he proceeds to aim the shaving cream nozzle at you.

10. T'Kenya (8) was sexually abused by a neighbor boy when she was 5 years old. She did not show any ill-effects at the time, but lately she has started sexually acting out with several of her nieces and nephews. In her six sessions with you, she has been relatively seductive but has done nothing overtly sexual. In the seventh session, she approaches you and starts rubbing her crotch against your knee.

11. Dermot (7) is a self-described "wild child." He loves to climb on things and jump from high places. He has broken several limbs this way and does not seem to have learned from these experiences. He begins to climb up the shelves in your playroom, saying, "I bet I can jump down from the top of this."

12. Jenny (9) is very good at sports but seems to be failing in every other aspect of her life. She is making poor grades in school, has no friends, and is disruptive at home. The first time she comes into the playroom, she wants to play pitch and catch with you, and you decide to comply. In subsequent sessions, this activity is all she wants to do. She has now been coming to you for 10 sessions. During every single session so far, she has insisted that you play catch with her the entire time. You decide that this is not particularly helpful, and in your 11th session, you decide to decline her invitation to play catch. She throws the ball at you.

13. Ajit (7) is a model student whose teacher referred him to play therapy because he is exhibiting the negative aspects of perfectionism. His teacher reports that he has very extreme reactions to what he perceives as personal "failures"—tearing up assignments that are not 100% accurate and refusing to take tests that he is not sure he will ace. His parents report that they have high standards and expect him to do his best but do not use corporal punishment when he does not succeed. In his first session, he is painting a picture and accidentally spills some paint on the floor. He starts to sob loudly and takes the paint container to the sink, ready to dump out the entire container.

Questions to Ponder

1. From your previous experience of being around children, describe your comfort level with managing children's misbehavior.

2. On the basis of your previous experience with children, your interactions with other adults, the practice exercises, and your sample sessions with children, what kind of misbehavior do you think will evoke the most anxiety for you? Explain your reasoning.

3. What will be the hardest part of limiting for you? Explain.

4. What purpose do you think limiting serves in the playroom? Explain.

5. What kind of impact will your possible work settings have on the way you limit? Explain.

6. What kind of impact will your own personality and/or issues have on the way you limit? Explain.

7. What is your position on conditional limits? Would you be comfortable negotiating certain limits with children, or would you be more comfortable with a binary (e.g., "Yes, you can do this." "No, you cannot do this.") position?

8. For each style of limiting, what appeals to you?

9. For each style of limiting, what do you think would be difficult for you?

10. If you were going to create your own strategy for limiting in the playroom, what steps would you include? Explain how each step would be helpful. Explain how each step fits into what you believe about people.

11. How do you feel about physically restraining children? How would you decide whether to use physical interventions with children?

12. What impact do think setting limits on children's behavior will have on your relationship with them?

13. How will you adapt your strategies for limiting depending on the ethnicity or cultural background of the child?

Chapter 9

Returning Responsibility to the Child

When working with children, it is relatively easy for the play therapist to get into the habit of taking care of them and making decisions for them that they could make themselves. Whenever possible, it is essential to refrain from this practice, because it can be potentially harmful to children's sense of self-confidence and self-efficacy. One of the main methods of avoiding doing things for children that they can (and should) do for themselves is the technique of returning responsibility to the child (Landreth, 1991). This skill involves letting children know, either directly or indirectly, that the play therapist believes that they have the capacity for successfully executing the behavior or making the decision in question.

The purpose of returning responsibility is to empower children. There are two components to this empowerment: (a) Children get the message that the therapist believes that they can be successful, and (b) they have the experience of trying something that they would not usually attempt. By returning the responsibility to children, the therapist attempts to imbue them with a sense of self-efficacy and convey that the task or choice is within their reach. The actual experience of trying is frequently empowering in and of itself. As children realize that they are in control of their own behavior and decisions, the very act of doing or choosing lets them experience a feeling of power that they may not regularly experience. It does not matter whether they are successful in the attempted behavior or make the "correct" decision. By allowing them to handle the consequences of their own choices, the therapist encourages independence, self-responsibility, and creativity (Landreth, 1991).

When to Return Responsibility to the Child

It is appropriate to apply the skill of returning responsibility to children in situations in which they explicitly or implicitly ask for help and in situations in which the therapist feels a need to help them even though they have not indicated a desire for assistance. Sometimes the responsibility relates to behavior, and other times it relates to decisions. Examples of each of these instances follow:

* Child <u>explicitly</u> asks for help with <u>behavior</u>

—"Can you tie my shoes?"

—"Will you turn the water on for me?"

—"Please button my coat for me."

* Child <u>explicitly</u> asks for help with <u>decisions</u>

—"Will you tell me what color I should paint this picture?"

—"What do you think I should do next?"

—"What kind of animal is this red puppet?"

—"What is this?"

* Child <u>implies</u> that he or she needs help with <u>behavior</u>

—"I can't tie my shoes."

—"How do you make this faucet work?"

—"I don't know how to tell time."

* *Child <u>implies</u> that he or she needs help with <u>decisions</u>*

—"I can't decide what color to paint this boat."

—"I am not sure what to do next." (looks at the counselor)

—"I wonder what kind of animal this little thing is."

* *Situations in which the therapist may feel a need to help the child with <u>behavior</u> without being asked*

—The child is jumping up and down trying to reach something on a high shelf.

—The child keeps on trying to tie his shoes but is not experiencing success.

—The child is trying to make the dart gun work but has not quite figured out how the mechanism catches.

* *Situations in which the therapist may feel a need to help the child with <u>decisions</u> without being asked*

—The child looks around the playroom, obviously having difficulty deciding what to do.

—The child touches a number of different toys, picking them up and then putting them down again.

—The child stands with the paint brush poised but does not paint anything on the paper.

How to Return Responsibility to the Child

There are two main styles of returning the responsibility to the children—the direct approach and the indirect approach. Whereas the direct approach has only one version, the indirect approach has at least four different variations: (a) using the child's metaphor; (b) using minimal encouragers; (c) restating content, reflecting feelings, or tracking; and (d) applying the whisper technique (G. Landreth, personal communication, March 1984). Sometimes, the therapist may decide to combine elements of the direct approach and the indirect approach.

Direct Approach

In the direct approach, the therapist expressly tells children that it is up to them to execute the behavior or make the choice without assistance. With situations in which children explicitly ask for help, the therapist can simply tell them that it is up to them to carry out the behavior or make the choice (e.g., "You can decide what you want to do with the baby doll.")

In situations in which the therapist believes that children are implicitly asking for help, he or she might initially want to make a guess about them wanting the therapist to do something or make a decision for them (e.g., "You seem like you want me to tell you what color to paint the flower."). After this, the therapist would tell them that they can take care of the situation or make the choice by themselves (e.g., "In the playroom, you can decide that for yourself."). When the therapist feels a need to help children with behaviors and decisions even though they have not asked, he or she might reflect a feeling before making an encouraging comment that suggests he or she has confidence that they can handle the situation themselves (e.g., "You seem a bit frustrated that you can't reach that puppet on the top shelf, but I bet you can figure out how to get it down.").

Indirect Approach

The other strategies for returning responsibility back to the child are more indirect. There are four different variations on this approach: (a) using the child's metaphor to return responsibility to the child; (b) using minimal encouragers or ignoring the child's desire for assistance; (c) using restatement of content, reflection of feelings, or tracking; and (d) using a variation of the whisper technique (G. Landreth, personal communication, March 1984).

Using the child's metaphor. The therapist can be indirectly direct by returning responsibility to the child through a metaphor. For example, if the child asks the therapist where the mouse should hide, the therapist would respond, "The mouse can decide for herself which is the best place to hide from the cat," or "Ms. Mouse, I bet you can figure out a place to hide." This method works only if the child has been communicating through a metaphor.

Using minimal encouragers. Another method of indirectly returning responsibility is to use minimal encouragers (e.g., "Mmmmm") or to not answer when the child asks for help (Landreth, 1991). By providing little feedback to the child, the therapist allows the child time to go ahead and make a decision or take action without interference or input from the therapist. This method seems to work best in situations in which the child is obliquely asking for assistance. It also works when the child is directly asking for help, but in these instances, this strategy may be relatively frustrating to the child.

Restating content, reflecting feelings, or tracking. By restating the content of the child's request (e.g., "You asked me what that little red thing is."), reflecting the child's feelings (e.g., "You seem a little anxious about knowing exactly what time it is."), or tracking (e.g., "You are touching all the toys."), the therapist can indirectly return the responsibility to the child. This approach works well with most situations in which the child is asking for or needing help.

Applying the whisper technique. The therapist can also use a variation of the whisper technique (G. Landreth, personal communication, March 1984). The whisper technique is usually used in role-playing (see chapter 13, "Advanced Play Therapy Skills") but can also work in returning responsibility to the child. For example, if Sigmund asks the therapist to tell him where to hide a ball, the therapist can use a whisper to ask the child for direction (e.g., "Where should I say the ball is?"). This technique would put the child in charge of generating an answer to his own question. Applying the whisper technique seems to work best when the child is directly asking for assistance or advice.

Combining the Direct Approach and the Indirect Approach

There are times when the therapist may want to use a combination of the indirect and direct approaches to return responsibility to the child. One example of such a time is when the therapist does not know if the child can actually accomplish the task but wants to gather more information. In this case, the therapist could start with an indirect approach by restating the content of the child's request or reflecting a feeling and watching the child's response. For example, if Wanpen asks the therapist to put a puzzle together, the therapist could reflect a feeling and then restate the content of her request by saying, "You seem to be afraid that maybe you won't be able to put the puzzle back together, so you are asking me to do it for you." When the child responds to this intervention, the therapist can make a decision about his or her next intervention. If Wanpen clarifies that she does know how to put the puzzle back but is feeling a little anxious about that skill, the therapist can use a direct response such as, "I have confidence that you can put it together if you work at it." If the child's response indicates that there is a good chance that the child will not be successful at the task at hand, the therapist may want to suggest a collaboration.

It is important to note that the combination of direct and indirect approaches with a suggestion of collaboration is appropriate only when the child is asking for help with behaviors. It is not appropriate with decision making because, although there may be behaviors the child cannot successfully accomplish, he or she will always be capable of making decisions in the playroom because there are no "right" or "wrong" decisions. This would make a collaboration inappropriate because it would involve the therapist in doing something for the child that the child can do alone.

When Not to Return Responsibility to the Child

It is not always appropriate to return the responsibility to the child. Although each therapist will need to decide whether to use this skill with an individual child in a particular situation, there are several circumstances in which returning the responsibility to a child might be contraindicated. These extenuating circumstances include situations in which (a) the therapist believes that the child is not capable of taking responsibility for the behavior; (b) the child is engaging in regressive behavior, and the therapist believes that this behavior is appropriate for that particular child; (c) the child's history indicates that the child may need someone to take care of him or her in certain situations; and (d) the child's life is not going particularly well and the child needs special nurturing.

Child Cannot Take Responsibility for That Behavior

It can be extremely discouraging to a child who truly cannot do something to be told by an adult that he or she really can do it. In cases in which the therapist does not know whether the child can actually do something, it is usually more helpful and encouraging to suggest that the therapist and the child work together on the project. The therapist can suggest that they collaborate on the activity (e.g., "Let's do it as a team. You hold the shoe lace in a circle, and I will loop the other one around it.") or ask the child to give directions on how the task could be accomplished (e.g., "Tell me how high you wanted it lifted and where it should go on the wall."). This strategy avoids any implicit suggestion that the inability to complete the task constitutes incompetence on the part of the child, which could be very discouraging to the child.

Regressive Behavior

If the therapist's theoretical orientation supports the concept that regression is therapeutically useful to children, the therapist may choose not to return responsibility to the child if he or she is engaging in regressive behavior. For example, when Sophia (9) uses a baby voice to ask, "Will you wrap this blanket around my baby?" the therapist may simply choose to do this for her.

Child's History

Sometimes a child's history will suggest that the child is not psychologically capable or ready to take care of himself or herself in certain situations. This may be due to a trauma or some element in the child's caretaking that has contributed to the child being unable to take responsibility at the current time. An example of a trauma that might affect the decision to return responsibility would be Frank (8), who broke both of his arms when he fell down a flight of stairs when he was 2 years old. Frank feels tremendous anxiety connected to stairs and has difficulty climbing stairs without holding an adult's hand. If Frank asked the therapist to hold his hand as they climbed the stairs to the therapist's office, the therapist might choose not to return this responsibility to him.

An example of an element in the child's upbringing that might affect the decision to return responsibility would be Lahti (7). Lahti's mother died when Lahti was 1 year old, and her father sank into depression, had to be hospitalized, and has never recovered. Lahti has been raised by a series of distant relatives who had multiple children of their own and could not spare very much attention for Lahti. She is extremely needy and frequently asks the therapist to do things for her that she could do herself. Lahti's therapist could decide that Lahti needs more nurturing than many other children, resulting in the therapist not always returning the responsibility to Lahti even in situations when the therapist believes that Lahti is capable of taking care of herself. Eventually, as Lahti begins feeling better about herself, the therapist could begin to return responsibility to her.

Child's Current Situation

If the therapist has information about the child's current life situation, there may be times when he or she decides that not returning the responsibility to the child is appropriate for the child at that particular point in time. This might involve the child having a particularly bad week or month, an anniversary of some kind of trauma, unusual family turmoil, and so forth. In such cases, a child who is usually very self-reliant might ask for help. When this happens, the therapist may decide to forgo returning the responsibility to the child. For example, ever since 6-year-old Greg started in therapy, he has always loaded the dart gun for himself. The week after his parents told him they are getting a divorce, he asks the therapist to load the darts into the gun for him. Greg's therapist might decide to just do this for him rather than returning the responsibility to him.

Applications in Different Theoretical Orientations

According to the information gathered from the experts in various approaches to play therapy, the skill of returning responsibility to the child seems to be a widely used play therapy strategy. All of the therapists who responded to the survey use this skill, and most of them seem to apply this skill in similar situations. However, the methods they use to return responsibility to the child sometimes vary, as do their explanations of the reasons why they use this skill.

All of the experts were relatively consistent in the situations in which they return responsibility to the child. They tend to return responsibility to the child when the child asks them to do something that the child can do without assistance or asks them to make a decision that the child has not attempted to make alone.

The replies from the nondirective play therapists suggested that they would generally use a relatively simple approach to returning responsibility to the child, seldom combining direct and indirect responses. With children who want help with decisions, most nondirective play therapists would probably use some variation of the direct format of saying to the child, "In here, you can decide." With children who want help with actions, most nondirective play therapists would use an indirect approach, usually reflecting the child's feelings, restating the content of the request for help, tracking the child's behavior, or using a minimal encourager.

Several of the more directive play therapists suggested that they would probably use more complex procedures for returning responsibility to the child. They may (a) make an interpretation to the child of why he or she has asked the therapist for help, directions, or permission before the therapist returns the responsibility to the child (K. O'Connor, personal communication, October 1997); (b) use "empowerment responses," including encouraging statements such as, "I bet you can fix that car if you try"; using asides such as asking the child, "What would the mommy say?"; and inviting the child to teach the therapist with comments like, "Can you show me how to do that?" (H. Benedict, personal communication, October 1997); and (c) use interpretation, goal disclosure, and encouragement (J. White, personal communication, October 1997).

Several of the play therapists made a special note that, although they do use the skill of returning responsibility to the child, they would never refuse to help a child asking for help, regardless of whether they felt that the child could do the task. This distinction seemed to be directed toward situations in which the child directly asks for help with behavior, rather than the other situations in which the therapist would return responsibility to the child.

Examples of Returning Responsibility to the Child

These examples include representative samples of each type of situation in which the therapist would return responsibility to the child. After each scenario, I have listed several different ways of returning responsibility. For each response, I have labeled the style of returning responsibility illustrated by that response.

Child *Explicitly* Asks for Help With *Behaviors*

* *Don sits on the ground and says, "Can you tie my shoes?"*

1. "I think you can tie them for yourself." (**direct**)
2. "You want some help with tying your shoes." (**indirect, restating content**)
3. "You seem a little nervous about whether you can tie your shoes. Want

to try it together?" (**combination of indirect and direct, with a suggestion of collaboration**)

* *Sally goes over to the water faucet and says, "Will you turn the water on for me?"*

1. "You can do that all by yourself." (**direct**)
2. "You'd like me to do that for you." (**indirect, restating content**)
3. "You wish I would turn the water on for you. You tell me what to do and we can help one another." (**combination of indirect and direct, with a suggestion of collaboration**)

* *Tyler, who buttoned his coat by himself last week, says, "Please button my coat for me."*

1. "I noticed that you did that all by yourself last week, and I am guessing that you can do it by yourself again this time." (**direct**)
2. Therapist smiles and nods encouragingly but does not move to help. (**indirect, minimal encourager**)
3. "Even though you did it last week, you're not feeling very confident that you can do it again. Why don't you show me how it gets started, and we can work together from there?" (**combination of indirect and direct, with a suggestion of collaboration**)

Child *Explicitly* Asks for Help With *Decisions*

* *Rowena looks up from her painting and asks, "Will you tell me what color I should paint this picture?"*

1. "In here, it can be any color you want it to be." (**direct**)
2. "You want me to tell you what color you should paint that picture." (**indirect, restating content**)
3. Whispering to the child, "What color should I say?" (**indirect, using the whisper technique**)

* *Sam Lone Eagle puts the dinosaurs away and asks, "What do you think I should do next?"*

1. "You can make that choice for yourself." (**direct**)
2. "Hmmmm." (waiting for him to go ahead and make a decision without giving an answer) (**indirect, minimal encourager**)
3. "You want me to tell you what to do." (**indirect, restating content**)

* *Ceyrah picks up a puppet and asks, "What kind of animal is this red puppet?"*

1. "In here, it can be whatever you want it to be." (**direct**)
2. "Let's ask her." Turns to the puppet and says, "What kind of animal are you?" (**indirect, using metaphor**)
3. "You wish I would tell you what animal that is, but in here, you can decide that for yourself." (**combination of indirect and direct**)

* *Lyle picks up a toy and asks, "What is this?"*

1. "That is up to you." (**direct**)
2. "You want to know what that is." (**indirect, restatement of content**)
3. Whispering, "What is that?" (**indirect, using the whisper technique**)

Child *Implicitly* Asks for Help With *Behavior*

* *Claire sits on the floor pouting and says, "I can't tie my shoes."*

1. "You sound like you want some help with tying your shoes, but I bet you can figure out a way to do that yourself." (**makes a guess about the underlying communication, then direct**)
2. "You're kind of feeling sorry for yourself and thinking that you just can't do that." (**indirect, reflecting feeling**)
3. "You sound a bit discouraged. Let's figure out how we can work together to get them tied." (**combination of indirect and direct, with a suggestion of collaboration**)

* *Liam walks over to the sink and asks, "How do you make this faucet work?"*

1. "Try it, and I bet you can figure it out." (**direct**)
2. "It sounds like you want me to show you how that works. Hmmmm." (**makes a guess about the underlying communication and then indirect, minimal encourager**)
3. "I'm thinking that you would like to figure that out, but you're not sure you can do it yourself. Why don't you put your hand on top of mine, and let's see if we can turn it on together?" (**makes a guess about the underlying communication and then combination of direct and indirect, with a suggestion of collaboration**)

* *Lessie asks, "What color does this flower want to be?"*
    1. "In here, the flower can choose any color to be." (indirect, using the child's metaphor)
    2. "You can pick a color for the flower." (direct)
    3. "I'm guessing that maybe you think there is a certain color that flower is supposed to be, but in here, you can decide on things like that because there is no 'right' color for flowers to be." (makes a guess about the underlying communication and then direct)

* *Scott looks really sad and says, "I don't know how to tell time."*
    1. "You can just make up a time, and that's what it will be in the playroom." (direct)
    2. "You sound kind of sad that you don't know how to tell time." (indirect, reflecting feeling)
    3. "I'm guessing you would like me to tell you what time it is. Mmmmm." (makes a guess about the underlying communication and then indirect, minimal encourager)
    4. "Well, sounds like you're not sure that you can figure out what the time is and you want some help with that. How can we figure out the time?" (makes a guess about the underlying communication and then suggests collaboration)

Child *Implicitly* Asks for Help With *Decisions*

* *Delaney says, "I can't decide what color to paint this boat."*
    1. "You sound like you wish I would decide that for you, but in here, that is your decision to make." (makes a guess about the underlying communication, then direct)
    2. "You feel like you can't decide, but I think you can." (combination of indirect and direct)
    3. "Let's ask the boat. 'Hey Boat, what color would you like to be?'" (indirect, whisper technique)

* *Kenisha looks askance at the therapist and whines, "I am not sure what to do next."*
    1. "I have confidence that you can figure that out for yourself." (direct)
    2. "You seem a bit confused about what you want to do now." (indirect, reflecting feeling)

3. "I am thinking that you wish I would decide that for you, but I know that you can make your own plan for what you do next." (**makes a guess about underlying communication, then direct**)

* *Ichiro says, "I wonder what kind of animal this little thing is."*
   1. "In here, it can be what you would like for it to be." (**direct**)
   2. "I wonder . . . ." (**indirect, minimal encourager**)
   3. "It sounds like you are thinking that I should tell you what that animal is, but in the playroom, you are in charge of making those decisions." (**makes a guess about underlying communication, then direct**)
   4. Whisper, "What would you like it to be?" (**indirect, whisper technique**)

Therapist Wants to Help Child With *Behavior* Without Being Asked

* *Shannon is jumping up and down trying to reach something on a high shelf.*
   1. "I know it is hard to reach that, but I bet you can think of a way you can get what you want." (**direct**)
   2. "That looks a bit frustrating, but you are continuing to try to get it." (**indirect, reflection of feeling**)
   3. Therapist says nothing, looks supportive, and thinks about why this is an issue for herself. (**indirect, minimal encourager**)

   * *Demetrius keeps on trying to tie his shoes but is not experiencing success with this task.*
   1. "You are determined to do that even though it is so hard. Shall we figure out a way we could work on it together?" (**indirect, reflection of feeling, then suggestion for collaboration**)
   2. "That seems really hard to do. I am thinking that we might work as a team to tie those shoes. What should I do first?" (**suggestion for collaboration**)

   * *Kamalah is trying to make the dart gun work but has not quite figured out how the mechanism catches.*
   1. Therapist nods, looks empathic, and does not say anything. (**indirect, minimal encourager**)

2. "Most of the kids who come here have trouble figuring out how to work that. What if we work on it together and get it to work?" (**suggestion for collaboration**)

Therapist Wants to Help Child With *Decisions* Without Being Asked

* *Juan looks around the playroom, obviously having difficulty deciding what to do, and says, "There's so much stuff."*

1. "There are a lot of things in here." (**indirect, restating content**)
2. "Wow, a guy might be overwhelmed with all the toys in here." (**indirect, reflecting feeling**)
3. Silence (**indirect, minimal encourager**)

* *Janette touches a number of different toys, picking them up and then putting them down again.*

1. "You look a little confused at having so many different choices." (**indirect, reflection of feeling**)
2. "You are touching many of the things in here." (**indirect, tracking**)
3. Silence (**indirect, minimal encourager**)

Practice Exercises

For each of the following scenarios, (a) label the type of situation (e.g., child explicitly asking for help, therapist wants to help with decisions), (b) generate two different ways of returning responsibility to the child in that particular instance, (c) identify the style of returning responsibility to the child (direct; indirect, reflecting feeling; etc.) for each response and explain why you chose that particular style in this situation, and (d) describe some set of extenuating circumstances in which you would decide not to return responsibility to that child for that particular behavior.

1. Jerome (4) stands with the paint brush poised but does not paint anything on the paper.
2. Natalia (6) asks, "Should I use red or green for this girl's hair?"
3. Colm (7) says, "I don't think I am supposed to get in the sandbox."
4. Jesus (5) says, "It is really hard to open this jar."
5. Leticia (9) tries to open the lid of a box, can't get it open, and sits down and begins to cry.

6. Patrick (8) looks at the therapist and says, "Is it against the rules to cuss in here?"
7. Taiwo (3) asks, "What is this little man's name?"
8. Logan (6) tries to get the lid off the sandbox and turns to the therapist saying, "This is just too hard for me to do by myself."
9. Charlotte (8) asks, "What do the other kids who come here use this for?"
10. Lyfong (9) says, "I want to jump off the top of the pile of pillows," and looks at the therapist without doing it.
11. Thomasina (6) picks up the cash register and asks, "How does this work?"
12. Santiago (5) climbs up to the top of the sandbox, starts falling off, and yells, "Help me. I can't save myself."
13. Sally (7) says, "I can't get the blocks back in the pile."
14. Saul (8) wants to know, "What do you do with this?" holding out the dart gun.
15. He tries to shoot it, unsuccessfully, and hands it to you, saying, "Why won't this work?"
16. He takes it back, saying, "Show me how to make it work."
17. Gigi (9) brings a doll to you and asks, "What is the mother supposed to do?"
18. Giovanni (6) says, "This wolf is wondering whether he is supposed to eat that bear."
19. Orin (4) asks, "How is this horse supposed to fly?"
20. Lucinda (6) is trying to comb her hair, but there are so many snarls in it that she is getting angry.
21. Taro (8) asks, "What is the right answer to this math problem I wrote on the piece of paper?"

Questions to Ponder

1. Explain your beliefs about the basic concept underlying the skill of returning responsibility to the child. Do you believe this can be helpful to children? Why or why not?
2. On the basis of your past experiences with children, your responses to the practice exercises, and your sample sessions with a child, which of the various ways of returning responsibility to the child will be comfortable for you to use? Explain your reasoning.

3. What are some situations in which you would not use the skill of returning the responsibility to the child? Why would this be the case in these situations?

4. Explain your thoughts on the best way to respond if a child asks you for help with behavior in the playroom.

5. Explain your thoughts on the best way to respond if a child asks you for help with decisions in the playroom.

6. What are some situations in which you would feel a need to help a child with a behavior or decision even though the child has not asked for help? What are your own personal issues connected to these situations?

7. How do you feel/what do you think about using encouraging statements, such as "I bet you can figure that out for yourself," or "You really know a lot about fixing things. I believe that you can fix that without my help," as a part of the procedure of returning responsibility to the child?

8. How do you feel/what do you think about using minimal encouragers or silence as a method of returning responsibility to the child?

9. How do you feel/what do you think about using the whisper technique to return responsibility to the child?

Chapter 10

Dealing With Questions

In play therapy, children frequently ask questions of the therapist. The therapist must have a strategy for dealing with these questions so that he or she can be consistent in the relationship with the child. There are several options for dealing with questions. The method of responding to children's questions depends partly on the nature of the question, partly on the personal inclination of the therapist, and partly on his or her theoretical orientation.

The Nature of Children's Questions in Play Therapy

Most questions that children ask in play therapy can fit into one of four distinct categories: practical, personal, relationship, or ongoing process of play therapy (Landreth 1991; O'Connor, 1991). In deciding which strategy to use in answering a particular question, one of the important factors for the therapist to consider is the type of question.

Practical Questions

Practical questions are those that ask for commonsense information. Although these questions can have an underlying hidden meaning, they are usually requests for simple data or feedback. Some examples of practical questions are as follows:

* "What time is it?"
* "What is this?"
* "Can I go to the bathroom?"
* "Where is my mother?"
* "Where is the glue?"
* "Is today the day we get out of school early?"
* "Can we play a game today?"
* "Is this a dog or a wolf puppet?"
* "Can I hit the mirror with the hammer?"

Personal Questions

Sometimes children in play therapy will ask the therapist personal questions about his or her life situation. In my experience, when children ask me personal questions, they are usually feeling a need to increase their knowledge of my life. They may do this because they are feeling exposed because I know more about them than they know about me. They may ask personal questions because they want to enhance their feeling of connectedness with me or because they wish to explore my "credentials." Sometimes the purpose of personal questions is to check out a hunch about who the therapist "really" is. Some examples of personal questions include

* "Do you have any children?"
* "Did you have to go to school to learn to play with kids?"
* "Where do you live?"
* "Why do you work with children?"
* "Are you married?"
* "Where is your mommy?"
* "Do you have any brothers or sisters?"
* "What is your favorite color (or food)?"
* "Why am I brown and you are white?"

Sometimes older children or more "streetwise" younger children may ask questions that are too personal as a way of shocking the therapist or gaining a sense of power over him or her (Kottman, 1995; O'Connor, 1991). Other children who have poor boundaries or have experienced sexual abuse may believe that this type of question is acceptable social interaction. Some examples of this type of inappropriate personal question include the following:

* "Do you like sex?"
* "Do you and your wife/husband 'do it?'"
* "What do you wear to bed?"
* "What kind of guy/girl do you think is cute?"
* "Would you like to touch my privates?"

Relationship Questions

With relationship questions, children ask about the therapeutic relationship and the personal relationship between them and the therapist. By asking relationship questions, children probe to see how the therapist feels about them from a professional perspective and from a private perspective. Children would rather have the therapist "really" care about them instead of caring about them because it is part of the job. The purpose of this type of query may be to determine the strength of the relationship. This information could help children avoid making an emotional commitment that is disproportionate to the therapist's emotional commitment (Kottman, 1995). In relationship questions, there are usually two different messages: an obvious, literal question and an underlying hidden question. For instance, in the question "Who else comes here?" the obvious, literal question is a request for the names of other clients, and the underlying hidden question is "Are there other children that you care for as much as you care for me?" Examples of relationship questions include

* "Do you like me?"
* "How many other children come here?"
* "Am I your favorite kid?"
* "Do you like me as much as your own little boy?"
* "Do you think I am special?"
* "Did you notice that I don't have arms like other kids?"
* "Are you happy to see me?"
* "Can I be your kid someday?"
* "Do you like Asian people?"
* "If you could, would you want to adopt me?"
* "Do you miss me when I'm not here?"
* "Don't you wish I could stay longer?"

Ongoing-Process Questions

Landreth (1991) listed questions that children frequently ask in play therapy. Many of these questions seem to focus on the ongoing process of therapy. In these questions, children wonder about "the parameters of the process of play therapy and the boundaries of the relationship between them and the play therapist" (Kottman, 1995, p. 67). These questions may be aimed at getting help from the therapist or exploring the rules in the play-room. Sometimes, ongoing-process questions are attempts by children to get the therapist to read their minds or make decisions for them. Again, in many cases, there is a blatant, factual question (e.g., "Can I shoot the dart gun at you?") and a more subtle subtext (e.g., "What are the rules in here?" or "Will you let me do something to hurt you?"). Examples of ongoing process questions include the following:

* "Would you like it better if I paint this barn red?"
* "Can I throw this ball in your face?"
* "How long do we have to stay in here?"
* "What do you think I am going to do now?"
* "Why do you talk like that?"
* "How come you always talk about feelings?"

* "Why don't you ever answer my questions?"
* "Don't you know how to play pitch and catch?"
* "What should I do next?"
* "Can you guess what I am drawing?"
* "Will you tie my shoes?"
* "When is my mom going to come in?"
* "What do you tell my dad about what we do in here?"
* "Can I spill paint on the rug?"

Dual-Category Questions

The categories presented here are not exclusive. A question that seems on the surface to be a practical question may also have a more subtle subtext that is really a relationship question or a question about the ongoing play therapy process. For example, when Jackie asks the question, "Do I know any of the other kids who come here?" she may be asking a straightforward, practical question about whether there is anyone in her school with whom she could get a ride to the clinic. She could also be asking a relationship question because she feels jealous about the possibility that the therapist has warm feelings about other children she might know.

This is not an "either/or" situation. If a particular question fits into more than one category, it could be that the child is aware of both aspects of the question and is intentionally asking a dual-purpose question. However, this would be too sophisticated for most young children. Usually when a question is double-edged, the child is focused on the literal meaning of the question, and the more hidden meaning is out of his or her awareness. When the therapist makes a guess about the underlying meaning, many times the child has a recognition reflex, which is an involuntary response acknowledging the accuracy of the guess and registering the new awareness on the child's part (Kottman, 1995).

Types of Responses (With Examples)

Although there are innumerable ways to respond to children's questions in play therapy, most of the possibilities will fit into one of eight categories. The therapist can (a) return the responsibility to the child, (b) ignore the question, (c) give a minimal encourager for an answer, (d) restate the question, (e) make a guess about the purpose of the question, (f) answer the question, (g) reply to the question with another question, or (h) decline to answer the question in a polite manner. For each of these choices, I explain the mechanics of the method, describe the kinds of questions for which such a reply would be appropriate, explore which theoretical approaches would use such a response, and give several examples when possible.

Return Responsibility to the Child

One method of handling questions is to return the responsibility back to the child (see chapter 9, "Returning Responsibility to the Child"). The therapist would usually do this with practical questions asking for specific information about toys, game procedures, or playroom rules or with questions about the ongoing process that ask the therapist to take care of or make decisions for the child. This response style would be appropriate for both nondirective and directive play therapists, although there are some formats for stating the return (e.g., encouraging comments) that would probably suit more directive therapists than nondirective therapists. Some examples of returning the responsibility to the child are as follows:

* "You can decide that for yourself."
* "I bet you can figure that out."
* "In here, it can be whatever you want it to be."
* "You are the only one who can know what you are going to do next."

Ignore the Question

In some cases, the therapist might choose to ignore the question, with the purpose of encouraging the child to discover or determine an answer on his or her own. This response can work with any of the categories of questions but is probably more appropriate with practical questions and ongoing-process questions because they are the queries most likely to be designed as a method for engaging the therapist in solving children's problems for them. This response style would be appropriate for therapists of any theoretical orientation.

When choosing this method of response, it is important for the therapist not to ignore the child while ignoring the question. The therapist should make eye contact and smile in a caring way, nonverbally conveying a confidence that the child can answer the question for himself or herself without the assistance of the therapist.

Use Minimal Encouragers

Minimal encouragers are counseling responses designed to convey interest and understanding to the client in as few words as possible. These include simple responses such as "Uh-huh," "Mmmmm," "I see," "Yes," "Well," and "Hmmmm." Another method of minimally encouraging the client is to repeat one or two words of the client's sentence or question (e.g., The child asks, "What color should I paint this picture?" and the therapist replies, "What color?"). The therapist can also smile and nod at the child. As in instances when the therapist chooses not to reply to the child's question, eye contact and a listening posture are important in the delivery of minimal encouragers so that the child realizes that the therapist is attending to what is happening in the playroom.

It is usually appropriate in play therapy for the therapist to avoid answering questions that the child could answer without any assistance. Using minimal encouragers is a way of letting the child know that the therapist is paying attention to what he or she is asking without answering the question. This technique works best as a stalling tactic, with the therapist hoping the child will answer the question in the interval provided by the minimal encourager. This strategy works with all four types of questions but is probably most appropriate with practical questions and questions about the ongoing play therapy process because they are the two categories most likely to involve the child asking questions that he or she can answer without any input from the therapist. Although nondirective play therapists are more likely to use this strategy for responding to questions than are more directive play therapists, either type of play therapist could comfortably deliver minimal encouragers and remain theoretically consistent.

Restate the Question

This response style uses replies that are a verbal mirror for the child's question. The purpose of this strategy is to return the initiative to the client so that he or she must then consider whether to reask the question, find his or her own answer to the question, or decide that the answer is not worth pursuing. Sometimes repeating the gist of the question to the child also helps clarify the purpose or intent of the question for the child. This strategy is appropriate for all four types of questions and is used most often in a nondirective approach.

When the therapist restates the question, it can be presented as a state-ment or as a question, depending on the intonation of the therapist's delivery and the words the therapist chooses. If the therapist decides to restate the question as a statement, he or she simply tells the child what the child was asking. Sometimes the therapist will want to paraphrase the question, and other times the child's exact words can best convey the meaning of the question. Some examples of restating the question as a statement are as follows:

* The child asks, "What time is it?"
  The therapist responds, "You want to know what time it is."

* The child asks, "Do you have any children?"
  The therapist responds, "You are curious about whether I have any children."

* The child asks, "Do you like me?"
  The therapist responds, "You're wondering how I feel about you."

* The child asks, " Do you like Asian people?"
  The therapist responds, "You would like me to tell you if I like Asian people like you and your family."

If the therapist decides to restate the question using a question, he or she can simply repeat the original question, changing only the words necessary to have the sentence make sense or changing the words to paraphrase the original question. Because many nondirective play therapists prefer to avoid asking questions, they would usually choose not to use this formulation to restate the question. Some examples of restating a question as a question are

* The child asks, "What time is it?"
  The therapist responds, "What time is it?" or "What is the time?"

* The child asks, "Do you have any children?"
  The therapist responds, "Do I have any children?"

* The child asks, "Do you like me?"
  The therapist responds, "Do I like you?" or "Do I care about you?"

* The child asks, " Should I paint this red?"
  The therapist responds, "Should you paint that red?"

There are some questions, especially those about race, culture, or ethnicity, that should not be answered using this strategy. If a child asks, "Do you like Asian people?" it would be culturally insensitive to restate with a question because the child could easily interpret such an answer as conveying a lack of acceptance of his or her cultural background.

Guess About the Purpose/Interpret

In some of the more directive approaches to play therapy, including Adlerian and ecosystemic, the therapist will make a guess about the purpose of the question, interpret the meaning of the question, or interpret the reason the child asked the question (Kottman, 1995; K. O'Connor, personal communication, October 1997). This process helps clarify the child's intention and assists the child in gaining an awareness of any underlying message communicated by the question. To avoid imposing the therapist's meaning onto the child's question, he or she might choose to deliver such responses in the form of tentative hypotheses. This process allows the child to give feedback about the accuracy and relevancy of the therapist's guess. Because the child may not give that feedback in verbal form, the therapist must closely observe the child's behavior and play during and after he or she shares the hypothesis.

Although this strategy can be effective with practical questions that have multiple interpretations, it is more useful with questions about the therapist's personal life, the relationship between the child and the therapist, and the ongoing therapeutic process. This is due to the dual nature of these three types of questions, with their frequent double messages. Making guesses helps children examine possible underlying meaning. The guess should reflect the therapist's best understanding about the messages conveyed by the child's nonverbal communication as well as the verbal component of the message. It should also reflect any other information or patterns of behavior that the therapist has observed in the child throughout the therapy process. Guesses should never come "out of the clear blue sky" but should grow naturally out of what the therapist has learned about the child in the ongoing relationship and from interactions with parents, teachers, siblings, and other sources of information about the child and his or her life.

Because interpreting goals and meaning depends on a theoretical perspective, the hypotheses generated by the therapist will reflect his or her views about people and their motivation. The depth of interpretations will also depend on the stage of therapy and on the particular child, his or her developmental level, and whether he or she is concrete or abstract, direct or indirect.

The following are examples of making guesses about the purpose of a question, interpreting the meaning of the question, or interpreting why the child asked the question:

Helen asks, "What is this?"

1. "You want me to decide that for you?"
2. "I am thinking that sometimes you are kind of scared to make decisions for yourself."
3. "It seems like sometimes you would like me to take care of you and tell you what things are."

Mario asks, "Can we play a game today?"

1. "You sound like you already have what you want to do today figured out."
2. "You would kind of like to decide what we are going to do in here today."
3. "It seems like you're wondering if we can play together this morning."

Cynthia asks, "Where do you live?"

1. "You seem to be very curious about me."
2. "I'm thinking you would like to know more about me and my life."
3. "It seems as if you are feeling a little uncomfortable with me knowing more about you than you know about me."

Dawud asks, "What do you think I am going to do now?"

1. "You seem as though you wish I would make a guess about your plans."
2. "I am wondering if you feel powerful knowing something that I don't know."
3. "It's almost as if you want me to tell you what to do next."

Answer the Question

Sometimes the most sensible strategy for dealing with children's questions in therapy is to simply answer them—especially those that the therapist believes are straightforward requests for information. This is particularly the case with practical questions that have no underlying meaning and personal questions that are designed to reassure the child by providing more information about who the therapist is. The exception would be questions designed to allow the child to avoid taking responsibility for his or her own behavior or decisions.

If the therapist decides to answer questions, replies should be brief and just as straightforward as the queries, conveying simple information such as time, dates, directions, and so forth. Sometimes the most factual answer is "I don't know," and the therapist must be comfortable with saying this.

Some relationship questions warrant answers, but with these questions, the therapist may want to get more creative than with the simple informational queries. With questions such as "Do you like me?" or "Can I be your kid some day?" or "Am I your favorite kid?" the therapist will need to convey a sense of caring without necessarily giving a straight, factual answer to the child. General responses that provide reassurance and caring tend to be more appropriate with questions for which the "real" answer could be hurtful to the child. The following responses are examples of general answers that provide reassurance and caring:

* "I care about all of the children I bring into the playroom."
* "I think kids are the greatest people in the world."
* "I care about you a great deal."
* "You are a very special person."
* "You are a really important person to me."

With these questions, sometimes the best answer combines a guess about the purpose or interpretation of the meaning of the query with a general caring response designed to convey acceptance and understanding to the child. Most nondirective play therapists would probably feel uncomfortable making this type of response, but many directive play therapists would find this a valuable strategy for responding to very difficult questions from a child.

I provide several examples of combining a guess about the purpose, meaning, or motivation of the child's question with a general reassuring answer after each of the following questions:

* *Maria asks, "Am I your favorite kid?"*

1. "You sound like you want to know if I like you. I care about you a lot."

2. "I'm thinking perhaps you are worried about whether I like the other kids I see in here better than I like you. To me, you are a very special person."
3. "It seems as if you may be a little jealous of the other children I work with. I think you are pretty wonderful."

* *Charlie asks, "Am I kind of like a son to you?"*
1. "It sounds like you really want me to feel close to you. You are an important and neat person to me."
2. "It seems like maybe you would like to be my son. Even though you can't really be my little boy, I feel very close to you."

* *Midori asks, "Will you remember me when I don't come here anymore?"*
1. "You seem like you're worried that I might forget what a wonderful and special person you are. I will never forget that."
2. "Might it be that you are afraid that you won't always have a place in my heart? You will always have a place there even after you stop coming to play therapy."

Answer With a Question

There are times when the therapist might choose to answer the question with another question. This could be done in a direct manner if the therapist wanted to gather more information about the topic addressed in the original question (e.g., "What did you want to use to hit the mirror?"), to clarify what the child is asking (e.g., "So you're asking if you can jump from the top of the pillows onto what?"), or to explore the purpose or underlying message of the question (e.g., "Do you really want to know if I like girls better than boys, or do you want to know if I like you or your brother best?").

This response style could work with any of the different types of question, depending on the content and context of the query and the theoretical orientation of the therapist. Most nondirective play therapists do not usually ask questions in their interactions with children because they believe that asking questions increases the potential for leading the child. Therefore, those who subscribe to these theoretical orientations would be less likely to use this response style than would those who are more directive and willing to lead the client.

Another strategy for answering a question with a question would be to use the whisper technique (G. Landreth, personal communication, March

1984; see chapter 9, "Returning Responsibility to the Child"). In this instance, when the child asks a question, the therapist uses a whisper voice to ask, "What should I say?" to get the child to dictate the contents and direction of the response.

This style works best with practical questions and ongoing-process questions. It would be a bit strange to use this strategy with personal or relationship questions because they truly require input from the therapist.

Both nondirective and directive play therapists can feel comfortable using this strategy. Although it does give control to the child, if a more directive therapist wanted to share the control of the session, he or she could choose to alternate using the whisper technique with other response styles.

Decline to Answer

There are some questions, such as personal questions that are too personal or simply inappropriate, the therapist will probably want to refuse to answer in an overt way. This refusal would usually be stated with a response such as, "I choose not to answer that question," "I would rather not tell you that," or "That is private and isn't for discussing with other people." The use of this type of reply is probably more dependent on the personal preference of the therapist and his or her need for strong boundaries than on the theoretical orientation of the therapist. This style of responding would be appropriate across all of the approaches to play therapy.

Practice Exercises

For each of the following questions, decide which type of question it is. If there is an underlying hidden message, explain your interpretation of that message, and describe how you arrived at this interpretation. Then decide on several possible appropriate responses, and explain how those responses would be helpful to the child.

1. Jennifer (7), in her first session, timidly asks, "Are you going to tell me what to do now?"
2. Shlomo (9), who is usually very shy, comes into the playroom and asks, "Do you think I am a nice person?"

3. Anneliese (4) likes to control the sessions in various ways. In the sixth session, she introduces the idea that you should play a guessing game with her. She asks, "What animal am I?"

4. Xing Wang (5) picks up a toy gun and says, "What sound does this make?"

5. Sharee (8) likes to play with the dolls and uses them to "talk" for her. She picks up the little girl doll and the mother doll. She turns the mother doll toward you and asks, "Do you think my daughter, little Sherelle, has been bad again today? Should I give little Sherelle a spanking?"

6. In his 10th session, Che (9), who plays exclusively with the bop bag, looks around the playroom and says, "What did you do with the punching bag? Don't you know it is my favorite thing to do in here?" (Bonus question: Would you answer differently if you had removed the bop bag so as to encourage Che to use some of the other toys than if the bop bag had broken?)

7. Othelia (6) is sitting in the corner looking sad/bored/miserable. Although she is usually quite excited about coming to play therapy, she says, "Do I have to keep coming here week after week?"

8. Jeremy (9), in his first session, says, "What can you tell me about yourself?"

9. Iofe (7) is painting a picture. Her presenting problem is that she is afraid to take risks and typically defers to others. Her mother is worried that she "just isn't creative." She has consistently asked you to make decisions for her. She asks, "Can I paint the tree leaves blue?"

10. Christopher (5) looks you straight in the eye and asks, "How are you going to stop me from throwing this paint on your pants?"

11. Ingrid (7) comes into the session like a whirlwind, with a list of ideas of what she wants to do today. She immediately asks, "How long before it is time to leave?"

12. Aidan's (6) mother is having a new baby in a month, her 10th child. He asks you, "Are you pregnant?" (Or, if you are a man, "Is your wife pregnant?")

13. Mary (9) likes the dragon puppet more than anything in the playroom. At the end of her third session, after repeatedly telling you how much she likes that particular puppet, she asks, "Are you good at sharing?"

14. Raul's (7) father is Mexican and his mother is Asian. When he comes to your office, he asks, "How am I supposed to tell if I am brown or yellow?"

15. Saralynne (6), in her second session, asks, "Why do you talk so funny?"

Questions to Ponder

1. Do you think knowing what kind of question the child is asking (personal, relationship, ongoing process, or informational) will help you to formulate your response? Explain.

2. Which category of question do you think will personally give you the most trouble? Explain why that type of question will be difficult for you.

3. How would you handle inappropriate personal questions?

4. Which method of dealing with questions do you think will be the most comfortable for you? Explain your reasoning.

5. Which method of dealing with questions do you think will be the least comfortable for you? Explain your reasoning.

6. What do you think your strategy will be for dealing with relationship questions in which the underlying message seems to reveal the child's need for your attention and approval? Explain your reasoning.

7. How do you feel/what do you think about the therapist asking children questions in therapy? What kinds of questions do you think are permissible to ask the child in play therapy? Explain.

8. As a follow-up question to the previous question, what is your stance on the therapist taking the lead in play therapy? Explain your reasoning.

Chapter 11

Integration of Basic Skills: The Art of Play Therapy

U
p until this point in this text, I have presented each of the basic play therapy skills in isolation. This strategy is the simplest way to teach the "science"—the "how tos"—of play therapy. The primary drawback of this method of training is that it misses the "art" of play therapy. The art of play therapy consists of (a) the process of deciding when to use a skill, (b) the integration of several different skills together to create a melange that works more smoothly and more efficaciously than an isolated skill would, and (c) the melding of the therapist's personality and interactional style with the play therapy skills. The purpose of this chapter is to explore these issues.

Deciding When to Use a Skill

It is important to choose appropriate skills to optimize the chances for a successful outcome in play therapy, but this is not a simple task. The process of selecting which skill to use in a particular situation is multifaceted. It depends on the therapist's theoretical orientation, the therapist's intuition and experience, the therapist's personal preferences and personality, the individual child, the child's life context, the course of the play, the phase of the therapy, and any number of other factors.

Unfortunately, there is no way to arrange these factors in some kind of hierarchical order or assign them specific weights in the process—remember, this is the "art" aspect of play therapy, and art is not quantifiable. The true key to the selection of the "correct" skill is to remember that there is no "correct" skill. Almost any of the play therapy skills will work in most situations in the playroom. There is no magical formula for deciding which one to use in any particular moment, so you should not spend a great deal of time and energy straining to generate the perfect skill for each and every situation.

What you *must* do is trust in the process of play therapy, trust yourself, and trust the children—they will be your best teachers. You must believe that the play therapy process will flow in a way that is helpful to children. You must believe that there is little you can do in the playroom that will do permanent damage to a child. You must believe that children will show you what you need to know to help them and that they will let you know when you make a mistake.

(I know—you were still secretly hoping for an easy set of rules that I was going to tell you sometime soon.) Having made that disclaimer, I now explain how each of these facets can affect the selection of skills.

Theoretical Orientation

Each of the theoretical orientations provides a certain degree of guidance about when and how to use specific skills. As you study play therapy, you should begin to narrow the field of possible approaches to play therapy and focus your investigations on the theoretical orientations that most interest you. You will need to read books, book chapters, and journal articles devoted to those particular theories so that you can learn more about specifications regarding the application of skills within those orientations. Appendix

A contains references for further exploration in this area. If you are considering doing eclectic prescriptive play therapy, you will need to know a great deal about many different theories so as to have a broad range of possible interventions from which to choose.

Therapist's Intuition and Experience

Many times, the decision to use a certain skill stems from the therapist's intuition about what will work best at that moment with a particular child. The therapist's intuition may be due to his or her ability to recognize almost undetectable nonverbal cues from the child; it may be due to the therapist's ability to put together clues about the child's attitudes, feelings, thoughts, and perceptions to form patterns of insight; or it may be due to a myriad of other factors.

You will need to hone your intuition and learn to listen to it. Intuition can be an excellent guide in deciding when and how to apply the available skills in play therapy. It can help you decide (a) when to track, restate content, or reflect a feeling; (b) whether to track the child or the play object; (c) which feeling to reflect; (d) whether to help a child or to return the responsibility to the child; and (e) when to use a skill in isolation and when to combine several skills for an integrated intervention.

Experience can also be helpful in this process. By observing and remembering how various children react to an intervention, you will begin to form general guidelines for when specific skills will work and when they will not. From experience, you will learn that some skills work wonderfully with certain types of children and that others do not. You will learn how to time your various interventions for optimal effect. You will learn what feels best for you in terms of the proportion of skills used in each phase of play therapy.

Experience can also guide you in deciding how each of the skills will work best for you. From past interactions with children, you will realize that there are some applications of the various skills that do not seem to work for you. You may have observed other play therapists successfully using these skills, but you may still not feel comfortable or confident using those skills.

For instance, I have trouble limiting with passive voice. Although children almost always abide by the limits I set when I use other styles of limiting, they tend to ignore me when I use passive voice to limit. I have seen this skill work very well for many other therapists, and I realize that it is a valuable skill—for other people.

Therapist's Personal Preference and Personality

Therapists' personalities and way of being in the world will have a major impact on their application of the various play therapy skills. These factors will influence the interventions they use and the ways they use them. For instance, individuals who are uncomfortable with feelings seldom reflect feelings—they concentrate on tracking and restating content and may ignore opportunities for reflecting emotions. Individuals who are given to caretaking others may have difficulty returning responsibility to children— they usually prefer to do things for children rather than watch children struggle with decisions and behaviors. Individuals who tend to be loquacious may choose the most long-winded method of presenting a particular intervention, and those who tend to favor complexity over simplicity may choose the most complicated method of applying a skill.

It is appropriate and acceptable for your personal preferences and your personality to have an impact on your therapeutic process, but you must avoid having their influence cloud your clinical judgment or prevent you from offering the best care for your clients. Because an interaction between how you counsel and who you are seems to be inevitable, it is imperative for you to know yourself well enough that you can monitor your use of techniques to make sure that you do not let your issues dominate your selection and application of skills to the detriment of clients.

The Individual Child

The personal preferences and personalities of the children with whom you work will also affect the process of play therapy. Certain children react better to some skills than they do to others. This is also true for the various methods of applying each of the skills. For instance, there are some children who simply hate it when you reflect feelings and reject any attempt to discuss emotions in a session. You will have several options with these children—you can avoid feeling reflections with them, decide that reflections are exactly what they need and increase the number of reflections you make in each session, or gradually phase in more reflections of feelings over a long period of time so that these children can learn to cope with having feelings bandied about the room. An innumerable number of factors will go into your decisions in this area, including your knowledge of child development and child psychopathology, your understanding of theory, your intuition and experience with children who have acted in similar fashions, and the interaction of your personality with the personality of the child.

It is essential to focus on the individual child in your play therapy sessions and to remember that the play is the communication. The child will let you know which skills are effective and helpful to him or her and which are not—partly through verbal feedback and nonverbal reactions to the various interventions, but mostly through the play. Your main job is to truly "listen," observe patterns, and be willing to adjust your interaction with the child and your choices of specific strategies to accommodate what works with him or her.

Context of the Child's Life

Another factor in making decisions about which techniques to use in a session is the context of the child's life. You will need to consider current and recent events in the child's life when making choices about intervention strategies because the child's reactions, feelings, attitudes, thoughts, and behaviors will vary depending on his or her situation and his or her cultural or ethnic background. You will also need to consider the interactional patterns that occur in the child's family because you will not want to duplicate any dysfunctional patterns in your relationship with the child. The presenting problem may also have an impact on the child's attitudes and interactional patterns in sessions, and you may need to adjust your interventions accordingly.

It is important for you to keep informed of the circumstances of each child's life. This will allow you to make adjustments necessary to accommodate intervention styles to situations that might have an impact on the child. These could include factors such as a death in the family, a birthday, a failing report card, special holidays, a lost pet, or any other kind of event that might result in the child behaving in a new or unusual manner in the playroom. For example, a child who has recently had some kind of traumatic event occur may need more reflections of feelings than other children. An overly dependent child whose mother recently returned to the workforce may initially need a lot of nurturing, which might preclude extensive returns of responsibility.

There are some presenting problems that influence the therapist's choice of skills or the way these skills are applied in sessions. The therapist's knowledge of the various aspects of specific diagnoses, developmental crises, relationship difficulties, and other reasons for coming to play therapy will help to individualize intervention strategies.

An example of this type of adaptation would be play therapy with children with ADHD who need a great deal of structure (Kaduson, 1997). In a playroom, this structure involves setting limits early and often. Because children with ADHD tend not to generalize cause-and-effect relationships, you might decide to explain the consequences for violations of limits at the same time you set the limits, even if you would not normally do so. Most children with ADHD do not read nonverbal cues well, and they tend not to heed indirect feedback, so you would probably use direct rather than indirect formulations for your interventions. You would probably not want to link several different skills so as to avoid overwhelming these children with too much input at once.

The Course of the Play

Again, the play *is* the thing, and you will need to adapt your application of the various skills to what is going on in the play. For example, if Daisy is working through a lot of very emotional issues and the themes are feeling-oriented, it will probably behoove you to increase the number of feeling reflections you are using in the session. If Julian is spending a great deal of energy describing how things are going in his life, you may want to switch into the mode of restating content to make sure that he realizes that you are listening to him and honoring his efforts at communication. If Padmini is challenging limits that she would usually never consider violating, you may want to give her some slack and let her attempt some behaviors she would not normally be brave enough to try. The list could go on forever. The important element is that each session, each moment in a particular session, is a world in and of itself. You must be alert to what is happening in the play in the here and now and be willing to adjust your choice of interventions on the basis of what is happening in the play at that particular moment in time.

The Phase of the Therapy

It makes intuitive sense that the therapist uses the least intrusive and least potentially threatening interventions early in the therapy process and the more intrusive and more potentially threatening interventions later in the therapy process. You, of course, must decide for yourself whether you believe this and if you wish to adapt your practice to accommodate for the possibility. If you do, you must also decide which skills you believe are the ones that children might perceive to be intrusive and potentially threatening.

Integrating Skills (With Examples)

As you gain mastery of each of the basic play therapy skills, you may notice that your application of the skills still feels rather stilted and artificial. There are two methods of skill integration that could help to change this. One of these methods is rather narrow and concrete—the integration of the various skills with one another. The other method is more global and abstract—the integration of the skills with your own natural way of communicating and interacting.

Although you can concentrate on both of these transformations at the same time, remember that the integration of skills will be an easier and quicker process and the integration of skills with your interactional style will be a slower and potentially more painful evolution. I would suggest that you begin by practicing blending skills with one another and later move to the gradual process of working toward congruence and confluence between you, the person, and you, the therapist.

Integration of Skills

To start the transformation from isolated skills to integrated skills, you must first learn the mechanics of how to blend the basic skills into intervention techniques. You must also decide which skills meld smoothly and which skills clash. There are several obvious natural combinations that work well together, but remember, what works for one play therapist may not suit another play therapist, so you will need to experiment.

It will also be helpful for you to practice using skills in isolation and in combination and experiment with making decisions about when to integrate and how to time your interventions. There is no formula for doing this either. It will depend on the child's developmental level; the child's situation; the child's standard way of processing information; the phase of therapy; and various factors related to your own comfort, personal style, and expertise.

Mechanics of blending skills. The procedure for blending one skill with one or more other skills is relatively simple. You take whatever you would have said or done for the first skill and decide how you can fit it into what you would have said or done for the second skill. The following are some suggestions for different methods of doing this blending:

1. The blended intervention can be a compound sentence that just combines the two different skills.
2. You can use one of the skills as an adjective, adverb, or other modifier.
3. You can use several different sentences for your intervention, with each one containing a different skill.
4. You can talk about or to the play object—sometimes using a metaphor and/or acting as if the play object is alive, has feelings, can talk, and so forth.
5. If you have enough information about the child and his or her situation, you can make a cause-and-effect attribution linking two different skills.

These are some basic strategies of combination, but this list of procedures is not exhaustive. Methods for different ways of integrating the various skills are limited only by your imagination and your willingness to experiment with your own creative process of generating new ways of combining two or more skills.

Most play therapists would probably be willing to use the procedures described in the first three methods of integrating skills. However, many nondirective play therapists would probably feel uncomfortable about the directive/interpretive nature of the last two methods described. These two strategies would perhaps be more comfortable for therapists who are willing to lead the client, rather than letting the client always take the lead.

The following examples illustrate several different ways of integrating various basic skills:

  * *You want to blend a reflection of feeling with a tracking intervention. Your reflection of feeling is "You seem angry today," and your tracking intervention is "You are hitting that bop bag." Possible combined interventions are as follows:*

1. "You are hitting that bop bag, and you seem angry today." (**compound sentence**)
2. "You seem to be punching that bop bag in an angry way today." (**using one skill as an adjective**)
3. "You are hitting that bop bag. You sure seem angry today." (**combining two different sentences**)
4. "I bet that guy (the bop bag) thinks you are pretty angry today; you are punching him so hard." (**referring to a play object, assuming it can think or has feelings**)
5. "You're hitting that bop bag because you are feeling angry today." (**attribution**)

* You want to blend a restatement of content with a tracking intervention. Your reflection of feeling is "It seems like you're kind of sad right now," and your restatement of content is "You are missing your grandmother." Possible integrated interventions include

1. "You're missing your grandmother, and it just seems like you are kind of sad about that right now." (**compound sentence**)
2. "You're feeling sad about missing your grandmother." (**using one skill as an adjective**)
3. "You are missing your grandmother. You seem sad right now." (**two sentences**)
4. "You're feeling sad because you miss your grandmother." (**attribution**)

* You want to blend a reflection of feeling with returning responsibility to the child. Your reflection of feeling is "You act like you're a little nervous about deciding that for yourself," and your returning responsibility to the child is "In here, you can choose for yourself." Possible integrated interventions include

1. "You act like you're a little nervous about deciding for yourself, but in here, you can choose." (**compound sentence**)
2. "In here, you can decide things for yourself, even though you might feel a little nervous about making a choice." (**using one skill as an adjective**)
3. "You act like you're a little nervous about deciding that for yourself. In here, you can choose for yourself." (**two sentences**)

Several important aspects of the generation and delivery of integrated interventions include limiting the length, monitoring the nonverbal elements of the communication, and avoiding hidden messages or underlying subtexts. Combining two different skills frequently expands the verbiage and complicates the message, which can result in an intervention that children do not understand. Probably the best solution to this possibility is to remember to keep all interventions as simple and short as possible. The longer the verbal communication of the therapist, the more potential for children not listening to or not comprehending the message.

The tone of voice that the therapist uses in this process and the emphasis on different words will affect the meaning conveyed by the intervention. Because integrated interventions are longer and more complex than isolated skills, they have a greater chance of being distorted by nonverbal communication. For example, depending on the tone of voice and the emphasis on different words, the integrated intervention, "You act like you're a little nervous about deciding that for yourself. In here, you can choose for yourself," can convey an extremely encouraging message or an extremely discouraging message. By stressing the word *you* in the second sentence in an upbeat, positive tone, the therapist can suggest confidence and a sense of empowerment to the child. In contrast, by stressing the words *in here* in a sarcastic or doubting voice, the therapist can convey doubt that the child could make decisions anywhere other than the playroom. The most practical solution to this problem is for the therapist to pay close attention to his or her patterns of nonverbal communication so as to avoid inadvertently delivering a message that could be potentially discouraging to the child.

Sometimes certain words, such as the conjunctions used in forming compound sentences, can convey a message the therapist does not intend to communicate. An example of this difficulty would be when the therapist combines a reflection of feelings with returning the responsibility to the child using the word *but*. This might result in an integrated intervention like, "You seem unsure about whether you will make the right decision, but in here, you can decide." To an insecure child, this might convey the message, "We are going to let you decide even though you will probably get it wrong." Using *and* instead of *but* usually prevents this from happening.

Because the therapist does not usually have the luxury of a great deal of time to analyze possible subtexts of his or her interventions before delivering them, it may not be practical to avoid every occurrence of this potential pitfall of integrated interventions. However, it is important to closely monitor children's reactions and responses to these therapeutic responses, especially when they are first introduced. The purpose of this careful observation is to provide the therapist with a chance to take corrective measures with the child and avoid this problem in similar integrated interventions in the future.

Deciding which skills meld and which skills clash. There are a few general guidelines about deciding which skills blend well and which skills do not. However, for the most part, this decision depends on personal inclination and experience.

Both tracking and restatement of content are simple, concrete skills. In combination, these two skills usually complement one another nicely and prevent an overabundance of isolated interventions that sound so obvious that they become insulting to the child. Integration of tracking and restatement of content can keep the therapist's statements more interesting than they are in isolation.

Reflections of feelings blend well with all of the other basic skills—tracking, restatement of content, limiting, returning responsibility to the child, and responding to questions. Most procedures for setting limits include a step for reflecting feelings if possible, so these skills tend to be integrated on a regular basis. Reflection of feelings can also add power to tracking and restatement of content, giving more depth to these rather superficial skills. By adding reflection of feelings to returning responsibility to the child, the therapist can quite frequently probe the underlying issues related to the child's wanting or needing help in making decisions or following through with action.

Tracking and restating content do not combine well with limiting, because they do not usually add anything to the limiting process. Depending on the limiting procedure, however, some therapists will feel comfortable adding returning responsibility to the child. For example, the direct, encouraging approach to returning responsibility to the child (e.g., "I bet you can figure out a way to do that.") works very well in Adlerian limit setting. This strategy can fit into the third step of Adlerian limiting by inviting the child to help generate appropriate behaviors and in the fourth step of deciding on logical consequences.

You will need to experiment with your application of skills to further explore which skills work well together for you and which skills clash when you use them in combination. Again, you will need to monitor children's reactions to your combinations and your feelings as you deliver the combinations to gather information about this process.

Integration of Skills With Your Personal Interactional Style

As you gain confidence in the mechanics of combining the basic skills, you will want to shift your attention to situations in which you still feel uncomfortable in the playroom—those times when you continue to feel as though your interventions are weak and your delivery does not flow in a smooth, natural way. As you start to recognize patterns in these feelings of discomfort, it will be helpful to work on the integration of your personal interactional style with your mastery of the basic play therapy skills.

The awareness of times when you are not comfortable in the playroom is actually the first step in this process, because in many cases this discomfort is the result of you not being yourself in the playroom. As your ability to recognize awkwardness in yourself while doing play therapy increases, you can consider the cause of your uneasiness. You will need to decide whether the uncomfortable feelings are related to (a) your efforts to do things "correctly," which frequently lead to an undermining of your natural way of interacting with others; (b) your own anxiety about particular topics or skills; (c) the normal awkwardness involved in learning a new skill; or (d) some other factor. As you begin to notice particular situations in which you feel that you are not really being yourself in the playroom, you must ask yourself how you could be more natural and comfortable. It might help to visualize yourself in the playroom using the skills in your own words or to visualize yourself using the skills in more comfortable situations, such as with your friends and family. Sometimes you can actually practice the basic play therapy skills with members of your family, other children you know, or your friends just to smooth out your delivery and develop a method of saying things that will feel more natural to you. It is also helpful to practice different, more familiar ways of phrasing the various interventions in the playroom to facilitate the development of your own personal style for being with children in play therapy.

The most important factor in you becoming an "artful" play therapist is acquiring experience being in a playroom with children, experimenting with the various play therapy skills, and learning to listen to and trust your own judgment and knowledge about children. Another essential factor is your willingness to continually work on your own growth, to notice and honor your own intuition about yourself and your own process—as a professional and as a person, both in and out of the playroom.

Practice Exercises

In each of the following scenarios, (a) write your intervention; (b) label which skills you used, and explain why you chose those skills; and (c) if you used an integrated intervention, describe the method you used to combine the isolated skills. You do not have to confine yourself to the methods described in this chapter. Please use your own imagination and your own personal way of communicating to adapt the skills in creative ways. Because I believe that it is easier to use combined interventions with children whom you know relatively well, I use continuing sagas of two children so that you have an ongoing session with which to work. It would be helpful to generate two or three different interventions for each scenario to explore different ways of handling a situation.

1. Jonah (9) comes into the playroom in his fifth session, looking very downcast, and says, "I don't want to be here. I don't like this place, and I don't like you."
2. Jonah stands up, looks around the playroom, and says, "I don't know what to do in here." He picks up the gun, aims in at the floor, and when it doesn't work, puts it back, saying (in a disgusted voice), "See, this place is so stupid."
3. Jonah looks at you and says, "Well, do you have anything that would be fun to do here? Should I paint a picture? That probably wouldn't be fun either."
4. After your response, he says, "Well, I knew you wouldn't help me out. You never do. You're just like my teacher." He turns his back and goes over to the sandbox, where he starts dumping sand on the floor.
5. When you set a limit on dumping the sand on the floor, he simply ignores you.
6. Jonah stands up and says, "You are really getting on my nerves today.

I am going out and see if my dad is here yet." He starts toward the door.

7. Jonah sits down on the floor and begins to cry and says, "I knew it. You just don't like me, and you won't let me do anything I want to do. I want my dad."

8. Suddenly, still crying, he gets up and gets a Lincoln Log, points it at you, and starts making machine-gun noises.

9. Jonah looks at you and says, "What's the matter? Don't you want to defend yourself? Get a gun and shoot back. What's wrong with you?"

10. Jonah laughs and says, "Hey, this is really fun. I want to do this for the rest of the time. OK, you are the police, and I am the robber. You have to stop me from getting away. I just robbed a bank."

11. In her 10th session, Alison (6), a foster child who was taken away from her birth parents for abuse, is playing with the dolls. She is usually a very talkative child but has said very little to you today. The mother doll says to the smallest child doll, "This is all your fault, you know. You will have to be punished."

12. Continuing her play, Alison moves the small doll child over to the corner and begins making whimpering noises. She turns away from you, and you realize she has started to cry.

13. Alison moves the small doll over to the bed and puts her in the bed. She picks up the mother doll and puts her right by the bed. In the mother doll's voice, she says, "You little brat. Were you trying to hide from me?"

14. Alison turns to you and says in a very slow, sad voice, "Where can she hide from her? How can she get away? She doesn't know."

15. Alison hands you the dolls; says, "You play it now"; and walks over and starts to paint a picture.

16. She says, "I am going to paint a picture for you. What should I paint?"

17. She paints a picture of a house burning with people hanging out of the window yelling, "Help, save me!" There are several people standing and watching the fire, but they do not seem to be trying to help the people in the burning house.

18. Alison turns to you and says, "Those people are just watching. They could help, but they are not going to."

19. She stops painting and goes over to the house and gets the mother

doll. She carries her over to the sandbox, gets a shovel, and buries her. She turns to you with a big grin on her face, turns back to the sandbox, and heaps more sand on the mother doll.

20. She looks over to see what kind of a reaction you have to the action in the sandbox and says, "I would like to leave her here. Can you help me bury her some more?"

Questions to Ponder

1. What role does intuition play in your life?
2. On a scale of 1–10 (with 1 being *none* and 10 being *more than anyone else I know*), how would you rate the strength of your intuitive sense of what is going on with other people? Explain your rating.
3. On a scale of 1–10 (with 1 being *none* and 10 being *more than anyone else I know*), how would you rate your ability to trust in your own intuition? Explain your rating.
4. How well do you understand yourself and your own issues? What are the main issues you think might interfere with your ability to work with children and their families?
5. As compared with the "science" of play therapy, how important do you think the "art" of play therapy is? Explain.
6. Which of the different elements in the "art" of play therapy are important to you? Explain your reasoning.
7. What will be your biggest obstacles in moving toward being more congruent in your interactions in the playroom and in other relationships in your life? Explain.
8. What do you think will be the most important strategies for integrating your own personal style of communicating and interacting with the skills of play therapy?

Part 3
Advanced Skills
and Concepts

Chapter 12

Recognizing and Communicating Through Metaphors

*A*lonzo *(6) has a Black mother and an Asian father. Both sets of grandparents have severed ties with the family, which has created a great deal of tension between his parents. Alonzo arranges all of the dolls in two different "camps" on the edges of the sandbox, sorted by skin color. He puts a small brown doll in an ambulance, moving it from camp to camp, but no one will let the doll out of the ambulance.*

Lois (8) comes to play therapy with a presenting problem of generalized anxiety. She tells you about a book her mother read her. The plot was that there was a family in which every member was afraid of something. The family adopted a dog that was also afraid of a bunch of different stuff. Each member of the family helped the dog stop being afraid of the thing that frightened that member.

Roger (7) has been diagnosed as having ADHD. His presenting problem is impulsivity and refusal to complete work in school. He comes into the playroom, scoots around the room, crashes into your chair, and says, "I am a locomotive, and I cannot stop. Even if a car gets in my way, I just run right over it."

These are just three examples of the myriad of metaphors that pervade the play therapy process. Metaphors are in play scenes that children act out alone or ask the therapist to role-play; they are in the stories that children tell about events that have happened to them or to others; they are in the fantasy stories that children make up; and they are in plot summaries from movies, television shows, and books. In play therapy, children use metaphors to explore and reveal the self, consider the world and how it works, investigate relationships with others, and communicate with the play therapist. It is the job of the play therapist to recognize each metaphor as it occurs, to listen to the metaphor and try to understand what it means for that particular child in that specific context, and to use the metaphor as a vehicle for communicating with the child.

Recognizing Metaphors

> Every story a child tells, acts out through play, or writes contributes to a self-portrait—a portrait that he can look at, refer to, think about, and change, a portrait others can use to develop an understanding of the storyteller. Each time a child describes an experience he or someone else has had, he constructs part of his past, adding to his sense of who he is and conveying that sense to others. Each time a child makes up a story about something that might have happened to himself or to another, he expands his world. (Engel, 1995, p. 1)

One of the primary jobs of the play therapist is to recognize clients' metaphors—noticing the various images and stories present in the play and acknowledging their metaphoric potential. By listening to stories in the playroom for their symbolic content, the play therapist can begin to see the child's world through the child's eyes, making the connections between the images and stories present in the play and the situations and relationships in the child's life.

Once you begin to listen and look for metaphors, you will find them everywhere in the play—they will be in children's stories, their puppet shows, their drawings and paintings, and their descriptions of their friends—everywhere. Your first mission is to just begin to notice them and acknowledge to yourself that there may be some kind of symbolic message in the play. When you have gotten into the rhythm of recognizing that there is frequently a "hidden" story in the play, you will need to consider what these metaphors mean in the context of your clients' lives.

Understanding the Meaning of Metaphors in Play Therapy

Metaphors are symbolic, not direct, so the meaning of the metaphor may be hidden inside the story or the play. It is the play therapist's job to try to understand the meaning of the metaphor to better comprehend the child's feelings, attitudes, relationships, and views about self, others, and the world.

Some play therapists, such as Norton and Norton (1997) and Allan (1988), believe that certain symbols have common meanings that are shared across different children. They contend that most of the time when a child tells a story using a specific symbol, that symbol has a particular universal interpretation. For instance, in a story about a bird, the bird would signify transformation, or in a description of a house, the house would symbolize the child's family. Although Allan (1988) suggested that caution must be used in interpreting the meaning of all symbols according to a universal standard, the play therapists who adhere to this perspective tend to view the meaning of certain symbols as being the same across children and cultures.

Other play therapists believe that metaphors are idiosyncratic and phenomenological (Kottman, 1995; Landreth, 1991; Oaklander, 1978/1992). For those who adhere to this view, symbols in metaphors are unique to that particular child at that specific moment in time. From this perspective, the only way the metaphor can be completely understood is to consider the child's history and culture, the time context of the storytelling, the developmental level of the child, and a multitude of other factors.

You will have to consider your own views about the interpretation of the meaning of metaphors. Regardless of your stance on this issue, it will be important for you to try to understand the message of the metaphor and to convey that desire to the child, in an accepting, patient way, without pressuring the child to communicate in more direct ways. With many children, the simple willingness on your part to listen and to try to understand the message of the metaphor is enough to produce a shift in the way they look at themselves, others, and the world.

Even when the meaning of the metaphor eludes you, consideration of possible meanings can be helpful. By thinking about the different possible messages that could be conveyed by that particular story or play sequence, you may gain a better understanding of the dynamics of the child. In many cases, there is not one "right" answer about the message of the play—by thinking about all the possible communications available in that metaphor, you can learn a great deal about the child and about his or her own way of looking at the world.

Sometimes the specific content of the metaphor is not that important. What the child is trying to convey may be a feeling or attitude, rather than concrete information about a certain situation—the affective tone of the story may be the message of the metaphor. For instance, if Sam tells you the story of his football team winning the Super Bowl, he may not really care who won the game—he may just be happy and optimistic that his life is going the way he wants it to go.

It is also important to remember that not every story or play scene has hidden dimensions. Many times there are no underlying layers of meaning in a narrative from a child—a story about a bird may just be a story about a bird.

Examples of Metaphors and Possible Meanings

After each of the following metaphors, there are several possible interpretations of the meaning of the metaphor. All or none of these interpretations could be correct for that particular child under those specific circumstances.

   * *Rashid (7) walks into the room, takes the family of dolls (with the exception of the little boy), buries them under a pile of sand, and says, "Nothing can ever save them."*

   1. Rashid's family is having difficulties, and he believes the situation is hopeless.

2. Rashid believes that family secrets are hurting the family but that it will never be acceptable to bring them out into the open and discuss them.
3. Rashid saw his family killed in a war.
4. Rashid believes that (because he is the identified patient) it is his job to fix the problems of the family, but he just does not know how to go about doing it.
5. Rashid saw a frightening movie in which an entire family was buried alive, with the son the only one who survived.

* John (6) tells you this story: "There once was a bird who lived in a cage and wanted to fly away. One day, the bird escaped, but an eagle saw him and attacked him. The bird fell from the sky and died."

1. The bird symbolizes John, and he feels as though he is trapped.
2. John believes that being trapped is still safer than dealing with the world. He is afraid that if he escapes from his current situation, his life will be even worse.
3. John believes that bigger, more powerful people are dangerous, especially if he tries to get what he wants.
4. John believes that trying to get his needs met is dangerous.
5. John saw a bird get attacked by a bigger bird.

* In his second session, Gino (4) uses the puppet theater to make a "fort." He places various puppets in between you and the fort, telling you they are the "guards." He goes to the basket of costumes and gets a suit of armor, gathers several swords, and hides inside the "fort."

1. Gino is afraid of you and feels a need to protect himself from you.
2. Gino has safety issues and believes that he needs to make sure he is protected.
3. Gino believes that there are people who are being overprotective in his life and keeping him shut away from the world.
4. Gino wants to convey the idea that he knows how to take care of himself.
5. Gino is afraid that you will learn things about him that he is not sure he wants you to know.

* Ayako's (5) mother died when Ayako was 4. Her father has never remarried and seems to have difficulty taking care of himself and his three children. Ayako tells you the story of a garden where the gardener took care of the flowers

and they were all happy and bright. However, the gardener decided to leave, and now the flowers are all droopy and the weeds are taking over the garden.

1. Ayako's mother was the "gardener," and now that she is gone, all the "flowers" (children) are struggling.
2. Ayako believes that her mother "decided" to leave.
3. Ayako does not believe her father has the skills to take care of the family.
4. Ayako's mother had a garden in their yard, and through neglect, the garden is now dying.
5. In the Japanese culture, gardens symbolize growth and a sense of well-being.

* Todd (9) describes the plot of a movie he watched recently. The way he tells the story, the hero is defeated by an overwhelming number of adversaries. You, having seen an action-thriller or two yourself, know that the "actual" plot resolution involves the hero defeating the overwhelming number of adversaries.

1. Todd believes that there are so many obstacles in his life that he cannot overcome them all.
2. Todd has a pessimistic view of the world and believes that heroes do not win, no matter how hard they try.
3. Todd feels as though everyone in his life is out to get him and that he has no friends or allies.

Using the Child's Metaphor to Communicate With the Child

I believe that it is essential to avoid "breaking" the metaphor—asking the child to explain the meaning of the metaphor or interpreting the meaning of the metaphor to the child. By "breaking" the metaphor, the therapist conveys a lack of respect for the child's decision to communicate indirectly and implies that the child should be direct and concrete. Instead of "breaking" the metaphor, I use the child's metaphor to indirectly communicate with the child.

Whether or not the therapist completely understands the underlying meaning of the child's metaphor, it is still possible to use the metaphor to communicate with the child. If the child is using indirect modes of expression, especially metaphors, the therapist will have a greater likelihood of the child positively responding if he or she is willing to use the same indirect mode of expression.

The therapist can use the child's metaphor as a vehicle for basic intervention skills, such as reflecting feelings or returning responsibility to the child, or for more complex interventions, such as teaching problem-solving techniques, conveying new information, making suggestions about alternative solutions to problem situations, or making interpretations. The therapist can also use the metaphor as a vehicle for asking questions about the child's life or relationships, using an indirect forum for asking.

In all of these situations, the therapist simply uses whatever is happening with the characters in the metaphor as an opportunity to apply that particular skill. For example, Brian is telling a story about a mouse that is being chased by a cat. The therapist could use basic skills to track the behaviors of the mouse, restate the content of the cat, and reflect the feelings of the mouse. The therapist could ask the mouse about the different ways she has tried to get away from the cat or make a suggestion about asking someone else to intervene with the cat for her.

When using the child's metaphor, you should consider which character in the story represents the child's point of view. This will guide you in making choices about which character to use as a focal point for the interventions. If you wish to convey empathic understanding to the child, it is better to concentrate on the character who represents the child in the metaphor. If you wish to facilitate the development of empathy in the client, it is frequently helpful to concentrate on other characters in the story.

Monitoring the Child's Reaction to Using the Metaphor

If the therapist decides to use the child's metaphor to communicate with the child, it is important for the therapist to monitor the child's reaction to the adaptation of the metaphor. Most of the time, the child will simply go along with the therapist's use of the metaphor and continue to use it to communicate more information. In cases in which both the therapist and the child feel comfortable with a particular metaphor, they may use the same metaphor over a number of different sessions as a recurring mode of communication.

Alternatively, the child may have a negative reaction to the therapist co-opting the metaphor. This negative reaction could be a subtle nonverbal response, such as a head shake or a frown at the therapist's use of the metaphor, or it could be a blatant rejection of the therapist's use of the metaphor, such as a repudiation of any changes the therapist has made in the story or a refusal to use that particular metaphor in future interactions.

When this happens, the therapist must examine whether the negative reaction was to the direction the therapist was taking the metaphor or to the co-opting of the metaphor. If the reaction was to the direction the therapist was taking the metaphor, the child may reject the particular part of the metaphor that he or she does not like (e.g., "The mouse wouldn't ask for help. What are you talking about?") or convey more generalized disapproval (e.g., "I don't want to tell this story anymore. You don't know what you are talking about."). When this happens, the therapist may just need to adjust his or her direction or use of the metaphor. For example, Brian may not like it when the therapist makes suggestions for ways the mouse can elude the cat. He is perfectly content for the mouse to be chased by the cat and tells the therapist that this is his story and she should leave it alone. After all, he identifies with the cat and sees nothing wrong with picking on smaller creatures. For future uses of Brian's metaphors, the therapist needs to be more careful to decide which character represents Brian.

Sometimes the therapist just "gets it wrong" in the metaphor just as he or she could make a mistake in a more direct form of communication. The therapist may have inaccurately reflected a feeling or missed the gist of a restatement of content. When this happens, the child's reaction is usually a relatively mild correction, such as "No, the mouse isn't scared. He likes being chased."

There are some children who do not wish to "share" their metaphors with the therapist. With these children, their negative reaction to the therapist using their metaphor is frequently a violent rejection of anything the therapist does with the metaphor. It is usually better with these children for the therapist to avoid adapting their metaphors. Instead, the therapist must generate other ways of making suggestions (both directly and indirectly) with them.

Examples of Using the
Child's Metaphor to Communicate

Using the metaphors from earlier in the chapter, I have written several different examples of the therapist using the child's metaphor to communicate with the child.

* Alonzo (6) has a Black mother and an Asian father. Both sets of grandparents have severed ties with the family, which has created a great deal of tension between his parents. Alonzo arranges all of the dolls in two different "camps" on the edges of the sandbox, sorted by skin color. He puts a small brown doll in an ambulance, moving it from camp to camp, but no one will let the doll out of the ambulance.

1. "Every time he stops, the others won't let him get out." (**tracking**)
2. "It seems like he might be lonely—like he is trying to find a place to stop and the others won't let him." (**reflection of feeling and interpretation**)
3. "He seems to just have to keep on moving. He must be getting kind of tired out." (**interpretation and reflection of feeling**)
4. "I wonder how the person in there feels." (**disguised question**)
5. "What are those people on the edges saying to the person in there?" (**question**)
6. "Why won't the other people let him stop?" (**question**)
7. "He does not seem to be able to find a place to stop." (**interpretation**)

* Roger (7) has been diagnosed as having ADHD. His presenting problem is impulsivity and refusal to complete work in school. He comes into the playroom, scoots around the room, crashes into your chair, and says, "I am a locomotive, and I cannot stop. Even if a car gets in my way, I just run right over it."

1. "You just feel like you cannot stop." (**restatement of content**)
2. "You believe that you cannot stop yourself." (**interpretation and cognitive reframe**)
3. "It must be kind of scary not being able to stop, Mr. Locomotive." (**reflection of feeling**)
4. "This train might just run over a car if it gets in its way." (**restatement of content**)
5. "If no one gives this train any help, it will crash." (**interpretation**)
6. "Mr. Locomotive, how are you feeling right now, not being able to stop?" (**question**)

7. "What could the train do to stop itself?" (**invitation to problem solve or generate alternative behaviors**)
8. "What would happen if someone helped the train put on his brakes?" (**invitation to problem solve or generate alternative behaviors**)

* Lois (8) comes to play therapy with a presenting problem of generalized anxiety. She tells you about a book her mother read her. The plot was that there was a family in which every member was afraid of something. The family adopted a dog that was also afraid of a bunch of different stuff. Each member of the family helped the dog stop being afraid of the thing that frightened that member.

1. "Everybody was scared of something, but the dog helped them even though he was scared too." (**restatement of content and reflection of feeling**)
2. "They found somebody to help them solve their problem." (**suggestion for problem-solving skill**)
3. "How did they feel about being able to find someone to help them with their fears?" (**question**)
4. "They figured out a way to stop being afraid." (**interpretation**)
5. "The dog helped everyone in the family. How did he feel when that happened?" (**interpretation and question about feeling**)
6. "I bet that dog felt very proud of himself for helping the members of the family stop being afraid." (**reflection of feeling**)

* Rashid (7) walks into the room, takes the family dolls (with the exception of the little boy), buries them under a pile of sand, and says, "Nothing can ever save them."

1. "They must be pretty discouraged knowing that nothing can ever save them." (**reflection of feeling**)
2. "I bet they are kind of scared way down there underneath all that." (**reflection of feeling**)
3. "The whole family got buried except the little boy. I wonder what the little boy thinks about that?" (**question**)
4. "They are buried and nothing can save them." (**tracking and restatement of content**)
5. "If someone wanted to help them, what would that someone have to do?" (**engagement of the child in problem solving**)
6. "I bet that little boy really misses them and wants them to know that he remembers them with love." (**reflection of feeling and interpretation**)

John (6) tells you this story: "There once was a bird who lived in a cage and wanted to fly away. One day, the bird escaped, but an eagle saw him and attacked him. The bird fell from the sky and died."

1. "The bird didn't want to live in the cage anymore. He felt trapped and wanted to get away." (**restatement of content and reflection of feeling**)
2. "The bird tried to take care of himself, but it didn't work out the way he wanted it to." (**interpretation**)
3. "He was excited because he got away, then he was scared that the eagle was after him." (**reflection of feeling**)
4. "He must have been so discouraged—thinking that he would get what he wanted and then having it snatched away from him." (**refection of feeling and interpretation**)

In his second session, Gino (4) uses the puppet theater to make a "fort." He places various puppets in between you and the fort, telling you they are the "guards." He goes to the basket of costumes and gets a suit of armor, gathers several swords, and hides inside the "fort."

1. "You figured out a way to make sure you are safe." (**encouragement of problem-solving skills**)
2. "The guards are in place to protect you." (**encouragement of problem-solving skills**)
3. "You feel safer having a fort, some armor, your guards, and some weapons to protect you." (**reflection of feeling**)
4. "Who lives in the fort?" (**question**)
5. "What are things that might be dangerous to the people who live in the fort?" (**question**)

Ayako's (5) mother died when Ayako was 4. Her father has never remarried and seems to have difficulty taking care of himself and his three children. Ayako tells you the story of a garden where the gardener took care of the flowers and they were all happy and bright. However, the gardener decided to leave, and now the flowers are all droopy and the weeds are taking over the garden.

1. "It sounds like the flowers feel pretty sad and lonely right now." (**reflection of feeling**)
2. "I am guessing that the flowers are kind of mad at the gardener for going away." (**interpretation and reflection of feeling**)
3. "What do the flowers need to be okay?" (**question and invitation to problem solving**)

4. "Is there anyone around who could take the gardener's place?" (question and invitation to problem solving)
5. "What are some things that the flowers could do to take care of themselves?" (question, invitation to problem solving, and returning the responsibility to the child)

Todd (9) describes the plot of a movie he watched recently. The way he tells the story, the hero is defeated by an overwhelming number of adversaries. You, having seen an action-thriller or two yourself, know that the "actual" plot resolution involves the hero defeating the overwhelming number of adversaries.

1. "I bet the hero was feeling pretty discouraged, after he tried so hard." (reflection of feelings)
2. "So even though he tried his best, things still didn't turn out the way he wanted them to." (restatement of content)
3. "What else could he have done to try to save himself?" (question and invitation to problem solving)
4. "What would have happened if he made a friend at the beginning of the movie and then asked for some help?" (problem solving and suggestion of alternative behaviors)
5. "What would you have done in his situation?" (question and invitation to problem solving)

Practice Exercises

For each of the following scenarios, write three possible explanations of the meaning of the metaphor. Write three different ways you could use the metaphor to communicate with the child, labeling the type of intervention you have made (reflection of feeling, interpretation, etc.).

1. DeWayne (9) tells you the following story: "I have a friend who was a very good baseball pitcher. He liked to throw fast balls that no one could hit. But one day, he went up against a great hitter, and no matter how hard he threw the ball, that hitter could always hit every pitch he threw. After that, he stopped playing baseball."
2. Mary Jo (4) is playing with the dolls in the dollhouse. The father doll starts yelling at the mother doll and hits her. The children dolls run and hide under the bed. The mother doll comes in and yells at the kids for messing up the stuff that is under the bed.

3. Jack (7) wants to play Power Rangers. He informs you that he will be the Green Power Ranger because he is the most powerful ranger and that you will be the Pink Power Ranger because she is not powerful at all. Then he says, "You know girls aren't as strong as boys are."

4. In the play with Jack, he tells you that you must help him attack the "Puddies," who are the bad guys. He hands you a sword and says, "Help me get them." After about 2 minutes, he takes your sword away and says, "You aren't very good at this. I guess I don't need your help. You go back and guard the fort, and I will get the Puddies by myself."

5. Saidah (8) has been expressing frustration with you because you continue to reflect her feelings even though she told you repeatedly that she does not like it when you talk about feelings. She begins to complain about her mother, saying, "She never does anything I tell her to. I try and try to get her to listen, but sometimes I just feel like a bug that she squashes. She just doesn't care about what I think."

6. Ho (6) takes all the pillows and makes a wall around himself. He looks at the wall, frowns, and starts getting other toys, stacking them on top of the pillows to make the walls taller. He gets in the middle of the walls, sits down, and smiles.

7. Bahati (4) has the mother doll rocking one of the baby dolls, singing to it. Suddenly, Bahati begins making crying noises that seem to emanate from the baby. The mother doll tries to comfort the baby, but it continues to cry. The mother doll seems to be getting frustrated, frowning, and muttering to herself. Finally, after all her efforts to comfort the baby fail, the father doll comes into the dollhouse and throws the mother doll on the floor.

8. Miles (9) relates a story of a television show he has watched in which the hero has a friend whom he really trusts, but the friend suddenly metamorphosizes into a monster who kills the hero.

9. Charlene (5) is painting a picture. She paints a house, some trees, some flowers, and a big bright sun. Then she takes the black paint and very carefully paints over the entire piece of paper until there is no picture or blank paper left.

10. Chuck (7) picks up the handcuffs and wants to put them on you, saying "You will be my prisoner." When you limit having your hands

handcuffed behind your back, he takes them and puts them on his own arms, takes the key, and buries it under the sand.

11. Latifa (8) has just found out her mother has terminal cancer. In the playroom, she carefully arranges a town in the sandbox, with every figure meticulously arranged. Then she picks up the magic wand and frantically stirs up the sand, saying, "This is a tornado. It is destroying the town."

12. Casey (7) has just been introduced to his father's fiancée and her two children. He comes into the playroom and begins to use the puppets to act out the story of Cinderella, with a major emphasis on the evilness of the stepmother and her daughters.

13. Cassandra (6) has a continuing story that she tells you about a busy bee who is always telling everyone what to do and how to live their lives. The bee has no friends, but it cannot seem to stop itself from being bossy and trying to get everyone to live their lives the way they are supposed to. No matter what feedback the other animals in the forest give the bee, it continues to engage in this self-defeating behavior.

14. Every time Felipe (5) gets frustrated or angry with you, he brings the dragon over and tries to bite your arm. When things are going smoothly in your relationship, he does not even seem to notice the dragon, but the minute he gets irritated with you, out comes the dragon—teeth at the ready.

Questions to Ponder

1. What will be the most difficult aspect for you of recognizing and using children's metaphors in play therapy? Explain.

2. What type of metaphor presentation (in the child's play, in the child's stories, in plot summaries by the child) might be the hardest for you to recognize? Explain.

3. Do you believe that there are certain universal meanings to specific symbols, or do you believe that each person formulates his or her own meaning for symbols? Explain your reasoning.

4. If you do not understand the meaning of a metaphor, how much discomfort will this cause for you? How will you deal with your discomfort?

5. What is your reaction to the suggestion that "breaking" the child's metaphor is disrespectful?

6. How do you think you will handle it if a child rejects your attempts to use his or her metaphor to communicate in a play therapy session?
7. How will you use your understanding of the child's ethnic or cultural background in your attempts to decipher his or her metaphors?

Chapter 13

Advanced Play
Therapy Skills

The number of different counseling techniques that can be adapted for use in the playroom is limited only by the imagination of the play therapist (Cerio, 2000; Gil, 1994; Kaduson & Schaefer, 1997; Kissel, 1990). If the therapist is willing to be creative and take some risks by experimenting with a variety of intervention strategies, he or she can generate a plethora of techniques that might be helpful in play therapy. It would be impossible in an overview such as this one to list and describe all of the possible play therapy techniques.

However, there are several other play therapy skills that are applicable to a wide range of different approaches to play therapy. I have chosen to cover metacommunication, therapeutic metaphors, mutual storytelling, and role-playing in this chapter because they can be used across a number of different theoretical orientations and they lend themselves to relatively simple and concrete description. For each of these play therapy skills, I describe the technique, explain the purpose for using that particular technique, provide several examples of how the technique can be used, and set up practice exercises so that the reader can experiment with the application of the skill.

Metacommunication

"In metacommunication, the counselor *meta* communicates; that is, the counselor steps outside the interaction that is occurring in the relationship between the counselor and the child and communicates *about* the communication" (Kottman, 1995, p. 152). There are several different types of situations in which metacommunication would be an appropriate response. The therapist can comment on the following:

1. Patterns in the interactions between himself or herself and the child (e.g., "I notice that you seem to get a little nervous when I move my chair close to you.").
2. Patterns in the way the child communicates (e.g., "It seems like whenever you want someone to do something your voice gets louder.").
3. Nonverbal communication on the part of the child (e.g., "You looked over here like maybe you were not sure it was okay to shoot the gun at the window.").
4. The child's reactions to the therapist's statements and questions (e.g., "You looked kind of mad when I asked you how your weekend with your dad went.").
5. Patterns in the child's behaviors, reactions, and/or attitudes across several sessions (e.g., "You seem to get very sad whenever you mention your parents' divorce.").
6. Patterns in the child's behaviors, reactions, and/or attitudes in the playroom that extend into other situations and relationships outside the playroom (e.g., "I have noticed that you like to be the boss in here with me. I am guessing that you also like to be the boss at home with your mom.").
7. Patterns in the child's behaviors, reactions, and/or attitudes that typify his or her personality, coping strategies, interpersonal interactional

style, approach to problem solving, approach to conflict resolution, and/or self-image (e.g., "It seems as though you use yelling to get other people to do what you want.").

Sometimes these situations may overlap. For example, the child's reactions to the therapist's statements and questions could be expressed through the child's nonverbal communication, or patterns in the interaction between the therapist and the child could manifest themselves in the patterns of the child's communication.

Purpose of Metacommunication

The purpose of metacommunicating is to help children begin to notice and understand their own patterns of communication. Many times, children are not aware that they are reacting in a certain way. Even when they are aware of their communication patterns, they may not have the abstract verbal-reasoning skills to conceptualize what these patterns mean about themselves and their interactions. By pointing out the patterns in children's behavior, the therapist can help children think about possible meanings in the patterns and help them gain insight into the issues related to underlying themes. Because the play therapy process frequently involves unspoken communication, it is important for the therapist to notice children's nonverbals, especially when they seem to be asking a question without words. It can also be helpful to notice and make comments about children's reactions to the therapist's interventions to give a voice to those reactions. Although adults give verbal feedback to the therapist about comments and questions, children do not usually do so. It becomes incumbent on the therapist to articulate those reactions so that children become aware of their own responses to therapeutic interventions and are able to use that information in the growth process.

How to Metacommunicate

Because metacommunication is concerned with patterns and reactions that are covert or implicit, this skill is speculative in nature. Therefore, it is better for the therapist to phrase metacommunication in a tentative way to avoid imposing his or her reality on the child. That way the child has a chance to correct or clarify what is happening with him or her without feeling a need to be defensive or to overpower the therapist who has made an incorrect guess about underlying issues or communication patterns. To maintain a tentative stance, the therapist includes conditional words and phrases like *might be, maybe, I would guess, I am thinking, kind of, seems as though,* and so forth.

There are three basic methods of metacommunicating. One is to simply describe the behavior or the pattern without adding any kind of speculation or guess about what the behavior or pattern means (e.g., "You frowned right after I said that about your mom.") The second method is to focus more on the meaning of the behavior or pattern, with little or no emphasis on the description of the behavior or pattern (e.g., "I am thinking when I say that your mom seems happy being married to your stepdad, you get kind of mad.") The third method is a combination of the first two—the therapist describes the behavior or pattern and speculates about what it might mean (e.g., "You frowned right after I said that your mom seems happy being married to your stepdad. I am thinking you got kind of mad when I said that.").

It is important to tailor the metacommunication to the child. There are some children who do not seem to understand or respond to metacommunication. This may be due to their developmental level or their cognitive ability, because understanding metacommunication requires a relatively high level of receptive language skills. It may also be due to the fact that they are reluctant to "own" certain feelings or acknowledge certain underlying issues. You may decide not to use metacommunication with children who do not have the abstract verbal-reasoning skills or the receptive language skills to comprehend the ideas you are trying to convey. However, it can be helpful to continue to metacommunicate with those who are simply reluctant to "own" certain feelings or acknowledge certain patterns so as to help them examine communication patterns and underlying issues.

With children who I believe have the capacity to understand the content of the metacommunication but who have some other reason for not responding in a constructive way, I may metacommunicate about their reactions to my original metacommunication. Other times, especially with children who have extremely negative reactions to my metacommunication, I simply say, "Well, it's something to think about," rather than getting into a power struggle with them about whether they accept my interpretation of a particular behavior.

Play therapists who tend to be nondirective will usually either avoid metacommunication or restrict themselves to the method of metacommunication that is a description of the behavior or the pattern that does not add any kind of speculation or guess about what the behavior or pattern means. Other, more directive play therapists may also use this method of metacommunicating but will be more likely to use the other two methods that involve making guesses about the meaning of the child's behavior.

Examples of Metacommunication

After each of the following scenarios, there are several possible metacommunications. I have tried to provide examples of the three methods of metacommunicating.

* Ajit (7) tends to be very aggressive with the female therapist whenever he does not get his way in a play session. He sometimes shouts at the therapist, gets very close physically, and does other things that seem intended to intimidate the therapist into doing what he wants. The therapist might metacommunicate by making comments such as

1. "You seem to get mad when I don't do what you want me to do."
2. "I have noticed that sometimes you yell at me and stand close to me when I don't do what you want."
3. "I am guessing that you think I will do what you want if you yell at me and stand really close to me."

* Elena (5) is a very warm and open child. She has always been very affectionate to her therapist, greeting her with hugs and kissing her on the cheek before she leaves a session. After the therapist announces that they have three more sessions left before they are done, Elena stops physically showing her affection and seems generally aloof in her sessions.

1. "It seems like you are feeling kind of sad because we only have three more times together."
2. "I have noticed that since I mentioned that we were going to have only three more times together it seems like you have stopped giving me hugs and you are not smiling very much when we are together."
3. "Since I mentioned that we have only three more times together, it seems like you have stopped giving me hugs and you don't smile very

much any more. I am thinking that you might be kind of sad and mad at me because we are going to stop our times together."

Ebony (6) is very quiet in her play therapy sessions. Whenever she has had a rough day at school or gotten in a conflict with one of her parents, she gets even more quiet in her sessions. This is especially true whenever her mother reports that she has had a problem to the therapist in the waiting room before Ebony's session.

1. "Ebony, I notice you are very quiet today."
2. "Ebony, it seems like you are especially quiet when you have had a hard day at school."
3. "I have noticed that you don't seem to talk much on the days when your mom tells me that you have had a rough day."
4. "I am guessing that you feel kind of bad about how your day went today, and you're just not feeling like talking very much. That happens sometimes when kids have had a hard day."
5. "I am thinking that you feel kind of embarrassed when your mom tells me that you guys haven't been getting along, and you just don't want to talk about that when it happens so you get really quiet."

Justine (4) is afraid of many different things in the world—for example, she fears snakes, bugs, fire trucks, and ambulances. Whenever she sees any of these items or discusses them in a session, her voice gets higher and louder and speeds up.

1. "I noticed that whenever you see a play fire truck or ambulance in the room that you get a little louder."
2. "You seem to be a little nervous whenever you look over there at the shelf with the fire truck and the ambulance."
3. "It sounds like your voice got louder when you saw the toy fire truck. I am thinking you feel a little nervous about having it in the playroom."

Alexander (7) was physically abused by his birth mother. He was taken away when he was 4 and placed with his grandmother. The therapist stands up to close the window in the playroom, and Alexander flinches.

1. "I noticed that when I stood up to close the window, you kind of got all scrunched up."
2. "It looked to me like when I stood up to close the window, you were a little scared about me coming over close to you."

3. "It seemed like you got kind of scrunched up when I stood up to close the window, like maybe you thought that I might hurt you."

* *Sven (6) tends to try to please the adults in his life and is highly anxious in this area. He is painting a picture. He originally asked the therapist what he should paint, and she returned the responsibility for making that decision to him. Every time he makes a stroke with the paint, he turns and visually checks the therapist's reaction.*

1. "I noticed that you were looking over here, kind of checking out what I was thinking."
2. "It seems like you are worried about whether I am going to like your painting or not."
3. "You seem to be looking over here like you are worried that I might not like your painting."
4. "I am thinking that you want to make sure that I like what you are doing over there on your painting."

* *Becka (9) does not like it when the therapist metacommunicates about her nonverbal reactions. Whenever the therapist does this, Becka says things like, "Don't talk about that" or "You don't know anything."*

1. "Whenever I mention something about what your body is doing, you tell me not to talk about it."
2. "It seems to me that you would like me to stop noticing it when you have a reaction in your body to what is happening in the playroom."
3. "I am thinking that you would like to get me to stop pointing it out when you shrug or smile or nod."

Therapeutic Metaphors

Metaphors in therapy constitute an indirect form of treatment. Like other forms of indirection, therapeutic metaphors do not engender the kind of resistance to considering new ideas that direct suggestions often can. They are experienced as a gentle and permissive, not a confrontive or demanding way to consider change. At one level, a metaphor is "just a story" that doesn't require any response, but at another level, it stimulates thinking, experiencing, and ideas for problem resolution. (Lankton & Lankton, 1989, pp. 1–2)

A therapeutic metaphor is a story designed specifically for a particular child and his or her situation. The therapist includes characters in the story who represent the various people in the child's life (both allies and obstacles) and puts the hero and the allies into situations in which they have to cope with problem situations similar to the difficulties that face the child. The characters express feelings that are parallel to those experienced by the child and the other people in the child's life. The therapist makes sure to explain the perspective of each of the characters in the story to shed light on different ways to view the problem. After struggling with the problem and trying different possible solutions, the main character comes to some kind of a resolution of the difficulties.

The purpose of including characters and circumstances similar to the child, other people in his or her life, and the child's situation is to help the child identify with the characters, explore the various perspectives presented in the story, and consider applying the potential solutions to problems in the story to his or her own situation. The therapist does not point out the parallels between the child's life and the story but lets the child decide whether to acknowledge the similarities or to act as if the story is "just a story."

How to Design and Deliver Therapeutic Metaphors

Several therapists who specialize in developing metaphors in their practice with children have suggested procedures for designing therapeutic metaphors (Brooks, 1981; Cerio, 2000; Lankton & Lankton, 1989; Mills & Crowley, 1986; Trottier & Seferlis, 1990). I have taken their ideas, combined them with my own experiences and the experiences of my students, and generated the following steps for designing metaphors for children in play therapy (Kottman, 1995).

1. Describe the setting and initial situation with enough detail so the child can visual them. The beginning scene should not be exactly the same as the child's circumstances but should have several similarities. The story can be set in a natural environment (e.g., "in the forest"), in a mythical environment (e.g., "once upon a time in the dragon's palace"), or in a realistic environment (e.g., "in a school where I used to work").

2. Describe the characters in enough detail so that the child gets a feel for what they are like. The cast of characters should include (a) the protagonist of the story—represents the child; (b) the antagonist of the story—represents someone or some situation that is giving the protagonist problems; (c) a resource person—someone wise or relatively uninvolved in the struggle who can provide advice, an alternative perspective, or possible solutions to difficulties encountered by the protagonist; and (d) one or two allies for the protagonist—someone who is willing to go through the difficulties with the protagonist and can provide support, encouragement, advice, an alternative perspective, or possible solutions. Depending on the setting and the interests and developmental level of the child, these characters can be realistic, fictional, or fantastic. I have found that it frequently helps the child's acceptance of the story if the protagonist and most of the other characters are the same sex as the child.

3. Describe the primary problem, dilemma, or struggle encountered by the protagonist and his or her allies concretely and in enough detail so that the child can visualize and understand the difficulty. The problem situation can have some parallels to the child's difficulty, but the correlation should not be so obvious that it precludes the opportunity for the child to continue in the belief that the metaphor is "just a story."

4. As the story progresses, the protagonist must make progress in his or her method of coping with the problem. This progress may involve trying some solutions that work, gaining some new coping skills that aid in handling the problem, or adopting a new perspective about the situation so that it does not seem insurmountable. The resolution should not come too easily, however. The protagonist may have setbacks or may simply have to try several different ways of dealing with the problem before the situation moves toward resolution. This ensures that the child does not see the progress as just a glib reassurance that "everything will be all right." It is important that the child feels that the protagonist has earned the final solution, rather than having it just happen. The protagonist must also be responsible for making the final decisions and for putting forth the majority of the effort toward the resolution. The resource person and the allies can help along the way, but they should not be responsible for overcoming obstacles or providing the solution to the problem.

5. Describe the resolution in a concrete manner that makes it clear what has changed in the protagonist's feelings, attitudes, perception, and/or behavior related to the problem situation. It is frequently helpful to leave some aspects of the original difficulty unsolved, so as to avoid implying that all problems can be resolved. However, at the end of the story, the protagonist must have made progress in learning how to cope with the situation. The resolution should include the protagonist (a) gaining insight into himself or herself and the situation; (b) gaining insight into others and the ways that they see themselves; (c) gaining insight into relationships and interactions with others; (d) developing improved attitudes toward himself or herself, others, and life; and/or (e) acquiring skills that can aid in coping with problem situations in the future. These gains should be related to gains the child needs to make in his or her life.

6. After the resolution, the protagonist and the other characters (sometimes including the antagonist) should have a celebration that affirms the changes that have taken place in the protagonist. This celebration usually involves a party, a ceremony, or simply a conversation in which the protagonist explains to the other characters what he or she has learned through the struggles and the other characters congratulate the protagonist on progress or changes made. Sometimes the therapist chooses to add a moral or message to the end of the story, but many children do not respond positively to this method of consolidation, perhaps because it can tend to be rather heavy-handed or sound judgmental.

In my experience, therapeutic metaphors seem to work better in play therapy if the therapist tailors the method of telling to the child's developmental age. Younger children (3–8 years old developmentally) seem to be more interested in animal characters rather than people. It also helps with these children to (a) act out the story with animal puppets or figures, (b) make a drawing or painting as you are telling the story to illustrate the metaphor, or (c) show them a "book" of the story illustrating the story that you have constructed prior to the session. A visual component is essential with most children in this age range because it seems to facilitate their understanding and acceptance of the story. With children in this age range,

I usually tell them that "the animals can talk in this story." Then I use different voices to tell the story, using a different voice for each animal.

With these children, you will also need to keep the story relatively short. I try to make stories for very young children (3–4 years old) just 2 to 3 minutes. For children in the 5–6-year-old range, I might have a story that is 3 to 4 minutes. With children who are 7 or 8 years old, the story can be a little longer, but it probably should not last more than 5 or 6 minutes, or you will lose the attention of your audience.

With older children who come to play therapy (older than 7 years developmentally), the therapist can decide whether to use animal characters; "real" people characters; cartoon characters; or fictional characters from books, television shows, or movies. The determination of the identity of the characters should be based on the child and his or her preferences and interests. With some children, the therapist can use characters that the child has already generated in stories the child has told. Other children may have a clear interest or hobby that could guide the therapist in character definition. Many children like to hear stories about "real" people—other children and their families and friends. I usually make up these "real" people or use acquaintances that have been heavily disguised to ensure that the child could not possibly recognize them.

Many older children do not need to have the visual input that is necessary with younger children. It is frequently helpful to experiment with this visual input—using visual aids with some metaphors and using none with other metaphors and watching how each child responds to the type of delivery used. Some older children like to help act out the metaphor, especially if you frame the story as a movie that you are going to videotape so that they can watch it later or as a radio show that you will audiotape so that they can listen to it at home. You can also do this with puppet shows or "plays" using the other toys in the playroom.

Developmentally older children can also tolerate longer stories. This is something you may also want to try with different variations for individual children, but most children 8 years or older can sustain interest in a metaphor that lasts as long as 8 to 10 minutes.

For therapists who do not wish to generate metaphors for individual children, there are sources of therapeutic metaphors designed for children with specific presenting problems or situations. The therapist can use these stories in exactly the form they were written or adapt them for individual children. Several sources for therapeutic metaphors are as follows:

* *Annie Stories: Storytelling for Common Issues* (Brett, 1988),
* *More Annie Stories: Therapeutic Storytelling Techniques* (Brett, 1992),
* *Cartoon Magic: How to Help Children Discover Their Rainbows Within* (Crowley & Mills, 1989),
* *Once Upon A Time: Therapeutic Stories to Heal Abused Children* (Davis, 1990),
* *Therapeutic Stories That Teach and Heal* (Davis, 1997).

Bibliotherapy is another way for the therapist to deliver metaphors without having to invent them. In bibliotherapy, the therapist can use therapeutic books that were specifically written for certain kinds of problems or can use books that just happen to cover topics related to an individual child's issues.

Although these generic metaphors can be extremely helpful, I would like to encourage you to try to design some metaphors for various children with whom you work. The prospect of this process can be a little intimidating. However, once you have delivered several metaphors you have designed especially for individual children and you see how excited and honored they feel at having a story made just for them, you may be willing to risk trying this intervention even if you do not feel that creativity is your strength.

Examples of Therapeutic Metaphors

The following examples present one possible metaphor for each of the children described in the scenario.

* *LaToya (6) lives in the projects, where she witnessed her babysitter getting shot in a drive-by shooting. Since that time, she is convinced that people and monsters are going to get her and hurt her. She clings to her mother and refuses to go with her new babysitter when her mother has to go to work. She has also expressed concerns about her mother's safety.*

A metaphor designed for LaToya:

Little Jackie was a bear who lived in a very dark and gloomy forest where lots of dangerous animals lived. These dangerous animals sometimes hurt the other animals in the forest, and the other animals were pretty scared—especially Little Jackie. Because she was so scared, Little Jackie would never go out and play in the forest, and she cried whenever her mother had to go out into the forest and hunt for berries. Her friends, Freddie the Fox and Olivia the Owl, told her that they could work together and help her stay safe if only she would come out and play with them, but she was still too scared.

One day, Little Jackie was talking with her mother's friend, Betty Big Bear. Betty was a very wise bear who sometimes babysat for Jackie. Betty reminded Jackie that the dangerous animals usually came out only at night and that they almost always stayed in certain parts of the forest. Betty told Jackie that she could probably keep herself safe in the forest if she made sure to stay in the safer parts of the forest, if she played outside only during the day, and if she had a plan for working with Freddie and Olivia to keep themselves safe. Jackie, Freddie, and Olivia made a plan that they could take turns watching out for any dangerous animals—one of them would watch while the other two played.

The next day they tried this plan. It was kind of boring being the one who kept watch, so they decided to switch more often. When Jackie was keeping watch, she saw a group of jackals coming down the path toward her friends. She whoofed really loudly to let Freddie and Olivia know that they needed to hide, but she did not know where to hide herself. Suddenly, she remembered that Betty had once told her a story about having climbed a tree when she was a cub to protect herself from a bigger, meaner bear. Jackie quickly climbed up a tree, and the jackals didn't even notice her. Jackie was really proud of herself for coming up with the idea of climbing the tree to keep herself safe.

After the jackals were gone, Freddie and Olivia came back to the clearing to play, but they could not find Jackie. Finally, she started laughing, and they looked up and saw her. They started laughing too. When she climbed down, both of her friends told her how they thought it was very smart of her to find a way to keep herself safe. They decided to go back to Jackie's house and tell her mother and Betty how they had come up with a plan that worked. Jackie told the grown-ups that she had figured out a way to keep herself safe and that she thought she would be all right playing in the forest. Jackie's mother and Betty were so proud of the way the three little animals had made a plan and protected themselves that they made honey cakes and had a party.

* *Rodrigo (9) was very embarrassed because he still wet the bed. His parents had tried all sorts of remedies, including waking him up several times during the night to go to the bathroom. His father had recently tried to shame him into going all night without wetting the bed, telling him he could never be a man until he stopped his "unmanly behavior." Rodrigo was convinced that it was impossible for him to stop wetting the bed, so no matter what anyone did, it didn't seem to help.*

A metaphor designed for Rodrigo:

When I was a school counselor, I had a kid in my school (his name was Antonio) who had a problem with spilling. No matter what happened, every time he had a glass of water or milk or juice, he spilled it—all over himself and everything else. He was very embarrassed about this behavior. Many of the other kids in his class were starting to make fun of him and that was even more embarrassing. His mother and father tried to help him think of a way to stop spilling, but nothing they suggested seemed to work. All three of them were very frustrated.

One day, Antonio came to my office to talk to me about his problem. I really wasn't sure what to suggest to him, so I asked two of his friends (Calvin and Darius) to help us come up with some ideas for how he could get over this problem. Calvin pointed out that when Antonio even picked up a glass, he got so worried that his hands shook, which made it hard to hold the glass. Calvin mentioned that he had heard Antonio mumbling to himself, "I just know I am going to spill this water," even before he had actually spilled anything. It seemed to me that maybe what was happening was that Antonio had already decided that he was going to spill, so it came true every time. I asked Antonio if he could come up with a way to change the way he thought about himself and spilling. Antonio told me that he did kind of always think he was going to spill, and then he got so nervous and worried that it was hard not to spill. Antonio decided that he would start telling himself, "I am going to drink this glass of water without spilling." Calvin and Darius suggested that he keep an empty glass nearby, so that if he thought he might spill he could decide to pour whatever was in the glass into the empty glass—to prove to himself that he could pour instead of spilling. Antonio decided to try both of these ideas.

The first day, it was hard for him to remember to tell himself, "I am going to drink this without spilling," but Calvin and Darius reminded him at lunch and his dad reminded him at dinner. He spilled a little bit one time during the day, but he managed to get most of it into the empty glass. The second day, it was easier for him to remember to tell himself that he was not going to spill, and he didn't even need the empty glass. Actually, he decided always having an empty glass was kind of stupid anyway and wanted to try just telling himself that he was going to drink without spilling. On the third and fourth days, the plan went perfectly. On the fifth day, Antonio spilled his drink twice. He was so upset that he was ready to give up the plan, but Calvin and Darius reminded him that not everything works out perfectly and that everybody has to practice when they learn something new. They also told him that they would be disappointed and a little mad if he didn't keep on trying to make the plan work that they helped to think up. So for the rest of that week and the next, Antonio continued to tell himself that he could drink without spilling, and it worked—most of the time.

At the end of the second week, Antonio came back to my office to tell me how things were going. He said, "You know, it isn't working perfectly, but things are a lot better than they used to be. I think I had just convinced myself that I could not drink without spilling, and now I know that I can. I just have to concentrate on telling myself that I can do it, and I have to give myself a break when I am not perfect." I was so impressed by Antonio's willingness to try a new way of thinking about himself and his not giving up that I invited Antonio, Calvin, and Darius to go out to McDonald's with me after school. Antonio drank an entire big drink without spilling a single drop.

Mutual Storytelling

Mutual storytelling is a counseling strategy developed by Richard Gardner (1971, 1986) in which the therapist asks the child to tell a story with a beginning, a middle, and an end. The therapist then tells a story using the same beginning—characters, setting, and dilemma—as the child's story. The new story should incorporate more constructive problem-solving skills and a more functional resolution than the original story. The idea behind mutual storytelling is that children's stories represent their worldview in some way. The stories might represent their ideas about relationships, their perception of problem situations in their lives, their ideas about appropriate ways to solve problems, or their view of themselves and others. The purpose of mutual storytelling is to use the children's stories as a springboard for offering (a) different views about relationships, themselves, and others;

(b) different ways to perceive the problem situations in their lives; and (c) more socially acceptable ways to solve problems. The therapist's story is usually intended to teach behaviors—new ways of coping with problem situations and different strategies for interacting with others.

How to Use Mutual Storytelling

The first step in this process is to ask the child to tell a story. Children like to tell stories to adults who are willing to listen to them, so usually this invitation to tell a story is sufficient introduction to get this process started. To make the story more concrete, the play therapist may want to suggest ways for the children to incorporate toys and other play media in the storytelling process (Frederiksen, 1997; Kottman, 1995; Kottman & Stiles, 1990; Stiles & Kottman, 1990). With younger children (7 years or younger), it is helpful to set the stage by asking the children to choose a group of puppets, animals, or other toys to be the characters in the story; pretend these characters can talk; and use them to tell a story (Kottman, 1995).

An older child (8 years or older) may balk at using the puppets and animals, but he or she may be willing to use miniature figures to tell stories. It can also encourage a child in this age range to tell stories if the therapist sets the scene by saying that he or she is the guest on a television or radio show who was invited to tell the audience a story (Gardner, 1986). The therapist will then play the host of the television or radio show and retell the story from that role. The therapist can add a certain amount of authenticity by audiotaping or videotaping the story. An additional advantage to this approach is that the child can take home the tape of the telling and retelling and listen to it as many times as he or she wishes.

Because it is important that the child be invested in the story, I usually suggest that the story be original—not the plot of a movie, book, or television show. However, there are some children who contend that they cannot make up a story by themselves. With these children, I let them use a borrowed plot because they almost always impose their worldview onto the way they recount the story. They filter the plot of the original story through their own way of looking at relationships and situations so that the story reveals more about them than it does about the movie, book, or television show (Kottman, 1995).

Many times, children will tell very short stories, without much detail or plot. These stories quite frequently have abrupt endings when the children run out of ideas and simply stop the narrative. Depending on how you believe they will react, you may choose to probe a bit to elicit more details of the story. Some children tolerate this probing well and even seem to enjoy your interest in the story. These children will frequently reengage themselves in the story after a couple of questions from you and will tell more of the story without further prompting. Other children will resent your probing and react as if you were criticizing their ability to tell a story. You must watch for their nonverbal responses to probes and adjust your own behavior accordingly. The second step in the process is to listen to the story metaphorically. As you listen to the child's story, you need to be thinking about how the story represents the child's worldview and situations and relationships in the child's life. It is helpful to consider the following questions as a way to structure your understanding of the story (Gardner, 1986; Kottman, 1995).

1. How does what the characters in the story do fit with what you already know about the client?
2. How does the situation in the story resemble situations the client normally encounters?
3. Which of the characters in the story represents the child?
4. How does the character who represents the client feel in the story?
5. Which of the characters in the story represent the important people in the child's life or the people involved in a particular situation with which the child is currently struggling?
6. How does the affective tone of the story represent the child's perceptions of the world? Does the affective tone convey the idea that the child is optimistic or pessimistic?
7. How does the story represent the child's perceptions of himself or herself?
8. What does the story tell you about the way the child thinks about his or her ability to cope with problem situations?
9. How does the story represent the child's attitudes toward other people?
10. What does the story reveal about the child's perceptions of patterns and themes in relationships and interactions?

11. How are the patterns and themes in relationships and interactions in the story similar to what you have observed in the child's patterns and themes in relationships and interactions?

12. What is the usual method of coping with conflicts or problem situations in the story?

13. How is the usual method of coping with conflicts or problem situations in the story similar to the child's usual mode of handling conflict or resolving problems?

14. What is your affective response to the story?

On the basis of thoughts generated by these questions and any additional questions you have that would help your understanding of the original story, you formulate some ideas about what the story reveals about the child, the child's life, relationships with others, self-image, and the usual method of dealing with difficulties. There may be theory-specific questions you would ask about the story as well. For instance, if you were a cognitive–behavioral play therapist, you might ask yourself how the story reveals the child's self-talk. If you were an Adlerian play therapist, you might want to think about what the story reveals about the goals of misbehavior, the Crucial Cs, and the child's personality priorities.

The third step in this process is the retelling of the story, with a more adaptive, socially appropriate middle and ending. In preparation for the retelling, you will want to consider the following questions.

1. Which character(s) would you leave in? Why?

2. Would you add any character(s)? If yes, what traits would you incorporate in any added character(s)?

3. Why would that (those) character(s) be important with this client?

4. What positive characteristics or traits would you want to encourage in your client through this story?

5. Do you want to incorporate some kind of consequences for negative behaviors in the story? If so, what kind of consequences would be appropriate without sounding moralistic or judgmental?

6. If the affective tone of the original story was negative or pessimistic, how can you incorporate a more positive, optimistic affective tone?

7. How can you incorporate more constructive patterns of interacting with others?

8. How can you include more socially appropriate methods of resolving conflicts or resolving any difficulties in the story?
9. How can you encourage the client to focus on his or her strengths?
10. How can you use the elements of the story to teach new ways of viewing other people?
11. How can you use the story to give the client feedback about how others see him or her?
12. How can you use the story to improve the client's faith in his or her ability to solve problems?
13. How can you incorporate more descriptions of the characters' feelings and reactions to use the characters to model the expression of feelings?

This seems like a lot of factors to consider as you listen to a child tell you a story that may last 30 to 60 seconds. As you begin using mutual storytelling, you may want to give yourself extra time to go through both of these lists before you retell the story. This extra time can involve making an audiotape or a videotape of the original story, listening to it outside of the session, and coming back to the next session with your modified version of the story. It can involve you simply thinking about the original story for several minutes and then retelling the story later in the session.

Just as with therapeutic metaphors, there are a number of ways to deliver the retelling. You can use the same modality the child did (puppet show, videotape, miniatures, animal figures, etc.), or you can use a different modality (painting or drawing a picture or mural, making a book, making a personalized audiotape, etc.). It is essential to present the retelling without emphasizing that you are *re*telling the story—you don't want to imply that there was anything wrong with the original version of the story. As you introduce your version of the story, it is helpful to tell the child that you were so interested in the story and the characters in his or her story that it reminded you of a story you wanted to tell about those same characters.

It is important to remember that every play therapist will probably have a distinct interpretation of the meaning and underlying messages of the original story and will design a completely different retelling than any other play therapist. There is no one perfect retelling for the story, so there is no reason to agonize over every nuance of the retelling in an attempt to get it "right." You may do one retelling in the session when the child tells the original story and then do several other retellings of the same story in subsequent sessions.

Examples of Mutual Storytelling

* Kareem (7) is referred to play therapy by his school counselor, who reports that he tends to be rather shy and withdrawn in the classroom but extremely aggressive on the playground. The school counselor speculates that this pattern is related to the fact that he struggles with academic subjects and the other students make fun of him for this. Kareem is very strong and physically powerful though, so he may be taking his revenge on the playground. Kareem uses the animal puppets to tell the following story:

There once was a fox, and he had a lot of trouble tracking other animals to eat. When he played with the other foxes, they made fun of him. They said, "You are so dumb; you can't do anything right. What is wrong with you?" He would jump on them and bite them on their ears. Nobody wanted to be friends with him. They said, "Go away and leave us alone."

A possible retelling of this story:

There once was a fox, named Jarome, and he had some trouble tracking small animals to eat. He was very frustrated by this, and he tried a lot of different ways to learn to track better. Jarome was still having trouble despite all his efforts to learn to track. When he would play with the other young foxes, they said, "Why do you have so much trouble tracking? What is wrong with you?" Jarome said, "I don't know, but I really want to learn how." Two of the other foxes (Sandy and Foxy) said, "We will help you learn." The other young foxes were still mean to him, saying, "You are not even a fox. You should know how to track." Jarome decided that it would be worth them making fun of him if he could finally learn how to track from Sandy and Foxy. They practiced every day together, and Jarome slowly began to get better and better at tracking. He felt very proud of himself, and he said to Sandy and Foxy, "Thank you so much for helping me. I don't think I could have learned to track without your help." Jarome tracked and caught several squirrels to give them in thanks. He ignored the other young foxes and decided to work on being better friends with Sandy and Foxy because they had helped him with his problem.

    * *Lindey (9) lived with her mother and stepfather. Although she had originally gotten along with her stepfather, the more he tried to impose rules and discipline on the family, the more angry Lindey became. Lindey's mother and stepfather were very willing to work things out, but they were at a loss for how to cope with Lindey's alternately defiant and clinging behavior. Lindey sat on a chair and told this story:*

There once was a kitten that nobody wanted. She tried to find a place to live, but her mother didn't want her to live with her and her father didn't want her to live with him. She went to her grandmother's house, and she didn't want her either. She was kind of sad, but then she got mad. She went back to each house and knocked them all down. The kitten thought that she would feel better when she did this, but she didn't. She felt worse than ever.

    A possible retelling of this story:

There once was a kitten named Saboo who thought that nobody wanted her. Saboo's father said that she couldn't live with him because he worked nights and he was afraid that he couldn't take good care of her. Her mother said that she could live with her, but Saboo did not get along with her mother's new husband, so that wasn't working out very well. The kitten's grandmother (Gram) was very old, and she had trouble taking care of herself. Even though Gram wanted Saboo to come and live with her, she decided that would not be best for the kitten.

Gram was also very wise, though, and she knew how much Saboo's father and mother and stepfather all loved her. Gram asked Saboo if she could help Saboo figure out some new ways that Saboo could try to get along with her stepfather. They had some good ideas, but the kitten was still not sure that it would work out for her to live with her mother and stepfather. Gram asked Saboo if she would be willing to come to a meeting with her mother, her stepfather, and her grandmother so they all could talk about the problems they had been having. Gram reminded Saboo that her stepfather had never been a parent before, so he might need some help from Saboo learning how to be a dad. The kitten knew that her grandmother would be on her side, so Saboo agreed to try to work it out.

They had the meeting, and they all decided that they would give it another chance. Saboo moved back in with her mother and stepfather and started training him how to be a good dad. Her stepfather really wanted to be a good dad, so he listened to what Saboo had to say. Things were still not perfect, but they got better every day.

* *Wen Ju (5) rules his family by using temper tantrums to get what he wants. Whenever his mother and father try to get him to comply with their requests or they say "no" to him, he throws himself on the floor, yells, screams, bites, cries, and throws things at them. He acts out the following story with the animal figures:*

This is the big lion. He says, "I am the king, and everybody has to do what I say." These are all the other animals who live in the woods. They say, "What will you do if we don't do what you say?" The big lion says, "I will roar at you and scratch you and make you do what I want." The other animals say, "Okay, we will do what you tell us to do."

A possible retelling of this story:

Leo, the big lion, was very powerful, and he had a lot of friends. Leo liked for the other animals in the woods to do what he wanted. However, when they didn't do what he wanted, he felt kind of confused and kind of mad. He decided to try to get them to do what he wanted by roaring at them and scratching them. He hurt several of the other animals, so all the animals hid when he came to their part of the woods. Leo was disappointed that no one wanted to be friends or play with him anymore, so he told the animals he had hurt that he was sorry. He asked them how he could be friends with them again. They said, "You cannot always be the boss. You will have to take turns. Sometimes you can be the boss, but sometimes we want to be the boss too. And you cannot roar or scratch just because you don't get your way." Leo decided to try their way and see how it worked. He didn't like letting the other animals get their way, but he did it anyway and he was pretty happy because he had a lot of new friends.

* *Carisa (8) has lived in several different foster families since she was taken away from her parents, who are both drug users. Some of the changes in placement were due to Carisa not getting along with the members of the foster families, and some of them were due to factors unrelated to Carisa's behavior. She uses the puppets to put on a "show." Carisa's story:*

There once was a raccoon who couldn't live with her mother and father because they got in trouble. She tried to live with a wolf family, but they sent her away for cussing. She tried to live with a family of bees, but they kept stinging her, so she ran away from home. She tried to live with a snail family, but they didn't want her because she wasn't slimy. She was afraid that she would never find a family of her own.

A possible retelling of this story:

There once was a raccoon named Black Eyes who couldn't live with her mother and father because they could not take care of her. She got a social worker (Mrs. Foxy), who tried to find the best place for her to live. Mrs. Foxy first put her with a family of wolves but realized that this was a mistake because wolves are only good at raising other wolves. Black Eyes thought that the problem with the wolf family was something she had done wrong and she was sad, but Mrs. Foxy told her that it wasn't a problem with her—it was a problem with the wolves. Mrs. Foxy moved Black Eyes to a family of bees. However, the family of bees had not had enough training in living with other animals who were not used to getting stung, and they kept accidentally stinging Black Eyes. Black Eyes thought maybe she was doing something to upset the bees and that was why they were stinging her. Mrs. Foxy explained that it wasn't anyone's fault, that the bees were just not ready to be foster parents yet. Mrs. Foxy moved Black Eyes to a family of snails, but that didn't work out either. The snails were not used to living with an animal who didn't have a lot of slime. Black Eyes felt sad that she wasn't slimy enough to fit into the snail family, but Mrs. Foxy said, "I think you are great just the way you are." Then Mrs. Foxy had a wonderful idea. She said, "I wish I had thought of this before." She put Black Eyes with a family of raccoons. The raccoon family thought that Black Eyes was a great little raccoon, and they all lived (mostly) happily ever after.

Role-Playing/Engaging in Play With the Child

There are a number of different ways to role-play or engage in play with the child, depending on the therapist's personal preference and theoretical orientation. These methods include the whisper technique (G. Landreth, personal communication, March 1985), role reversal, and behavior rehearsal.

Whisper Technique

The whisper technique consists of an interaction between the therapist and the child in which the therapist gives control of the direction and the contents of the play (or the role-playing) to the child. This method of playing ensures that the child has input into what happens in the interaction; it can also be a strategy for returning responsibility to the child.

How to use the whisper technique. In using the whisper technique for role-playing, the therapist uses at least three different voices: (a) his or her own voice, (b) a character voice, and (c) a whisper voice. The therapist uses his or her own voice to make therapeutic comments—tracking, restating content, reflecting feelings, metacommunicating, and so forth. The therapist uses the character voice (or voices) to represent the characters he or she is playing. The whisper voice is used by the therapist to ask the child for directions. By whispering, "What should I say?" or "What should I do?" the therapist involves the child in the decision-making process in a way that encourages engagement and taking responsibility.

In my interactions with children, I have noticed that most of them are much more likely to respond with directions when I ask for them in a whisper. I am not really sure why, but this strategy works very well. When the therapist initially uses the whisper, some children are not sure what to do. However, they will usually begin to respond if the therapist persists in asking and gives them a prompt or two by saying things in a continued whisper like, "Now you are supposed to tell me what to say" or "I am going to wait to do something until you tell me what to do." If they do not respond even with these prompts, the therapist may want to metacommunicate about what could be going on with them. They may be afraid to take a risk and tell an adult what to do, they may think that the therapist is trying to trick them in some way, they may not be in the practice of controlling anything and have no ideas for what should happen next in the role-play, and so forth.

Beginning therapists tend to struggle with remembering to use their own voice to continue to interact in a therapeutic way with the child. They get so caught up in the playing that they let that particular aspect of the whisper technique lapse. It will be important for you to remember that you are still the therapist even when you are a partner in the child's play.

When the child is "stuck." There will be certain circumstances in which the therapist might feel that the child is "stuck." These are situations when the child plays the exact same role over and over and over again with the same behaviors, talk, and so forth, without seeming to gain insight or learn new behaviors. This repetition may stem from the child using the play for abreaction—as a way to gain a sense of mastery over a certain experience or relationship or as catharsis—or for the expression of painful feelings.

When this is the case, the child will tend to be relaxed and calm after the play scene has ended.

At other times, though, the child will seem agitated and confused after the play has ended. In these cases, the child may be exhibiting posttraumatic play (Gil, 1991; Terr, 1983, 1990)—play in which the child feels retraumatized rather than helped toward a sense of mastery.

When the therapist feels as though the child is "stuck," it is essential for him or her to consider how the play is affecting the child. If the play actually seems to be soothing the child in some way, it is probably appropriate to let the child continue to be stuck until he or she feels a need to move somewhere else with the play. The therapist should not interfere with the child's quest for mastery simply because the therapist is bored with the play.

However, if the therapist believes that the child is engaging in repetitive posttraumatic play, he or she can make the decision to take the role-playing in a different direction and not use the whisper technique to ask the child for the next set of instructions. When this happens, the therapist can just do or say something to move the play past the stuck part. This may involve alternate endings to the story, different coping strategies for dealing with problem situations, new characters that provide help or advice to the other characters, and so forth. Most nondirective, child-centered play therapists would probably choose not to be this directive. They would most likely deal with this issue in another way—perhaps by choosing not to participate in a role-playing or playing situation that seems to be evoking a posttraumatic response.

If you are in this situation and are struggling with whether the child is stuck in a productive, useful way or in a nonproductive, self-destructive way, you might want to consider getting supervision about the case or consulting with an experienced play therapy colleague. Sometimes the reason you are "stuck" with the child's "stuckness" is related to one of your own issues, rather than the child's issues.

Other Methods of Role-Playing or Playing With the Child

There are several other methods of role-playing or playing with the child that are frequently used in play therapy. Some therapists use puppets or costumes to present metaphors or mutual storytelling, assigning parts to themselves and the child. Other therapists structure role-playing to help the child practice new behaviors, or they use "instant replay" to experiment with a variety of ways to handle problem situations. "Instant replay" is a technique in which the therapist asks the child to repeat a recent interaction—with a different attitude or style of approaching the situation. The therapist would use this technique for giving a child feedback that his or her usual way of interacting with others is not appropriate and inviting the child to practice more appropriate interactional patterns.

To increase a child's empathy, understanding of the feelings of others, and ability to comprehend different perspectives, sometimes the play therapist will set up role-reversal situations. In role reversal, the therapist pretends to be the child, and the child pretends to be some important person in the child's life, usually one with whom the child has a pattern of conflict or misunderstanding. Because the purpose in these methods of role-playing is to teach the child new perspectives or skills, the therapist will not usually use the whisper technique to ask for directions. He or she will decide what to do or say without letting the child control the interaction.

In some cases, the therapist may be working with a variation of release therapy, in which the child acts out a particularly traumatic event over and over until the event loses its impact on the child. By participating in this play, the therapist can have a certain amount of control over how the event gets played out and what kinds of processing the child does.

Examples of Role-Playing and Engaging in Play With the Child

In the following examples, I have tried to demonstrate several different methods of setting up role-playing and engaging in play with children, including the whisper technique, "instant replay," teaching and practicing new behaviors, and role reversal.

Whisper Technique

Richard: "Let's play cops and robbers."

Therapist: "Okay." (In a whisper:) "Who do you want me to be?"

Richard: "You be the robber, and I will be the cop."

Therapist: "So you decided that you want to be the cop and you want me to be the robber." (In a whisper:) "What should I do?"

Richard: "You go over there and grab the money. Then you hide behind those pillows."

Therapist: "You want me to steal the money and then hide." (In a rough "robber" voice:) "I am going to get all this money and hide."

Richard: "Just crouch down over there behind the pillows. Now, I say, 'I am a great detective. I bet I will be able to find that robber who stole all the money.'"

Therapist: "You have a lot of confidence in yourself, Mr. Detective. You are sure you will be able to find that robber." (In a whisper:) "What should I be doing?"

Richard: "You think I can't find you."

Therapist: (In a rough, "robber" voice) "That cop will never find me. He thinks he is a good detective, but I have a great hiding place where he won't find me."

Richard: (Walking over to the pillows) "Ah ha!!! You thought I wouldn't find you, didn't you. I am going to take you to jail."

Therapist: "Wow, even though that robber thought she had a good hiding place, you found her anyway. You sound very proud of yourself." (In a whisper:) "What should I do?"

Richard: "Try to get away."

Therapist: (In rough voice:) "I am going to escape."

Richard: "That's what you think. I am taking you to jail." (Grasps therapist's arm and pulls her toward another part of the room.)

Therapist: "You knew just how to keep the robber from getting away. You really are a great detective." (In a whisper:) "What should I say?"

Richard: "Say, 'The End.'"

Therapist: "So the story is finished now. The end!"

Instant Replay

Richard: (In a very bossy voice:) "I want to play with that game up there on the shelf. Get it for me right now."

Therapist: "I would be glad to help you get that game, but when you talk to me like that it hurts my feelings, and I don't feel like doing favors for you. Let's try that again. Try asking me to get the game in a different way."

Richard: (In a more neutral voice:) "I want to play with that game up there on the shelf. Could you get it for me?"

Therapist: "I would be delighted to get it for you. Thank you for asking in such a polite way."

Teaching/Practicing New Behaviors

Therapist: "Okay, Richard, the next time your brother tries to get you into trouble, what are you going to do?"

Richard: "Ignore him, and go tell my mom in a nonwhiny voice that James hit me or whatever he did."

Therapist: "Let's practice that. I will be James and your mother, and you be yourself. I am James, and I come up and push you. What do you say?"

Richard: "Nothing. I turn and walk away. Then I go to my mom and say, 'Mom, I just wanted you to know that James pushed me. I walked away and didn't do anything back.'"

Therapist: (In a high-pitched "mom" voice:) "Wow, Richard. That's great. I am proud of you." (Switches to regular voice:) "How did that feel? Let's try it again using a different strategy."

Role Reversal

Therapist: "Richard, from what you have told me, sometimes you seem to get yourself into trouble with your teacher when you use a crabby voice or you try to tell her what to do. Let's pretend that you are the teacher and I am you, just to give you an idea of how she feels when you speak to her that way. (In a crabby voice:) "I can't believe you gave me a *C* on this work. I want you to change this grade right now." (In a regular voice:) "Now, what would the teacher say?"

Richard: "I can't change the grade. You missed all these problems."

Therapist: (In a crabby voice:) "You are so mean. You never do what I want. I hate you." (In a regular voice:) "What would the teacher say if you said that?"

Richard: "Richard, I am sorry that you feel that way, but we don't talk that way to people in our room. You need to go to the office."

Therapist: "How did that feel when you were being the teacher and I talked to you that way?"

Richard: "Bad. I didn't like it. I got mad, but I didn't think the teacher would yell at me. She never has before."

Therapist: "Let's try it now, and I will talk in a more polite way about the same situation. Let's see how you feel."

Practice Exercises

Metacommunication

For each of the following scenarios, write two different responses involving metacommunication.

1. Luke (7) was referred to play therapy because he has "low self-esteem." Every time the therapist returns responsibility to him, he shakes his head, looks sad, and says, "I can't do that. You know I can't."
2. Yvonne (5) is in foster care because her mother is in a drug rehabilitation program. She comes into the session, smiling, chattering, and bouncing. She told you last week that she was going to get to visit her mother this afternoon before your session.
3. Gunther (9) does not like talking about his incarcerated father. Every time the therapist brings up a comment or a question about his father, he moves to the other side of the room and sits with his arms crossed.
4. Raisa (6) tells you that her stepfather yelled at her this afternoon. She seems really sad, so you reflect that feeling by saying, "You seem very sad about that." She says, "No, he can't do anything to make me sad."
5. Whenever the therapist asks Gavin (8) a question, he shrugs and frowns.
6. Raylene (4) has always had an excellent relationship with her play therapist. After her play therapist tells her that she is pregnant, Raylene seems to withdraw from the relationship—no longer making eye contact or chatting informally with the therapist. Several times, the therapist has noticed Raylene staring at her abdomen with animosity.
7. Fergus (8) is a pleaser, but he has trouble following the playroom rules. Whenever the therapist sets a limit with him, he gets compliant and quiet for the next 5 or 10 minutes. After that time, he gradually escalates—getting louder and more defiant, until the therapist sets another limit. When this limit setting has happened several times in a session, he asks the therapist if she still likes him.

8. Earlene (7) tells her school counselor that the other African American kids on the playground are picking on her because her skin is very dark. Even though she has never gotten into trouble at school before, she has been sent to the principal's office six times in 3 days for cussing and spitting on the playground.

Therapeutic Metaphors

Following the guidelines outlined in this chapter, design a therapeutic metaphor for each of the following children.

1. Alan (8) has a history of getting into fights with other children on the playground and in the neighborhood. He is a very small child, and he tends to pick on children who are much bigger than he is. He usually gets beaten up, but he prides himself on not letting other people intimidate him. He has told you several times that the only way to get any respect is to "show them they can't push me around."

2. Sita (5) has been in three foster families in the past 4 years. None of the moves has been the result of her behavior, as she is a sweet and compliant child. However, she has incorporated these experiences into her self-image as proof that no one will ever like her. She frequently does puppet shows for you about a little rabbit no one loves who has to move around the forest because her neighbors are always telling her that they do not want her to continue to live by them.

3. Joselyn (9) hates his name. He gets teased a lot by the other children in school about "having a girl's name." He is getting increasingly sullen and angry both at home and at school. He told you last session that he thinks his parents gave him this name because they did not want him—that he is their youngest child and his sister recently told him that he was an "accident."

4. Annie (3) is about to have a baby brother or sister. She has been acting out in various ways to destroy the baby dolls in the playroom—smothering, drowning, burying in the sand, and so forth.

5. Grady (7) is encopretic at school. He was potty-trained at age 3, but when he began kindergarten, he started soiling his pants on a regular basis. His kindergarten teacher was extremely harsh and would not let children use the restroom except at recess and lunch, but his first and

second grade teachers have been very nurturing and supportive, encouraging him to go to the bathroom whenever he has a need. Grady refuses to use the bathroom at school and may have a bowel movement in his pants two or three times a day.

6. Subira's (8) mother died 2 years ago of cancer. Subira adjusted reasonably well to this loss but has recently been having nightmares and clinging to her father and crying for "no apparent reason." Her father started seriously dating a woman 4 months ago and is talking about marriage. Although Subira initially seemed to like the woman, in the past month she has refused to have anything to do with her. In a session, she cries as she mentions that her father told her that if they were living in Nigeria, his country of origin, then he could have more than one wife.

Mutual Storytelling

Use the two lists of questions to formulate an understanding of the client and his or her issues and to design a retelling of the original story. If you wish, you can develop several different retellings for each story.

1. Bethesda (7) has had a series of losses in her life over the past year—her dog died, her best friend moved away, two other friends dumped her, and her grandmother moved into a retirement community. Although she is basically an optimistic child, Bethesda has developed a rather pessimistic attitude lately. This has affected her relationships with her classmates, her teacher, her younger brother, and her parents. She paints a picture and tells the following story:

This is an apple tree. It is sick. First, its apples all fall off, except for one. Then its leaves all fall off, except for one. It starts to get very droopy, and the gardener thinks it is going to die. The day even gets cloudy, and you can't see the sun anymore. There's no rainbow either.

2. Garrin (9) was sexually and physically abused by his aunt when he was 6. He tried to tell his parents about the situation, but they initially did not believe him. He is angry with his mother and father for not believing him and for not stopping his aunt. Garrin has nightmares and frequent crying outbursts. He also has a short temper and often hurts his two younger brothers. Recently, his parents caught him fondling one

of his brothers. He tells you that he cannot think of a story but will tell you the plot of a movie he saw instead. His story:

There was this guy, and he saw some guys robbing someone's house. He tried to tell the police, but no one listened to him. Then the police decided that it was really him that robbed the house. It turned out that someone got killed in the robbery, and the police blamed him. They started chasing him to try to catch him, but he got away. I don't think the police ever believed him though that he didn't do anything wrong.

3. Sabrina (5) is a selective mute. She talks to her parents and her younger sister but not to anyone else. She does not talk at school at all. Her kindergarten teacher has tried various interventions, but none of them have worked. She has never talked to you in the seven sessions you have worked with her. You ask her to tell her mother a story using the puppets while you leave the room and audiotape it. She consents to do this. Here is her story:

Robbie, the rabbit, liked to hop around in his yard, but he didn't like to go outside the yard. He said, "I am afraid that someone outside the yard will hurt me if I go out there." So, he just stopped going out of the yard. His mother tried to get him to go out of the yard. She said, "Don't be afraid. No one will hurt you." But he just would not do it. He told his mother, "You can't make me go out there."

4. Nine-year-old Harvey's mother has bipolar disorder. She frequently stops taking her medication and leaves him with his grandmother while she disappears for days at a time. She has been hospitalized twice in the past 3 years. Harvey's grandmother is trying to get legal custody of him, but she is afraid that his mother will take him and disappear with him. Harvey is struggling in school and seems to have rather erratic mood swings. Harvey's grandmother is afraid that he may be "working on being nuts like his mom." Harvey uses the miniatures to tell the following story. He does it all through dialogue, rather than having any kind of narrative.

One of the female figures says, "Hi. My name is Nelly. I am a crazy nut."
One of the other female figures replies, "My name is Jane. Nelly, you just have to shape up. I can't believe all the things you do. You just have to stop."

One of the smaller male figures says, "I don't have a name, and I hate you both. Why don't you just leave me alone?"

Nelly says, "Okay. I will leave you alone, but I am never coming back. You just don't know what I will do."

Jane says, "We don't care. Just get out of our lives."

The male figure says, "I do care. No, I don't care. I just don't know. I hate you both. I wish you were dead, and I wish I was too."

5. Jan (7) has asthma. Her parents tend to let her have her way rather than provoking an asthma attack. She is extremely bright but is not performing up to her potential in school. She makes an elaborate tableau with animal figures and puppets and tells the following story:

This is the Princess. She had once been asleep for a long time, and she was so beautiful that all the other people and animals in the kingdom came to look at her. Now that she is awake, she is in charge of the kingdom, and everybody has to do what she wants. Sometimes they don't like it, but that doesn't matter. When they don't do what she says, like this horse, she puts them into a cage and doesn't give them any water or food. Pretty soon, they promise to do what she wants.

6. Marvin's (6) little brother died of sudden infant death syndrome last year. Since then, his parents have been extremely protective of him, to the point that they do not let him out of their sight. He has begun to develop nightmares and seems unusually anxious for a child his age. He uses three animals to tell the following story:

This is the father sheep, this is the mother sheep, and this is the baby sheep. The baby sheep says to the mother and father sheep, "I am going out of the fence to see what else is on the farm." The father sheep says, "No, you cannot do that because you might get hurt." The mother sheep says, "We have to make sure you are safe." The baby sheep says, "But I am tired of being in the fence. I want to go and look around the farm." The mother and the father sheep still say, "No. You have to stay here with us so we will know you are safe."

Role-Playing

For the following scenarios, make up two different ways you could use role-playing with the child. Label the technique you used.

1. In his first session, Jesus (8) looks around the room for a little while and says, "Let's play with the army men."
2. Ginger (5) was sexually abused by her mother's boyfriend, who is now in jail. She loves to play with puppets. She asks you if you will play with her. You know that she has some issues about being able to say "no" to others and about whether her mother will continue to love her since she "caused" the boyfriend to be incarcerated.
3. Nine-year-old Guillermo's father died when he was a baby. He has always assumed the role of the "man" in the house. His mother has recently started dating again, and Guillermo treats all of his mother's dates with aggression and contempt. This behavior has caused a rift between him and his mother. In this session, they both come into the playroom.
4. Iseult (7) is the youngest of seven children. All of her older brothers and sisters have alternately spoiled and bossed her. She tends to think that she must be in charge of every situation, and she uses both her charm and her temper to get what she wants. She comes into the session and says, "I don't care what you want to do. Today, we are going to play house."
5. Martin (4) has just had a temper tantrum in the waiting room because his mother took a drum stick away from him when he hit her with it. He comes into the playroom mad at her and prepared to be mad at you. He says, "Let's do a puppet show."

Questions to Ponder

1. On the basis of the descriptions, examples, and practice exercises, what is your reaction to the skill of metacommunication?
2. Of the three methods of metacommunication (simple description, focus on the meaning, and describe behavior and speculate about the meaning), which do you think would be the most comfortable for you? Explain your reasoning.

3. Do you think you will use therapeutic metaphors in your play therapy practice? Explain your reasoning.

4. If you think you might use therapeutic metaphors, explore the types of situations in which you think you will be most likely to use this technique in your play therapy sessions.

5. What do you think will be the most problematic factor in your designing and delivering of therapeutic metaphors?

6. Do you think you will use mutual storytelling in your play therapy practice? Explain your reasoning.

7. On the basis of the examples and your own experience, might there be a certain type of child with whom you would be more likely to use mutual storytelling? Explain your reasoning.

8. What kinds of pressures will you put on yourself to be able to retell a child's story immediately after he or she tells the original story? How can you give yourself permission to retell the story either later in the same session or even in another session?

9. Do you think you will use role-playing or playing with a child in your play therapy practice? Explain your reasoning.

10. Which method of role-playing or playing with the child (whisper technique, "instant replay," teaching/practicing new behaviors, or role reversal) appeals to you the most? Explain.

11. Of the techniques described in this chapter, which would you be the most comfortable using? Which would you be the least comfortable using? Explain.

12. What will scare you the most about using these techniques in your work with children? What is your strategy for making sure these fears do not prevent you from using any techniques you feel would be appropriate in your work?

13. How will you adapt your strategies depending on the ethnicity or cultural background of the child?

Chapter 14

Professional Issues
in Play Therapy

There are many issues currently facing mental health and school counseling professionals who use play therapy as a treatment modality. These issues include (a) public awareness and understanding of the value of play therapy, (b) strategies for working with managed health care companies, (c) research into the efficacy of play therapy, (d) interventions for specific clients and/or disorders, (e) cultural awareness and sensitivity among play therapists, and (f) professional identity. In this chapter, I have attempted to explore each of these issues and to encourage you in considering how these issues could affect you and what you can do to respond to the professional challenges they present. I have also included some advice for beginning play therapists gleaned from the survey of selected experts in play therapy.

Public Awareness of Play Therapy

Schaefer (1998) contended that the practice of play therapy is "endangered by current economic and political pressures, particularly managed care" (p. 1). He suggested that, because many people do not know what play therapy is and do not understand that it can be helpful to children, health care policymakers can disallow play therapy as a service available to their customers. In an article predicting the state of play therapy in the 22nd century, I described several different avenues the future can take (Kottman, 1999a). In one possible future, play therapy had disappeared as a viable approach to working with children because the world had become so rigidly regimented that play was not allowed. It is difficult for people who are not familiar with play therapy (even those in the mental health and school counseling professions) to understand how "just playing with kids" could possibly be helping children deal with their problems. Both Schaefer and I believe that it is imperative for the survival of the profession of play therapy that members of the profession begin to conduct a campaign of public education and public advocacy.

Personal Application

You must consider how comfortable you are with the idea that you can be a powerful advocate for the field of play therapy. If you decide to respond to this challenge, you must make it a priority to disseminate information— to consumer groups, the media, politicians, and health care policymakers— about what play therapy is and how it can help children and their families. Holmberg and Benedict (1997) developed an excellent resource handout for parents and other consumers, explaining the process and possible outcomes of play therapy. You could also just adapt the description of play therapy that you developed in chapter 4 to design a brochure for the general public.

Managed Health Care

> It is our opinion that any therapist, group of therapists, or facility that rigidly refuses to adapt its thinking, its busi-

ness, and its clinical practices to the constraints of today's PPO, HMO, EAP [employee assistance program], and Managed Care "real world" will be unable to sustain independent practice due to financial reversals, and its story will eventually be told in the mental health practice obituary columns. (Browning & Browning, 1996, p. 15)

According to presentations at professional conferences devoted to play therapy (Anderson, 1997; Borkan, 1995; Krull, 1997; Krull & Welch, 1999), the survey of contemporary experts in play therapy, and conversations with play therapists in practice, managed health care is not going to disappear in the near future, and play therapists must learn strategies for managing the managed health care system

Many practitioners see the emergence of managed care as having the potential for making a positive impact on the field of play therapy (Borkan, 1995; Krull, 1997; Schaefer, 1998; Stone, 2000). They believe that the managed care system can help the profession to develop more creative interventions and to increase efforts toward establishing empirical support for the efficacy of play therapy. These play therapists suggest that the influence of managed health care companies will support the refinement of structured short-term play therapy strategies and promote prescriptive eclectic approaches to play therapy based on empirical data about treatment efficacy.

Other play therapists have a more pessimistic perception of the impact of managed health care on the professional practice of play therapy (Anderson, 1997; V. Oaklander, personal communication, October 1997). These practitioners believe that, by requiring therapeutic work with children be short term (usually six to eight sessions), managed health care companies have had a deleterious effect on the profession. The focus of their concern seems to be the need for educating those who make decisions for managed health care companies in an effort to expand their understanding of play therapy and the process of building relationships with children.

To optimize the positive impact and minimize the negative impact of managed care, play therapy practitioners and the professional organizations that represent them must work to educate the public and the decision makers in the managed health care system (especially those who conduct prospective and concurrent utilization reviews) about what play therapy is and how it can help children (Borkan, 1995; Krull, 1997; Krull & Welch, 1999; Schaefer, 1998).

Personal Application

Regardless of your stance on managed health care and the impact it has had on play therapy, when you get ready to begin practicing as a play therapist (unless you are a school counselor or are working for some other system that exempts you from this necessity), you will have to make some decisions related to managed health care. The first choice you will have to make is whether to try to manage without managed health care.

There is a movement among some mental health providers to opt out of the system and focus on working with out-of-pocket payers (Ackley, 1997; Browning & Browning, 1996). Browning and Browning suggested that this would not be an optimal move unless you wish to have a small part-time practice to supplement your other sources of income or you are a very skillful marketer and wish to work almost exclusively with upper-middle-class and upper-class clients. In contrast to this perspective, Ackley was very optimistic about establishing a practice that does not rely on third-party payment, outlining concrete steps for developing a private-pay practice.

If you decide that you are going to work within the managed health care system, you will need to learn as much as you can about "maneuvering the maze of managed care" (Corcoran & Vandiver, 1996). This will include gaining more knowledge and experience in the delivery of time-limited therapy and integrating the concepts and techniques from brief therapy into your practice of play therapy. You will also need to learn about working cooperatively with case managers, getting preferred-provider status, writing treatment plans, and measuring outcomes in therapy (Browning & Browning, 1996). Selected resources on brief therapy that can be of help in learning to work with the managed health care system are as follows:

* *A Brief Guide to Brief Therapy* (Cade & O'Hanlon, 1993),
* *A Primer of Brief Psychotherapy* (J. Cooper, 1995),
* *Brief Therapy and Managed Care: Readings for Contemporary Practice* (Hoyt, 1995),
* *The Child and Adolescent Psychotherapy Treatment Planner* (Jongsma, Peterson, & McInnis, 1996),
* *How to Partner With Managed Care* (Browning & Browning, 1996),

* *Maneuvering the Maze of Managed Care: Skills for Mental Health Practitioners* (Corcoran & Vandiver, 1996),
* *Planned Short-Term Psychotherapy: A Clinical Handbook* (2nd ed.; Bloom, 1997),
* *Short-Term Play Therapy for Disruptive Children* (Bodiford-McNeil, Hembree-Kigin, & Eyberg, 1996),
* *Successful Private Practice in the 1990s: A New Guide for the Mental Health Professional* (Beigel & Earle, 1990).

Research Support for Play Therapy Efficacy

One strategy for increasing public credibility for play therapy and making a case for third-party payment for play therapy from insurance companies and managed health care companies would be to provide more empirical evidence for the efficacy of play therapy. Over the past 50 years, many authors have been critical of the infrequent empirical research studies designed to investigate the process and outcome of play therapy. Lebo (1952) suggested that the body of play therapy research was "propaganda" that was "meager, unsound, and more frequently of a cheerful, persuasive nature" (p. 177). Pumfrey and Elliott (1970) suggested that there was little evidence for the efficacy of play therapy because "experiments so far conducted . . . have been neither large enough nor sophisticated enough in their design to provide the unequivocal generalizations sought" (p. 183). Phillips (1985), in a review of the play therapy research conducted up until that date, found that studies investigating the effectiveness of play therapy had yielded mostly insignificant results. He stated that "what play therapy needs is a systematic program of research that clearly sets out its hypotheses, designs well-controlled studies, carefully selects subjects, measures meaningful outcome, and uses appropriate and informative statistics" (Phillips, 1985, p. 757). In 1994, Hellendoorn, van der Kooij, and Sutton-Smith stated that "as a serious scientific enterprise, play therapy is still in poor shape" (p. 217). LeBlanc and Ritchie (1999) suggested that play therapy research "does not answer the basic questions that should be posed to all therapeutic interventions, namely does play therapy have a positive effect with children, how effective is play therapy, and what conditions or processes lead to effective play therapy?" (p. 21).

A survey of the articles in *The International Journal of Play Therapy* suggests that some researchers have responded to these criticisms and injunctions, but there is still little recent empirical support for the efficacy of play therapy. Schaefer (1998) contended that play therapists have not generated sufficient empirical evidence to convince others that play therapy should be the treatment of choice for many childhood disorders and problems. He urged the leadership of the Association for Play Therapy to encourage members to conduct more empirical research and to develop scientifically based practice guidelines for treatments proven effective with specific disorders and problems.

Personal Application

Most play therapists choose to focus on delivery of services to clients without engaging in research activities. If you wish to expand your professional goals to include research as well as practice, you can make an invaluable contribution to the field in a myriad of ways. To actuate this desire, you would have to acquire the knowledge and skills necessary to conduct well-designed research studies investigating the outcome and process of play therapy interventions. If you decide to become a researcher/practitioner, you can design studies to help determine which treatment strategies are effective with specific disorders and problems and to explore new and creative play therapy approaches that might prove efficacious.

Interventions for Specific Children

If research lends support for the efficacy of certain play therapy approaches or techniques, this may lead to a trend away from the application of a particular theory and toward the use of an eclectic prescriptive strategy that matches the most effective treatment or strategy to the specific client and/or disorder. This approach would encourage play therapists to weave together an assortment of interventions to formulate a comprehensive treatment program that is tailor-made for a specific child (Faust, 1993; Kaduson et al., 1997; Schaefer, 1998).

Kaduson et al. (1997) contended that "there is an unfortunate tendency for professionals with a strong theoretical bent to apply personally preferred techniques despite the fact that some children may not benefit from them" (p. xi). Their suggested solution to this difficulty is for practitioners to consider the strengths and weaknesses of specific theoretical orientations for treating various disorders and choose the intervention that has the most potential for positive results with that particular client. Faust (1993), Schaefer (1998), and Kaduson et al. (1997) urged play therapists to explore research that supports the idea that certain treatment strategies are more effective in treating specific disorders and client characteristics (e.g., Barlow, 1981; Burke & Silverman, 1987; Rappaport, 1991).

Play therapists who decide to follow through with this recommendation must work to acquire the experience, education, and training that will enable them to effectively integrate many different theoretical approaches and interventions into an internally consistent, interactive, and coordinated modality of working with clients. This method of conceptualizing clients and conducting play therapy sessions might be the best way of working, but the degree of training and experience required may pose difficulties for the average play therapist to realistically achieve.

Personal Application

Part of becoming an effective practitioner of prescriptive eclectic play therapy is avoiding "kitchen-sink" eclecticism—using whichever technique the therapist feels like using that particular moment with no understanding of the child and his or her issues (Norcross, 1987). To do this, you must work to acquire the knowledge and skills necessary to effectively apply the appropriate intervention and conceptualization of each client in the therapy process. It is also important to develop a referral network of qualified professionals trained to work with specific populations of children. As long as you can recommend several other clinicians who have the training and expertise for helping specific populations of children, you do not have to be an expert on every diagnostic category applied to children.

If you wish to pursue becoming a synthetic eclectic play therapist, it will be essential to develop a plan of action for acquiring the necessary knowledge base and experience base. Your plan should include the following elements:

1. Read about the various theoretical orientations and their philosophical underpinnings. Part of this process should involve going to the primary sources and reading the original works of the founders of each of the schools of thought on which the approaches to play therapy are based.

2. Read about the therapeutic interventions typically used by play therapists who ascribe to the various approaches.

3. Discuss the application of this wide range of theoretical constructs and treatment strategies with experienced play therapists to expand your understanding of the various concepts and interventions.

4. Integrate the numerous philosophical ideas about people, people's motivation, the change process, the role of the therapist, and a myriad of other aspects of psychological theory formation into an internally consistent model of personality development and therapeutic process.

5. Read about the various psychological and emotional issues related to common childhood disorders and discuss them with experienced play therapists so that you gain a practical understanding of the issues, how they affect children's lives, and how they are manifested in play therapy sessions.

6. Read enough about the short- and long-term needs of children with specific diagnoses and presenting problems so that you can formulate treatment plans based on these needs. It would probably also help to consult with experienced play therapists and other professionals who work with children to explore the practical implications of your reading.

7. Read enough about the specific developmental, biological, psychological, and social variables unique to individual children so that you know what to look for when you interact with specific children. Consultation with other professionals and interactions with children will also help you apply your knowledge.

8. Read the research literature related to each common childhood disorder and presenting problem to evaluate the efficacy of various intervention strategies with specific populations. Consultation with other professionals who work with children will supplement your reading with practical information about how specific play therapy interventions work.

Cultural Awareness and Sensitivity

Socioeconomic, cultural, racial, ethnic, religious, and political factors all have a tremendous impact on children and how they view and interact with the world (Canino & Spurlock, 1994). With the rapidly shifting population of the world, it is essential for play therapists to be able to work with children from a wide range of diverse backgrounds.

Glover (2001), Kao and Landreth (2001), Schaefer (1998), and Coleman et al. (1993) argued that both practicing play therapists and play therapy students must acquire knowledge about and experience in working with children from a variety of different backgrounds. They suggested that play therapists must increase their cultural sensitivity to avoid misdiagnosis and mistreatment and to increase the likelihood of building strong therapeutic alliances across cultures.

Developing effective play therapy strategies that work with a wide variety of different clients is essential (Coleman et al., 1993; Martinez & Valdez, 1992; Schaefer, 1998). Coleman et al. suggested the following guidelines for conducting play therapy with multicultural populations:

1. The play therapist must respect the historical, psychological, sociological, and political dimensions of the child's particular culture and/or ethnic group. This may mean that the play therapist would gather information about and experience with the child's culture and/or ethnic group. In the playroom, the play therapist would include materials and toys that conveyed this respect, such as dolls with ethnic features, pictures that show images of diversity, crayons with a variety of skin tones, and so forth.

2. The play therapist must investigate (through reading and interaction with knowledgeable individuals) the role of play in diverse populations to gain an understanding of the attitudes toward play of children from different ethnic groups and cultures. Children's play can be deeply influenced by cultural factors such as gender role stereotyping and attitudes toward expression of emotions. By learning more about various cultures and the role of play in those cultures, the play therapist can stock his or her playroom with toys and materials that are appropriate for children's self-expression. Enhanced understanding can also prevent the therapist from making comments or interpretations that violate children's cultural identities.

3. The play therapist must be familiar with the values, beliefs, customs, and traditions of the child's culture. It is also essential that the play therapist understands and appreciates the "idiosyncrasies and nuances peculiar to multicultural children" (Coleman et al., 1993,

p. 68). This is especially true in regard to language. The play therapist must avoid any type of bias against children who do not speak standard English.

4. The play therapist must remember that truly becoming knowledgeable about other cultures is an ongoing process that cannot be accomplished with one class or a weekend workshop. It is essential to continuously seek out more information and experience with a multicultural focus.

5. The play therapist must examine the appropriateness of the philosophy underlying his or her approach and the efficacy of various intervention strategies for specific children. The therapist must seek to find a "match" between children and their cultural backgrounds and the techniques used with them in play therapy. This would involve investigation of the psychological and multicultural literature and interaction with other mental health professionals and the children's support systems.

6. The play therapist must avoid taking either a Eurocentric or an Afrocentric perspective on play therapy interventions. One method of evaluating various interventions and deciding which one is optimal is pluralcentrism (Coleman et al., 1993). Pluralcentrism acknowledges the impact of the mainstream culture but encourages acceptance of diverse cultural and ethnic perspectives.

7. The play therapist has to be aware of his or her own culturally based biases, values, beliefs, and attitudes. It can be extremely helpful for a counselor who wishes to learn to appreciate a diversity of cultures to first learn to appreciate his or her own culture—this helps to eliminate cultural encapsulation and widen the counselor's own worldview.

8. The play therapist must make an effort to actively interact with multicultural populations. This can include attending religious ceremonies, visiting ethnic community centers, watching movies and theater productions with a focus on specific cultures, visiting children's homes and schools, and so forth.

It is essential for play therapists who are working with children from diverse cultural and ethnic groups to explore the following issues for each potential play therapy client and his or her family (R. Clemente, personal communication, November 15, 2000; Fascoli, 1999; A. Stewart, personal communication, September 29, 2000):

1. Country of origin and cultural identity;
2. Generation of family to emigrate;
3. Languages spoken and where those languages are spoken;
4. Parents' knowledge of English—understanding of written word, receptive vocabulary, and expressive vocabulary;
5. Eating and sleeping patterns and arrangements at home;
6. Expectations of children in the culture;
7. Level of acculturation;
8. Important holidays, celebrations, and cultural responsibilities;
9. Attitude of the family toward play;
10. Playmates of the child at home and in the neighborhood;
11. Usual play materials and activities;
12. Family members' attitude toward discipline;
13. Parents' patterns of discipline;
14. Responsibilities and expectations of child at home.

Coleman et al. (1993) and Schaefer (1998) also suggested that it is imperative to increase play therapy research with children from various cultures, races, socioeconomic statuses, religions, ethnicities, and geographical locations. It would be extremely useful to investigate the types of toys that are more likely to be helpful to multicultural children and specific strategies that work with particular populations.

Personal Application

You will need to consider how much of a priority becoming culturally sensitive is in your personal and professional life. If the acquisition of the knowledge and skills necessary to effectively interact with people from backgrounds that are different than yours is important to you, you will read books about working with a culturally diverse population, take courses on counseling a wide range of clients, and seek out experiences in which you interact and build relationships with people from diverse cultures and backgrounds.

With each child from a minority culture, you will want to think about the following issues as you decide whether play therapy is the best approach with that child (Glover, 2001; Kao & Landreth, 2001; A. Stewart, personal communication, September 29, 2000): (a) family and cultural attitudes toward receiving mental health care, (b) verbal expressiveness, (c) willingness to talk directly about problems, (d) availability of culture-specific intervention strategies, (f) family and cultural explanations of causes of "abnormal" behavior, (g) family and cultural attitudes toward individual versus group approach to problem solving, (h) willingness of the family to wait for symptom alleviation, and (i) family and cultural attitudes toward and expectations of "expert" professionals. You may want to tailor your approach to the child and his or her family on the basis of your understanding of the dynamics involved in these issues.

To convey a positive and proactive attitude toward working with a wide range of populations of children and their families, you should make sure to have a selection of the following items in your office (Bowers, 1996; A. Stewart, personal communication, September 29, 2000):

1. Posters, notices, and other information and welcome notices in relevant community languages;
2. Multilingual information leaflets for parents;
3. Photographs and other art reflecting different ethnic and cultural groups and various family structures and arrangements.

Your playroom should contain the following materials:

1. Puppets and boy and girl dolls that have skin tones, features, clothing, and equipment that represent a variety of cultures, ethnic groups, and disabilities;
2. Crayons, paints, markers, chalk, and paper in a range of colors, including different shades of brown, tan, and black;
3. Utensils and food from different cultures.

Professional Identity

For the field to flourish, it will be necessary to expand the professional identity of play therapists. Two methods of promoting the professional identity of play therapists are to establish a code of ethics for professionals who work therapeutically with children and to encourage some type of professional credentialing process for play therapists.

Establishing a Code of Ethics for Play Therapists

Because play therapists come from a wide range of professional disciplines (mental health counselors, school counselors, social workers, psychologists, psychiatrists, and nurses), they do not have a standard code of ethics that covers their professional behavior. Professional associations for play therapists have advocated that practitioners adhere to the code of ethics that pertains to their specific discipline (e.g., counselors follow the guidelines set up by the American Counseling Association and psychologists follow the guidelines set up by the American Psychological Association). Although this practice does provide some ethical standards for clinicians to follow, these ethical codes are not specifically designed to guide professionals who work with children. Jackson (1998) and Sweeney (2001) suggested that this is a potential pitfall because the legal status of children as minors prevents them from being able to provide legally binding informed consent for treatment and prevents them from legally holding the right to confidentiality. The child's parent or legal guardian has both of these rights (DeKraai, Sales, & Hall, 1998). Because the parent or guardian is the legally identified client at the same time the child is the direct recipient of most play therapy services, this may lead to ethical conflicts of interest between the parent, the child, and the play therapist (Jackson, 1998; Sweeney, 2001).

To avoid the difficulties presented by the practice of play therapy, Jackson (1998) suggested that the members of play therapy professional organizations must develop a unique code of ethics that can provide guidelines for their practice. She outlined specific ethical considerations for inclusion in a play therapy ethical code.

1. The nature of treatment must be clearly defined, with the play therapist

    a. Considering the parent or adult guardian as the client and informing him or her of possible conflicts of interest with the child or other interested parties.

    b. Determining if play therapy is the most efficacious intervention strategy by considering the presenting problem, published outcome studies, generally accepted professional practice, and the client's resources.

c. Explaining other possible treatment strategies to the client, including factors such as treatment duration, cost, comfort, and demonstrated effectiveness.

d. Describing his or her theoretical orientation and goals for treatment based on theoretical orientation to the client.

e. Considering both the child's needs and the adult client's needs in determining the goals for treatment.

f. Discussing the treatment plan and goals for therapy with both the child and the adult client in developmentally appropriate language. The client must agree with the therapist about the treatment goals.

g. Ensuring that the client is voluntarily participating in the play therapy process.

h. Ensuring that the client understands what play therapy is and is not, including risks and benefits, as compared with other treatment approaches.

2. With regard to confidentiality, the play therapist must

a. Discuss who has access to the client's treatment records.

b. Ensure that the only people who have access to therapy records are authorized to do so by the client.

c. Recognize that the child does not have a legal right to confidentiality—that only the adult client has this legal right.

3. To establish the adequacy of play therapy as a treatment modality, the play therapist should

a. Establish quantitative methods for measuring the problem and progress in treating the problem.

b. Share these measures with the client to document change in the child.

4. The play therapist should explain to the client what steps he or she will take if the play therapy treatment does not prove effective with the child.

5. The play therapist should refer the client to another therapist if the play therapy treatment is unsuccessful.

6. The play therapist should make a concerted effort to obtain the required hours of instruction and supervision necessary to become qualified to use a particular treatment modality and should report any deficits in his or her training to the client.

Other sources for information about the legal and ethical issues related to counseling children are provided by Daniels and Jenkins (2000), Salo and Shumate (1993), Sweeney (2001), and Thompson and Rudolph (2000).

Professional Play Therapist Credentialing

One of Jackson's (1998) recommendations is the establishment of standards for education and supervision of play therapists. By creating standards for the credentialing of play therapists, professional organizations can promote the acceptance of play therapy as a legitimate professional specialty in the fields of mental health and school counseling. There are two different sources for registration or certification as a professional play therapist: the Association for Play Therapy and the Canadian Association for Child and Play Therapy/International Board of Examination of Certified Play Therapists. Each of these organizations has a set of standards consisting of educational requirements and clinical experience that are required before an individual can attain this professional milestone (Association for Play Therapy, n.d.; Barnes, 1996). They have also established standards for continuing education. For information about each of these sets of standards, see Appendix C.

Personal Application

If you believe that play therapists should have a professional code of ethics that is separate and distinct from those of other clinical practitioners, you will need to provide input about this issue to the professional organizations that represent play therapists. By lobbying for such a code of ethics and by volunteering to submit your input about the contents of a code of ethics, you can make a contribution to the promotion of the professional identity of play therapy. You must also decide if you wish to pursue a play therapy credential. This decision will depend on the value you place on professional credentialing. Professional credentialing increases the credibility of the profession, so it is a professionally responsible action to take. Becoming registered or certified in play therapy can also give you recognition as an expert in working with children in your community, which can lead to more referrals from the public and from other professionals. Having the continuing education requirements of a professional credential not only encourages practitioners to stay current in their field, which otherwise might not be a priority, but can also help legitimize play therapy as a professionally viable area of specialization.

Advice to Beginning Play Therapists

As part of the survey that I sent to the contemporary experts in play therapy, I asked them, "What advice would you give to beginning play therapists?" Arranged in alphabetical order according to the therapists' last names, here is their advice to you.

"Learn it and learn it well. Be sure not to mix up treatment and diagnostic goals. Diagnostic protocols that have been validated should be chosen. Stick with methods that have empirical support and don't be pulled into methods that somebody made up one day that sound 'like they ought to work.' A theoretical base for the methods really is in order also. Without a good theoretical and empirical base, a therapist flips around techniques without a genuine rationale or understanding of effects." Louise Guerney—child-centered and filial therapy

---

"* Learn to listen (with your ears and eyes).
* Understand normal child development in order to understand when it has gone awry.
* Spend time with 'normal'/nonreferred children.
* Be flexible.
* Be able to 'get down' and play with kids at their level (physically, cognitively, etc.).
* Observe as much play therapy as you can (videotapes, one-way mirrors).
* Learn from your mistakes." Susan Knell—cognitive–behavioral

---

"Get as much supervision as possible." Garry Landreth—child-centered

---

"Whatever theory you learn and to which you are aligned, do it well, and substantiate your technique in good theory. Do not be lazy. Think about what is unfolding before you." John Paul Lilly—Jungian

---

"I'm a big proponent of people experiencing the power of the projective techniques I use; to remember what it is like to be a child; to work through some of their own childhood issues. Beginning therapists need to relax and trust themselves. And they need to continue to go to workshops, training, read, etc." Violet Oaklander—Gestalt

---

"Trust the process." Lessie Perry—child-centered

"Get good supervision with a knowledgeable play therapist." Chris Ruma-Cullen—cognitive–behavioral

---

"Become skilled in a variety of approaches and techniques, particularly short-term interventions." Charles Schaefer—eclectic prescriptive

---

"* Get lots of training and supervision.
 * Gradually learn the whole spectrum of nondirective and directive play therapies.
 * Know the foundations/principles of play therapy so you can make informed decisions regarding methods and not just be using a 'cookbook' approach." Rise Van Fleet—filial therapy, family systems, psychoeducational, child-centered, and cognitive–behavioral

---

"The best ways to learn are to watch someone who is competent and to practice yourself and get constant supervision. Other ideas are to:

1. Observe seasoned play therapists in the playroom.
2. Practice encouragement, tracking, and logical consequences on a daily basis—not just in the playroom.
3. Develop a theory base that you believe in and live by.
4. Attend Association for Play Therapy workshops and conferences in addition to taking classes.
5. Spend time with children.
6. Develop a strong foundation in child development." JoAnna White—Adlerian

Practice Exercises

1. Plan a short (3–6-minute) explanation of what play therapy is and how it can help children. You could actually practice giving this explanation to fellow students or colleagues.

2. Choose a child of your professional acquaintance and make a brief treatment plan for him or her that you could share with a managed care provider. Be sure to list both long- and short-term goals, using concrete, measurable behavior changes as your objective. Describe play therapy intervention strategies in clear and concrete language.

3. Design a research project you could do to measure play therapy process or outcome. Include a statement of the problem, the population of participants, any intervention strategies you would use, possible measurement instruments, potential research designs, your hypotheses about what you will find, and any limitations of the study you can imagine.

4. Design a plan for becoming more culturally aware and sensitive, including a rationale for why growth in this area is important to you.

5. Design a plan for enhancing your professional identity as a play therapist, including a rationale for why growth in this area is important to you.

6. For each of the following ethical dilemmas in play therapy, explain what the ethical issues are, how you would deal with the situation, and your reasoning. Use the ethical suggestions in this chapter and the ethical code of your professional organization.

   a. You have been working with a mother for 3 years on some very intense issues from her childhood. She wants you to continue to work with her but also to see her daughter.

   b. You are a school counselor, and a fourth grader wants to start seeing you for play therapy. She adamantly tells you that she will never speak to you again if you tell her parents that she is coming for play therapy.

   c. You are working with a schizophrenic child whose parents do not want him to continue on his medication. They want you to treat the problem with play therapy and no other medical intervention.

   d. You are a client-centered play therapist, working with a child who has been diagnosed with Asberger's syndrome. His insurance will no longer pay for your services because the company says that play therapy will not help him. His family cannot afford your services.

e. Your theoretical orientation is Gestalt, and a parent calls you, asking if you can do systematic desensitization on a child with a snake phobia.

f. You are a school counselor, working with a kindergarten child who is very active. The teacher wants you to "get him to stay in his seat and be quiet." The child is perfectly content to continue in his current path, and his parents are not dissatisfied with his behavior. How will you determine your goals for working with this child?

g. You have a 9-year-old client who is so reluctant to come to therapy that her parents have carried her into your playroom every week for a month.

h. You have a client who is dealing with some issues related to his parents' attitude toward him, and his parents want to observe his sessions.

i. You have an 8-year-old client who has specifically asked you not to tell her parents about some problems she is experiencing at school.

j. You do not have a release to talk to a client's school counselor, who calls wanting information about how your sessions are going.

k. You believe that a child is making significant progress, but her parents think that nothing is happening. They want to see your notes on the case so they can prove that "you are just wasting our time and money."

l. You have no training in play therapy but really like children and have some toys in your office. You have the reputation in your community of being a play therapist and get many professional referrals.

m. You are a Registered Play Therapist but have no training in clinical supervision. Someone in your community calls and asks you to serve as his play therapy supervisor.

Questions to Ponder

1. What do you think about the need for increasing public awareness of the value of play therapy?
2. What is your reaction to Kottman's prediction that the world is becoming so rigidly regimented that play will not be permitted in the 22nd century?
3. What is your attitude toward working with managed health care companies?
4. Do you support the contention that there needs to be more empirical research into the efficacy of play therapy? Why or why not?
5. What is your reaction to the argument that play therapy interventions should be developed for specific clients and/or specific disorders?
6. What stance do you take on the need for increased cultural awareness and sensitivity among play therapists?
7. How important do you think the development of a professional identity as a play therapist is?
8. What are your plans related to registration/certification as a play therapist?
9. If you had access to experts in play therapy, which ones would you want to question? What would you ask them?

Appendix A

Selected References on Different Theoretical Orientations to Play Therapy

Adlerian Play Therapy

Kottman, T. (1993). The king of rock and roll. In T. Kottman & C. Schaefer (Eds.), *Play therapy in action: A casebook for practitioners* (pp. 133–167). Northvale, NJ: Jason Aronson.

Kottman, T. (1994). Adlerian play therapy. In K. O'Connor & C. Schaefer (Eds.), *Handbook of play therapy* (Vol. 2, pp. 3–26). New York: Wiley.

Kottman, T. (1995). *Partners in play: An Adlerian approach to play therapy*. Alexandria, VA: American Counseling Association.

Kottman, T. (1997). Adlerian play therapy. In K. O'Connor & L. M. Braverman (Eds.), *Play therapy theory and practice: A comparative presentation* (pp. 310–340). New York: Wiley.

Kottman, T. (1998). Billy, the teddy bear boy. In L. Golden (Ed.), *Case studies in child and adolescent counseling* (2nd ed., pp. 70–82). New York: Macmillan.

Kottman, T., & Johnson, V. (1993). Adlerian play therapy: A tool for school counselors. *Elementary School Guidance and Counseling, 28*, 42–51.

Kottman, T., & Stiles, K. (1990). The mutual storytelling technique: An Adlerian application in child therapy. *Journal of Individual Psychology, 46*, 148–156.

Kottman, T., & Warlick, J. (1989). Adlerian play therapy: Practical considerations. *Journal of Individual Psychology, 45*, 433–446.

Child-Centered Play Therapy

Axline, V. (1969). *Play therapy* (Rev. ed.). New York: Ballantine Books.

Axline, V. (1971). *Dibs: In search of self.* New York: Ballantine Books.

Ginott, H. (1961). *Group therapy with children: The theory and practice of play therapy.* New York: McGraw-Hill.

Guerney, L. (1983). Client-centered play therapy. In C. Schaefer & K. O'Connor (Eds.), *Handbook of play therapy* (pp. 419–435). New York: Wiley.

Landreth, G. (1991). *Play therapy: The art of the relationship.* Muncie, IN: Accelerated Development.

Landreth, G., & Sweeney, D. (1997). Child-centered play therapy. In K. O'Connor & L. M. Braverman (Eds.), *Play therapy theory and practice: A comparative presentation* (pp. 17–45). New York: Wiley.

Perry, L. (1993). Audrey, the bois d'arc and me: A time of becoming. In T. Kottman & C. Schaefer (Eds.), *Play therapy in action: A casebook for practitioners* (pp. 133–167). Northvale, NJ: Jason Aronson.

Van Fleet, R. (1994). Filial therapy for adoptive children and parents. In K. O'Connor & C. Schaefer (Eds.), *Handbook of play therapy* (Vol. 2, pp. 371–386). New York: Wiley.

Van Fleet, R. (1997). Play and perfectionism: Putting fun back into families. In H. Kaduson & C. Schaefer (Eds.), *The playing cure* (pp. 61–82). Northvale, NJ: Jason Aronson.

Cognitive–Behavioral Play Therapy

Knell, S. (1993). *Cognitive–behavioral play therapy.* Northvale, NJ: Jason Aronson.

Knell, S. (1993) To show and not tell: Cognitive–behavioral play therapy. In T. Kottman & C. Schaefer (Eds.), *Play therapy in action: A casebook for practitioners* (pp. 169–208). Northvale, NJ: Jason Aronson.

Knell, S. (1994). Cognitive–behavioral play therapy. In K. O'Connor & C. Schaefer (Eds.), *Handbook of play therapy* (Vol. 2, pp. 111–142). New York: Wiley.

Knell, S. (1997). Cognitive–behavioral play therapy. In K. O'Connor & L. M. Braverman (Eds.), *Play therapy theory and practice: A comparative presentation* (pp. 79–99). New York: Wiley.

Knell, S., & Moore, D. (1990). Cognitive–behavioral play therapy in the treatment of encopresis. *Journal of Clinical Child Psychology, 19,* 55–60.

Knell, S., & Ruma, C. (1996). Play therapy with a sexually abused child. In M. Reinecke, F. M. Datillio, & A. Freeman (Eds.), *Cognitive therapy with children and adolescents: A casebook for clinical practice* (pp. 367–393). New York: Guilford Press.

Ecosystemic Play Therapy

O'Connor, K. (2000). *The play therapy primer: An integration of theories and techniques* (2nd ed.). New York: Wiley.

O'Connor, K. (1993). Child, protector, confidant: Structured group ecosystemic play therapy. In T. Kottman & C. Schaefer (Eds.), *Play therapy in action: A casebook for practitioners* (pp. 245–282). Northvale, NJ: Jason Aronson.

O'Connor, K. (1994). Ecosystemic play therapy. In K. O'Connor & C. Schaefer (Eds.), *Handbook of play therapy* (Vol. 2, pp. 61–84). New York: Wiley.

O'Connor, K. (1997). Ecosystemic play therapy. In K. O'Connor & L. M. Braverman (Eds.), *Play therapy theory and practice: A comparative presentation* (pp. 234–284). New York: Wiley.

O'Connor, K., & Ammen, S. (1997). *Play therapy treatment planning and interventions: The ecosystemic model and workbook.* Boston: Academic Press.

Gestalt Play Therapy

Carroll, F., & Oaklander, V. (1994). Gestalt play therapy. In K. O'Connor & L. M. Braverman (Eds.), *Play therapy theory and practice: A comparative presentation* (pp. 184–203). New York: Wiley.

Oaklander, V. (1992). *Windows to our children: A Gestalt approach to children and adolescents.* New York: Gestalt Journal Press. (Original work published 1978)

Oaklander, V. (1993). From meek to bold: A case study of Gestalt play therapy. In T. Kottman & C. Schaefer (Eds.), *Play therapy in action: A casebook for practitioners* (pp. 281–299). Northvale, NJ: Jason Aronson.

Oaklander, V. (1994). Gestalt play therapy. In K. O'Connor & C. Schaefer (Eds.), *Handbook of play therapy* (Vol. 2, pp. 143–156). New York: Wiley.

Jungian Play Therapy

Allan, J. (1988). *Inscapes of the child's world.* Dallas, TX: Spring.

Allan, J. (1994). Jungian play psychotherapy. In K. O'Connor & L. M. Braverman (Eds.), *Play therapy theory and practice: A comparative presentation* (pp. 100–130). New York: Wiley.

Allan, J., & Bertoia, J. (1992). *Written paths to healing: Education and Jungian child counseling.* Dallas, TX: Spring.

Allan, J., & Brown, K. (1993). Jungian play therapy in the elementary schools. *Elementary School Guidance and Counseling, 28,* 30–41.

Allan, J., & Levin, S. (1993). "Born on my bum": Jungian play therapy. In T. Kottman & C. Schaefer (Eds.), *Play therapy in action: A casebook for practitioners* (pp. 209–244). Northvale, NJ: Jason Aronson.

Psychodynamic Play Therapy

Cangelosi, D. (1993). Internal and external wars: Psychodynamic play therapy. In T. Kottman & C. Schaefer (Eds.), *Play therapy in action: A casebook for practitioners* (pp. 347–370). Northvale, NJ: Jason Aronson.

Esman, A. (1983). Psychoanalytic play therapy. In C. Schaefer & K. O'Connor (Eds.), *Handbook of play therapy* (pp. 11–20). New York: Wiley.

Freud, A. (1965). *Normality and pathology in childhood: Assessments of development.* New York: International University Press.

Freud, A. (1968). Indications and counterindications for child analysis. *Psychoanalytic Study of the Child, 23,* 37–46.

Gordetsky, S., & Zilbach, J. (1993). The worried boy. In L. Golden & M. Norwood (Eds.), *Case studies in child counseling* (pp. 51–62). New York: Macmillan.

Klein, M. (1932). *The psycho-analysis of children.* London: Hogarth Press.

Lee, A. (1997). Psychoanalytic play therapy. In K. O'Connor & L. M. Braverman (Eds.), *Play therapy theory and practice: A comparative presentation* (pp. 46–78). New York: Wiley.

Provus-McElroy, L. (1993). Healing a family's wounds. In L. Golden & M. Norwood (Eds.), *Case studies in child counseling* (pp. 121–132). New York: Macmillan.

Thematic Play Therapy

Benedict, H., & Mongovern, L. (1997). Thematic play therapy: An approach to treatment of attachment disorders in young children. In H. Kaduson & C. Schaefer (Eds.), *The playing cure* (pp. 227–316). Northvale, NJ: Jason Aronson.

Benedict, H., & Narcavage, C. (1997). *Healing children through play therapy: Therapeutic responses available to the clinician.* Unpublished manuscript, Baylor University, Waco, TX.

Theraplay

Jernberg, A. (1979). *Theraplay: A new treatment using structured play for problem children and their families.* San Francisco: Jossey-Bass.

Jernberg, A. (1991). Assessing parent–child interactions with the Marschak Interaction Method. In C. Schaefer, C. Gitlin, & K. Sundgrun (Eds.), *Play diagnosis and assessment* (pp. 493–515). New York: Wiley.

Jernberg, A. (1993). Attachment formation. In C. Schaefer (Ed.), *The therapeutic powers of play* (pp. 241–265). Northvale, NJ: Jason Aronson.

Jernberg, A., & Jernberg, E. (1993). Family Theraplay for the family tyrant. In T. Kottman & C. Schaefer (Eds.), *Play therapy in action: A casebook for practitioners* (pp. 45–96). Northvale, NJ: Jason Aronson.

Koller, T. (1994). Adolescent Theraplay. In K. O'Connor & C. Schaefer (Eds.), *Handbook of play therapy* (Vol. 2, pp. 159–188). New York: Wiley.

Koller, T., & Booth, P. (1997). Fostering attachment through family Theraplay. In K. O'Connor & L. M. Braverman (Eds.), *Play therapy theory and practice: A comparative presentation* (pp. 204–233). New York: Wiley.

Munns, E. (Ed.). (2000). *Theraplay: Innovations in attachment-enhancing play therapy.* Northvale, NJ: Jason Aronson.

Rubin, P., & Tregay, J. (1989). *Play with them—Theraplay groups in the classroom.* Springfield, IL: Charles C Thomas.

Appendix B

An Explanation of Play Therapy: Handout for Parents

Young children frequently have difficulty talking about what is bothering them. This difficulty is not because they don't want to discuss their thoughts and feelings, but because they haven't yet developed the vocabulary or the thinking skills that they need to be able to do this.

Play therapy is an approach to counseling children that allows them to use toys and other play and art materials to express their thoughts and feelings. In a play session, children can use their play to *show* the counselor what they are thinking and feeling. The counselor can use the play to communicate with children about what is happening in their lives and to help them explore alternative behaviors and attitudes.

Before the first session, parents and/or teachers will need to explain the details of how often children will be coming to play therapy, where it is, and basically what happens. Children seem to feel more comfortable if adults let them know that they do not have to talk to the counselor if they do not want to do so and that the main thing they will be doing is playing. I also think that it is important for adults to give children a simple explanation of their perception of the presenting problem and to suggest that children generally feel better about themselves and other people after going to play therapy for a while. This explanation helps get rid of children's fears about coming to counseling.

Because children frequently play in the sand or paint, they should wear comfortable play clothes, rather than "good" clothes, to play therapy. It is a fun process, and sometimes it is messy.

After a session, although it is appropriate for parents and teachers to let children know that they are interested in the children's experience in the play session, they should not question children about the experiences. If children draw or paint pictures or produce other artwork, parents and/or teachers should avoid questioning them about the art or praising or criticizing them.

To help build trust in the relationship with children, the counselor keeps what they say and do in the play therapy sessions private. Instead of talking about specifics, the counselor consults with parents and/or teachers about different ways to understand children and strategies to help them get along better with others and feel better about themselves.

A book that can help parents, teachers, and children learn more about play therapy and what happens in play sessions is *A Child's First Book About Play Therapy* by Marc A. Nemiroff and Jane Annunziata. It is published by the American Psychological Association, APA Order Department, P.O. Box 2710, Hyattsville, MD 20784.

Appendix C

Information About
Play Therapy
Certification/Registration

Professional Play Therapy
Associations and Certifying Boards

The Association for Play Therapy (APT)
2050 N. Winery, Suite 101
Fresno, CA 93703

Telephone number: (559) 252-2278
Fax number: (559) 252-2297
E-mail address: info@iapt.org
Web site: www.iapt.org

A s of 1998, the APT had two different levels of registration: Registered Play Therapist (RPT) and Registered Play Therapist–Supervisor (RPT-S); (APT, n.d.). The academic training required to become an RPT includes a master's degree from a regionally accredited institution of higher education in an "appropriate Medical or Mental Health profession" (APT, n.d., p. 1). The applicant must have graduate study in the following content areas: (a) child development; (b) theories of personality; (c) principles of psychotherapy; (d) child and adolescent psychopathology; and (e) legal, ethical, and professional issues. The applicant must also have received at least 150 clock hours of instruction in play therapy, with the following content areas covered: (a) history of play therapy, (b) theory related to play therapy, (c) techniques and method of play therapy, and (d) applications of play therapy to special settings or populations.

There are two distinct facets of clinical experience required for registration as a play therapist by APT. The applicant must have 2 years of supervised experience, including 2,000 clock hours of direct clinical experience in the area in which the applicant received his or her master's degree. At least 1 year of this experience (1,000 clock hours) must be completed after the applicant received his or her master's degree. The ratio of supervision to direct service time is supposed to be at least 1:10.

Either as part of the 2,000 hours of clinical experience or separate from them, the applicant for registration as a play therapist must have provided a minimum of 500 direct contact hours of play therapy under supervision. Again, the ratio of supervision to direct service time is required to be at least 1:10—so the applicant must have at least 50 hours of play therapy supervision during this time. The educational requirements to become an RPT-S are the same as those for becoming an RPT, as are the number of hours (500) of direct contact hours of play therapy under supervision. In addition to these requirements, applicants for the RPT-S must be licensed or certified by a national or regional board in a medical or mental health profession and have a minimum of 5 years (5,000 hours) of related clinical practice in the field of the applicant's current license after the receipt of the master's degree in that field. The applicant must also have provided at least 500 direct hours of play therapy in addition to the 500 hours provided under supervision.

After becoming registered, both play therapists and play therapist–supervisors must stay current in the field. To remain current in the field, APT requires them to complete 36 hours of APT-approved continuing education every 3 years.

****

The Canadian Association for Child and Play Therapy (CACPT)
2 Bloor St. West, Suite 100
Toronto, Ontario
Canada M4W 3E2
Telephone number (only valid in Canada): 1-800-361-3951

****

The International Board of Examiners
   of Certified Play Therapists (IBECPT)
11E 900 Greenbank Rd., Suite 527
Nepean (Ottawa), Ontario
Canada K2J 4P6
Telephone number: (613) 634-3125

The IBECPT specified course work and clinical experience required to become a certified play therapist (Barnes, 1996). The educational requirements are a master's or medical degree in an appropriate profession, including psychology, pediatrics, psychiatry, education, recreation therapy, child life, creative arts, occupational therapy, speech/language therapy, and social work. The applicant must have taken university courses in the following areas: (a) one full university year course (two semesters or three trimesters) in child and human development, (b) one full university year course in childhood and adolescent behavioral disorders and psychopathology, (c) one semester course in theories of personality, (d) two full university year courses in marriage and family issues, (e) one full university year course in principles of the therapeutic process, (f) a course in ethics and legal issues, (g) two full university year courses in research and evaluation methods, and (h) two full university year courses in child psychotherapy and play therapy.

The clinical experience required by the IBECPT involves a minimum of 2,500 hours of direct clinical experience in child psychology and play therapy. Five hundred of these hours can be focused on work other than child play therapy. A minimum of 200 hours of direct supervision (100 of which must be in individual supervision) with a supervisor preapproved by the IBECPT are also required.

As part of the certification process, applicants must participate in a certification interview and submit a minimum of three unedited videotapes of their work with children. They may also be required to take a written examination in specified areas of knowledge in which the board has determined that their background is lacking.

After certification, Child Psychotherapists and Play Therapists must complete 48 hours of continuing education approved by the IBECPT. Thirty of these hours must be in play therapy, and the other 18 hours can be in related therapeutic interests.

REFERENCES

Ackley, D. (1997). *Breaking free of managed care: A step-by-step guide to regaining control of your practice.* New York: Guilford Press.

Alger, I., Linn, S., & Beardslee, W. (1985). Puppetry as a therapeutic tool for hospitalized children. *Hospital and Community Psychiatry, 36,* 129–130.

Allan, J. (1988). *Inscapes of the child's world.* Dallas, TX: Spring.

Allan, J. (1994). Jungian play psychotherapy. In K. O'Connor & L. M. Braverman (Eds.), *Play therapy theory and practice: A comparative presentation* (pp. 100–130). New York: Wiley.

311

Allan, J., & Lawton-Speert, S. (1993). Play psychotherapy of a profoundly incest abused boy: A Jungian approach. *International Journal of Play Therapy, 2*(1), 33–48.

Allen, F. (1942). *Psychotherapy with children.* New York: Norton.

Anderson, J. (1997, October). *Play therapy in the real world: A survival kit.* Paper presented at the Third Annual Conference of the Iowa Association of Play Therapy, Iowa City, IA.

Anderson, J., & Richards, N. (1995, October). *Play therapy in the real world: Coping with managed care, challenging children, skeptical colleagues, time and space constraints.* Paper presented at the First Annual Conference of the Iowa Association of Play Therapy, Iowa City, IA.

Association for Play Therapy. (n.d.). *Registered play therapist/registered play therapist–supervisor: Minimum application criteria.* Fresno, CA: Author.

Association for Play Therapy. (1997). Play therapy definition. *Association for Play Therapy Newsletter, 16*(2), 4.

Auerbach-Walker, L., & Bolkavatz, M. (1988). Play therapy with children who have experienced sexual assault. In L. Auerbach-Walker (Ed.), *Handbook on sexual abuse of children: Assessment and treatment issues* (pp. 249–269). New York: Springer.

Axline, V. (1947). *Play therapy: The inner dynamics of childhood.* Boston: Houghton Mifflin.

Axline, V. (1969). *Play therapy* (Rev. ed.). New York: Ballantine Books.

Axline, V. (1971). *Dibs: In search of self.* New York: Ballantine Books.

Bandura, A. (1977). *Social learning theory.* Englewood Cliffs, NJ: Prentice Hall.

Barlow, D. (Ed.). (1981). *Behavioral assessment of adult disorders.* New York: Guilford Press.

Barlow, K., Strother, J., & Landreth, G. (1985). Child-centered play therapy: Nancy from baldness to curls. *School Counselor, 32,* 347–356.

Barlow, K., Strother, J., & Landreth, G. (1986). Sibling group play therapy: An effective alternative with an elective mute child. *School Counselor, 34,* 44–50.

Barnes, M. (1996). *The healing path with children: An exploration for parents and professionals.* Kingston, Ontario, Canada: Viktoria, Fermoyle & Berrigan.

Beck, A. (1976). *Cognitive therapy and the emotional disorders.* New York: International Universities Press.

Beigel, J., & Earle, R. (1990). *Successful private practice in the 1990s: A new guide for the mental health professional.* New York: Brunner/Mazel.

Benedict, H., & Mongoven, L. (1997). Thematic play therapy: An approach to treatment of attachment disorders in young children. In H. Kaduson, D. Cangelosi, & C. Schaefer (Eds.), *The playing cure: Individual play therapy for specific childhood problems* (pp. 277–315). Northvale, NJ: Jason Aronson.

Benedict, H., & Narcavage, C. (1997). *Healing children through play therapy: Therapeutic responses available to the clinician.* Unpublished manuscript, Baylor University, Waco, TX.

Berg, B. (1989). Cognitive play therapy for children of divorce. In P. Keller & S. Heyman (Eds.), *Innovations in clinical practice: A source book* (Vol. 4, pp. 143–173). Sarasota, FL: Professional Resource Exchange.

Bertoia, J., & Allan, J. (1988). Counseling seriously ill children: Use of spontaneous drawings. *Elementary School Guidance and Counseling, 22,* 206–221.

Bettner, B. L., & Lew, A. (1996). *Raising kids who can: Using family meetings to nurture responsible, capable, caring, and happy children* (Rev. ed.). Newton Center, MA: Connexions.

Bevin, T. (1999). Multiple traumas of refugees—near drowning and witnessing of maternal rape: Case of Sergio, age 9, and follow-up at age 16. In N. B. Webb (Ed.), *Play therapy with children in crisis* (2nd ed., pp. 164–182). New York: Guilford Press.

Bixler, R. (1949). Limits are therapy. *Journal of Consulting Psychology, 13,* 1–11.

Bleck, R., & Bleck, B. (1982). The disruptive child's play group. *Elementary School Guidance and Counseling, 17,* 137–141.

Bloom, B. (1997). *Planned short-term psychotherapy: A clinical handbook* (2nd ed.). Boston: Allyn & Bacon.

Bluestone, J. (1999). School-based peer therapy to facilitate mourning in latency-age children following sudden parental death: Cases of Joan, age 10½, and Roberta, age 9½, with follow-up 8 years later. In N. B. Webb (Ed.), *Play therapy with children in crisis* (2nd ed., pp. 225–251). New York: Guilford Press.

Bodiford-McNeil, C., Hembree-Kigin, T., & Eyberg, S. (1996). *Short-term play therapy for disruptive children.* King of Prussia, PA: Center for Applied Psychology.

Boley, S., Ammen, S., O'Connor, K., & Miller, L. (1996). The use of the Color-Your-Life Technique with pediatric cancer patients and their siblings. *International Journal of Play Therapy, 5*(2), 57–78.

Boley, S., Peterson, C., Miller, L., & Ammen, S. (1996). An investigation of the Color-Your-Life Technique with childhood cancer patients. *International Journal of Play Therapy, 5*(2), 41–56.

Booth, P., & Lindaman, S. (2000). Theraplay for enhancing attachment in adopted children. In H. Kaduson & C. Schaefer (Eds.), *Short-term play therapy for children* (pp. 194–227). New York: Guilford Press.

Borkan, T. (1995, October). *Play therapy adapts to the new world of managed care: Playful managed care.* Paper presented at the 12th Annual International Conference of the Association for Play Therapy, San Francisco, CA.

Bowers, E. (1996). *Directory of culturally diverse art and play therapy materials for children and adolescents.* Orangevale, CA: Author.

Bradway, K. (1979). Sandplay in psychotherapy. *Art Psychotherapy, 6*(2), 85–93.

Bratton, S., & Ray, D. (2000). What the research shows about play therapy. *International Journal of Play Therapy, 9*(1), 47–88.

Brett, D. (1988). *Annie stories: Storytelling for common issues.* New York: Workman.

Brett, D. (1992). *More Annie stories: Therapeutic storytelling techniques.* New York: Magination Press.

Briesmeister, J. (1997). Play therapy with depressed children. In H. Kaduson, D. Cangelosi, & C. Schaefer (Eds.), *The playing cure:*

Individual play therapy for specific childhood problems (pp. 3–28). Northvale, NJ: Jason Aronson.

Brody, V. (1978). Developmental play: A relationship-focused program for children. *Journal of Child Welfare, 57,* 591–599.

Brody, V. (1997). *The dialogue of touch: Developmental play therapy* (Rev. ed.). Northvale, NJ: Jason Aronson.

Brooks, R. (1981). Creative characters: A technique in child therapy. *Psychotherapy, 18,* 131–139.

Browning, C., & Browning, B. (1996). *How to partner with managed care.* New York: Wiley.

Brunskill, S. (1984). Play therapy for the hospitalized child. *American Urological Association Journal, 5*(2), 17–18.

Buber, M. (1958). *I and thou.* New York: Scribner.

Burke, A., & Silverman, W. (1987). The prescriptive treatment of school refusal. *Clinical Psychology Review, 7,* 353–362.

Cabe, N. (1997). Conduct disorder: Grounded play therapy. In H. Kaduson, D. Cangelosi, & C. Schaefer (Eds.), *The playing cure: Individual play therapy for specific childhood problems* (pp. 229–254). Northvale, NJ: Jason Aronson.

Cade, B., & O'Hanlon, W. (1993). *A brief guide to brief therapy.* New York: Norton.

Cangelosi, D. (1993). Internal and external wars: Psychodynamic play therapy. In T. Kottman & C. Schaefer (Eds.), *Play therapy in action: A casebook for practitioners* (pp. 347–370). Northvale, NJ: Jason Aronson.

Cangelosi, D. (1997). Play therapy for children from divorced and separated families. In H. Kaduson, D. Cangelosi, & C. Schaefer (Eds.), *The playing cure: Individual play therapy for specific childhood problems* (pp. 119–142). Northvale, NJ: Jason Aronson.

Canino, I., & Spurlock, J. (1994). *Culturally diverse children and adolescents: Assessment, diagnosis, and treatment.* New York: Guilford Press.

Carey, L. (1990). Sandplay therapy with a troubled child. *Arts in Psychotherapy, 17,* 197–209.

Carroll, F., & Oaklander, V. (1997). Gestalt play therapy. In K. O'Connor & L. M. Braverman (Eds.), *Play therapy theory and practice: A comparative presentation* (pp. 184–203). New York: Wiley.

Carter, S. (1987). Use of puppets to treat traumatic grief: A case study. *Elementary School Guidance and Counseling, 21,* 210–215.

Cerio, J. (2000). *Play therapy: A do-it-yourself guide for practitioners.* Alfred, NY: Alfred University.

Cockle, S., & Allan, J. (1996). Nigredo and Albedo: From darkness to light in the play therapy of a sexually abused girl. *International Journal of Play Therapy, 5*(1), 31–44.

Coleman, V., Parmer, T., & Barker, S. (1993). Play therapy for a multicultural population: Guidelines for mental health professionals. *International Journal of Play Therapy, 2*(1), 63–74.

Cook, J. A. (1997). Play therapy for selective mutism. In H. Kaduson, D. Cangelosi, & C. Schaefer (Eds.), *The playing cure: Individual play therapy for specific childhood problems* (pp. 83–115). Northvale, NJ: Jason Aronson.

Cooper, J. (1995). *A primer of brief psychotherapy.* New York: Norton.

Cooper, S., & Blitz, J. (1985). A therapeutic play group for hospitalized children with cancer. *Journal of Psychosocial Oncology, 3*(2), 23–27.

Corcoran, K., & Vandiver, V. (1996). *Maneuvering the maze of managed care: Skills for mental health practitioners.* New York: Free Press.

Crowley, R., & Mills, J. (1989). *Cartoon magic: How to help children discover their rainbows within.* New York: Magination Press.

Daniels, D., & Jenkins, P. (2000). *Therapy with children: Children's rights, confidentiality and the law.* Thousand Oaks, CA: Sage.

Davis, N. (1990). *Once upon a time: Therapeutic stories to heal abused children* (Rev. ed.). Oxon Hill, MD: Psychological Associates of Oxon Hill.

Davis, N. (1997). *Therapeutic stories that teach and heal.* Oxon Hill, MD: Psychological Associates of Oxon Hill.

DeKraai, M., Sales, B., & Hall, S. (1998). Informed consent, confidentiality, and duty to report laws in the conduct of child therapy. In R. J.

Morris & T. P. Kratochwill (Eds.), *The practice of child therapy* (3rd ed., pp. 540–559). Boston: Allyn & Bacon.

Dinkmeyer, D., & McKay, G. (1989). *The parent's handbook: Systematic training for effective parenting (STEP)* (3rd ed.). Circle Pines, MN: American Guidance Service.

Doyle, J., & Stoop, D. (1999). Witness and victim of multiple abuses: Case of Randy, age 10, in a residential treatment center, and follow-up at age 19 in prison. In N. B. Webb (Ed.), *Play therapy with children in crisis* (2nd ed., pp. 131–163). New York: Guilford Press.

Dreikurs, R., & Soltz, V. (1964). *Children: The challenge.* New York: Hawthorn/Dutton.

Ellerton, M., Caty, S., & Ritchie, J. (1985). Helping young children master intrusive procedures through play. *Children's Health Care, 13,* 167–173.

Ellis, A. (1971). *Growth through reason: Verbatim cases in rational-emotive therapy and cognitive–behavioral therapy.* New York: Lyle Stuart.

Engel, S. (1995). *The stories children tell: Making sense of the narratives of childhood.* New York: Freeman.

Erickson, E. (1950). *Childhood and society.* New York: Norton.

Esman, A. (1983). Psychoanalytic play therapy. In C. Schaefer & K. O'Connor (Eds.), *Handbook of play therapy* (pp. 11–20). New York: Wiley.

Fascoli, L. (1999). Developmentally appropriate play and turtle hunting. In E. Dau (Ed.), *Child's play: Revisiting play in early childhood* (pp. 53–59). Sydney, Australia: Maclennan & Petty.

Faust, J. (1993). Oh, but a heart, courage and a brain: An integrative approach to play therapy. In T. Kottman & C. Schaefer (Eds.), *Play therapy in action: A casebook for practitioners* (pp. 417–436). Northvale, NJ: Jason Aronson.

Fornari, V. (1999). The aftermath of a plane crash—helping a survivor cope with deaths of mother and sibling: Case of Mary, age 8. In N. B. Webb (Ed.), *Play therapy with children in crisis* (2nd ed., pp. 407–429). New York: Guilford Press.

Frederiksen, J. (1997). Storytelling with objects. In H. Kaduson & C. Schaefer (Eds.), *101 favorite play therapy techniques* (pp. 50–52). Northvale, NJ: Jason Aronson.

Freud, A. (1928). *Introduction to the technique of child analysis* (L. P. Clark, Trans.). New York: Nervous and Mental Disease.

Freud, A. (1946). *The psychoanalytic treatment of children.* London: Imago.

Freud, A. (1965). *Normality and pathology in childhood: Assessments of development.* New York: International University Press.

Freud, A. (1968). Indications and counterindications for child analysis. *Psychoanalytic Study of the Child, 23,* 37–46.

Freud, S. (1938). *The basic writings of Sigmund Freud.* New York: Modern Library.

Freud, S. (1955). *Analysis of a phobia in a five year old boy.* London: Hogarth Press. (Original work published in 1909)

Frey, D. (1993). I brought my own toys today! Play therapy with adults. In T. Kottman & C. Schaefer (Eds.), *Play therapy in action: A casebook for practitioners* (pp. 589–606). Northvale, NJ: Jason Aronson.

Gardner, R. (1971). *Therapeutic communication with children: The mutual storytelling technique.* Northvale, NJ: Jason Aronson.

Gardner, R. (1973). *The talking, feeling, and doing game.* Cresskill, NJ: Creative Therapeutics.

Gardner, R. (1986). *The psychotherapeutic technique of Richard A. Gardner.* Northvale, NJ: Jason Aronson.

Gil, E. (1991). *The healing power of play: Working with abused children.* New York: Guilford Press.

Gil, E. (1994). *Play in family therapy.* New York: Guilford Press.

Ginott, H. (1959). The theory and practice of therapeutic intervention in child treatment. *Journal of Consulting Psychology, 23,* 160–166.

Ginsberg, B. (1984). Beyond behavior modification: Client-centered play therapy with the retarded. *Academic Psychology Bulletin, 6,* 160–166.

Glasser, W. (1975). *Reality therapy.* New York: Harper & Row.

Glazer-Waldman, H., Zimmerman, J., Landreth, G., & Norton, D. (1992). Filial therapy: An intervention for parents of children with chronic illness. *International Journal of Play Therapy, 1*(1), 31–42.

Glover, G. (2001). Cultural considerations in play therapy. In G. Landreth (Ed.), *Innovations in play therapy: Issues, process, and special populations* (pp. 31–41). Philadelphia: Brunner–Routledge.

Golden, L. (1983). Play therapy for hospitalized children. In C. Schaefer & K. O'Connor (Eds.), *Handbook of play therapy* (pp. 213–233). New York: Wiley.

Goodman, R. (1999). Childhood cancer and the family: Case of Tim, age 6, and follow-up at age 15. In N. B. Webb (Ed.), *Play therapy with children in crisis* (2nd ed., pp. 380–406). New York: Guilford Press.

Gopaul-McNicol, S., & Thomas-Presswood, T. (1998). *Working with linguistically and culturally different children: Innovative clinical and educational approaches.* Needham Heights, MA: Allyn & Bacon.

Guerney, B. (1964). Filial therapy: Description and rationale. *Journal of Consulting Psychology, 28,* 304–310.

Guerney, L. (1983a). Client-centered (nondirective) play therapy. In C. Schaefer & K. O'Connor (Eds.), *Handbook of play therapy* (pp. 21–64). New York: Wiley.

Guerney, L. (1983b). Play therapy with learning disabled children. In C. Schaefer & K. O'Connor (Eds.), *Handbook of play therapy* (pp. 419–435). New York: Wiley.

Guerney, L. (1991). Parents as partners in treating behavior problems in early childhood settings. *Topics in Early Childhood Special Education, 11,* 74–90.

Guerney, L. (1997). Filial therapy. In K. O'Connor & L. M. Braverman (Eds.), *Play therapy theory and practice: A comparative presentation* (pp. 130–159). New York: Wiley.

Guerney, L., & Welsh, A. (1993). Two by two: A filial therapy case study. In T. Kottman & C. Schaefer (Eds.), *Play therapy in action: A casebook for practitioners* (pp. 561–588). Northvale, NJ: Jason Aronson.

Hall, P. (1997). Play therapy with sexually abused children. In H. Kaduson, D. Cangelosi, & C. Schaefer (Eds.), *The playing cure: Individual play therapy for specific childhood problems* (pp. 171–196). Northvale, NJ: Jason Aronson.

Hambridge, G. (1955). Structured play therapy. *American Journal of Orthopsychiatry, 25,* 304–310.

Hammond-Newman, M. (1994). Play therapy with children of alcoholics and addicts. In K. O'Connor & C. Schaefer (Eds.), *Handbook of play therapy* (Vol. 2, pp. 387–408). New York: Wiley.

Harvey, S. (1993). Ann: Dynamic play therapy with ritual abuse. In T. Kottman & C. Schaefer (Eds.), *Play therapy in action A casebook for practitioners.* (pp. 371–415). Northvale, NJ: Jason Aronson.

Harvey, S. (1994). Dynamic play therapy: Expressive play interventions with families. In K. O'Connor & C. Schaefer (Eds.) *Handbook of play therapy* (Vol. 2, pp. 85–110). New York: Wiley.

Hayworth, M. (1964). *Child psychotherapy: Practice and theory.* New York: Basic Books.

Hellendoorn, J. (1994). Play therapy with mentally retarded clients. In K. O'Connor & C. Schaefer (Eds.), *Handbook of play therapy* (Vol. 2, pp. 349–370). New York: Wiley.

Hellendoorn, J., & DeVroom, M. (1993). Gentleman Jim and his private war: Imagery interaction play therapy. In T. Kottman & C. Schaefer (Eds.), *Play therapy in action: A casebook for practitioners* (pp. 97–132). Northvale, NJ: Jason Aronson.

Hellendoorn, J., van der Kooij, R., & Sutton-Smith, B. (Eds.). (1994). *Play and intervention.* Albany: State University of New York Press.

Hofmann, J., & Rogers, P. (1991). A crisis play group in a shelter following the Santa Cruz earthquake. In N. B. Webb (Ed.), *Play therapy with children in crisis* (pp. 379–395). New York: Guilford Press.

Holmberg, J., & Benedict, H. (1997). Play therapy: How does that work anyway? A resource handout for parents. *Association for Play Therapy Newsletter, 16*(2), 4–6.

Hoyt, M. (1995). *Brief therapy and managed care: Readings for contemporary practice.* San Francisco: Jossey-Bass.

Hug-Hellmuth, H. (1921). On the technique of child analysis. *International Journal of Psychoanalysis, 2,* 287–305.

Jackson, Y. (1998). Applying APA ethical guidelines to individual play therapy with children. *International Journal of Play Therapy, 7*(2), 1–15.

James, O. O. (1997). *Play therapy: A comprehensive guide.* Northvale, NJ: Jason Aronson.

Jernberg, A. (1979). *Theraplay: A new treatment using structured play for problem children and their families.* San Francisco: Jossey-Bass.

Jernberg, A., & Booth, P. (1999). *Theraplay* (2nd ed.). San Francisco: Jossey-Bass.

Jernberg, A., & Jernberg, E. (1993). Family Theraplay for the family tyrant. In T. Kottman & C. Schaefer (Eds.), *Play therapy in action: A casebook for practitioners* (pp. 45–96). Northvale, NJ: Jason Aronson.

Johnson-Powell, G., & Yamamoto, J. (Eds.). (1997). *Transcultural child development: Psychological assessment and treatment.* New York: Wiley.

Jongsma, A., Peterson, L., & McInnis, W. (1996). *The child and adolescent psychotherapy treatment planner.* New York: Wiley.

Joyner, C. (1991). Individual, group and family crisis counseling following a hurricane: Case of Heather, age 9. In N. B. Webb (Ed.), *Play therapy with children in crisis* (pp. 396–415). New York: Guilford Press.

Kaduson, H. (1997). Play therapy for children with Attention-Deficit Hyperactivity Disorder. In H. Kaduson, D. Cangelosi, & C. Schaefer (Eds.), *The playing cure: Individual play therapy for specific childhood problems* (pp. 197–228). Northvale, NJ: Jason Aronson.

Kaduson, H., Cangelosi, D., & Schaefer, C. (Eds.). (1997). *The playing cure: Individualized play therapy for specific childhood problems.* Northvale, NJ: Jason Aronson.

Kaduson, H., & Finnerty, K. (1995). Self-control game interventions for Attention-Deficit Hyperactivity Disorder. *International Journal of Play Therapy, 2*(1), 15–30.

Kaduson, H., & Schaefer, C. (Eds.). (1997). *101 favorite play therapy techniques.* Northvale, NJ: Jason Aronson.

Kaduson, H., & Schaefer, C. (Eds.). (2000). *Short-term play therapy for children.* New York: Guilford Press.

Kale, A., & Landreth, G. (1999). Filial therapy with parents of children experiencing learning difficulties. *International Journal of Play Therapy, 8*(2), 35–56.

Kalff, D. (1971). *Sandplay: Mirror of a child's psyche.* San Francisco: Browser.

Kao, S., & Landreth, G. (2001). Play therapy with Chinese children. In G. Landreth (Ed.), *Innovations in play therapy: Issues, process, and special populations* (pp. 43–49). Philadelphia: Brunner–Routledge.

Kaplan, C. (1999). Life threatening blood disorder: Case of Daniel, age 11, and his mother. In N. B. Webb (Ed.), *Play therapy with children in crisis* (2nd ed., pp. 356–379). New York: Guilford Press.

Kissel, S. (1990). *Play therapy: A strategic approach.* Springfield, IL: Charles C Thomas.

Klein, J., & Landreth, G. (1993). Play therapy with multiple personality disorder clients. *International Journal of Play Therapy, 2*(1), 1–14.

Klein, M. (1932). *The psycho-analysis of children.* London: Hogarth Press.

Knell, S. (1993a). *Cognitive–behavioral play therapy.* Northvale, NJ: Jason Aronson.

Knell, S. (1993b). To show and not tell: Cognitive–behavioral play therapy. In T. Kottman & C. Schaefer (Eds.), *Play therapy in action: A casebook for practitioners* (pp. 169–208). Northvale, NJ: Jason Aronson.

Knell, S. (1994). Cognitive–behavioral play therapy. In K. O'Connor & C. Schaefer (Eds.), *Handbook of play therapy: (Vol. 2.,* pp. 111–142). New York: Wiley.

Knell, S. (1997). Cognitive–behavioral play therapy. In K. O'Connor & L. M. Braverman (Eds.), *Play therapy theory and practice: A comparative presentation* (pp. 79–99). New York: Wiley.

Knell, S. (2000). Cognitive–behavioral play therapy for childhood fears and phobias. In H. Kaduson & C. Schaefer (Eds.), *Short-term play therapy for children* (pp. 3–27). New York: Guilford Press.

Knell, S., & Moore, D. (1990). Cognitive–behavioral play therapy in the treatment of encopresis. *Journal of Clinical Child Psychology, 19,* 55–60.

Kohut, H. (1971). *The analysis of the self.* New York: International Universities Press.

Kohut, H. (1977). *The restoration of the self.* New York: International Universities Press.

Koller, T. (1994). Adolescent Theraplay. In K. O'Connor & C. Schaefer (Eds.), *Handbook of play therapy* (Vol. 2, pp. 159–188). New York: Wiley.

Koller, T., & Booth, P. (1997). Fostering attachment through family Theraplay. In K. O'Connor & L. M. Braverman (Eds.), *Play therapy theory and practice: A comparative presentation* (pp. 204–233). New York: Wiley.

Kottman, T. (1993). The king of rock and roll. In T. Kottman & C. Schaefer (Eds.), *Play therapy in action: A casebook for practitioners* (pp. 133–167). Northvale, NJ: Jason Aronson.

Kottman, T. (1994). Adlerian play therapy. In K. O'Connor & C. Schaefer (Eds.), *Handbook of play therapy* (Vol. 2, pp. 3–26). New York: Wiley.

Kottman, T. (1995). *Partners in play: An Adlerian approach to play therapy.* Alexandria, VA: American Counseling Association.

Kottman, T. (1997a). Adlerian play therapy. In K. O'Connor & L. M. Braverman (Eds.), *Play therapy theory and practice: A comparative presentation* (pp. 310–340). New York: Wiley.

Kottman, T. (1997b). Building a family: Play therapy with adopted children and their parents. In H. Kaduson, D. Cangelosi, & C. Schaefer (Eds.), *The playing cure: Individual play therapy for specific childhood problems* (pp. 337–370). Northvale, NJ: Jason Aronson.

Kottman, T. (1999a). Play therapy in 2100: Precognitions and prognostications. *International Journal of Play Therapy, 8*(1), 1–8.

Kottman, T. (1999b). Using the Crucial Cs in Adlerian play therapy. *Individual Psychology, 55,* 289–297.

Kottman, T., & Ashby, J. (1999). Using Adlerian personality priorities to custom-design consultation with parents of play therapy clients. *International Journal of Play Therapy, 8*(2), 77–92.

Kottman, T., & Stiles, K. (1990). The mutual storytelling technique: An Adlerian application in child therapy. *Journal of Individual Psychology, 46*, 148–156.

Kottman, T., Strother, J., & Deniger, M. (1987). Activity therapy: An alternative therapy for adolescents. *Journal of Humanistic Education and Development, 25,* 180–186.

Kraft, A., & Landreth, G. (1998). *Parents as therapeutic partners: Listening to your child's play.* Northvale, NJ: Jason Aronson.

Kranz, P., Kottman, T., & Lund, N. (1998). Play therapists' opinions concerning the education, training, and practice of play therapists. *International Journal of Play Therapy, 7*(1), 33–40.

Krull, T. (1997, October). *Managing more than before: Play therapy, the clinician and managed care . . . how to make it all work.* Paper presented at the 14th Annual International Conference of the Association for Play Therapy, Orlando, FL.

Krull, T., & Welch, B. (1999). How to create good relationships with managed care companies. *International Association for Play Therapy Newsletter, 18*(4), 9.

Landreth, G. (1978). Children communicate through play. *Texas Personnel and Guidance Association Journal, 1,* 41–42.

Landreth, G. (1988). Lessons for living from a dying child. *Journal of Counseling and Development, 67,* 100.

Landreth, G. (1991). *Play therapy: The art of the relationship.* Muncie, IN: Accelerated Development.

Landreth, G., & Sweeney, D. (1997). Child-centered play therapy. In K. O'Connor & L. M. Braverman (Eds.), *Play therapy theory and practice: A comparative presentation* (pp. 17–45). New York: Wiley.

Lankton, C., & Lankton, S. (1989). *Tales of enchantment: Goal-oriented metaphors for adults and children in therapy.* New York: Brunner/Mazel.

LeBlanc, M., & Ritchie, M. (1999). Predictors of play therapy outcomes. *International Journal of Play Therapy, 8*(2), 19–34.

Lebo, D. (1952). The present status of research on nondirective play therapy. *Journal of Consulting Psychology, 17,* 177–183.

Ledyard, P. (1999). Play therapy with the elderly: A case study. *International Journal of Play Therapy, 8*(2), 57–75.

Lee, A. (1997). Psychoanalytic play therapy. In K. O'Connor & L. M. Braverman (Eds.), *Play therapy theory and practice: A comparative presentation* (pp. 46–78). New York: Wiley.

Leland, H. (1983). Play therapy for mentally retarded and developmentally delayed children. In C. Schaefer & K. O'Connor (Eds.), *Handbook of play therapy* (pp. 436–455). New York: Wiley.

LeVieux, J. (1990, December). Issues in play therapy: The dying child. *Association for Play Therapy Newsletter, 9*(4), 4–5.

LeVieux, J. (1994). Terminal illness and death of father: Case of Celeste, age 5^1/$_2$. In N. B. Webb (Ed.), *Helping bereaved children: A handbook for practitioners* (pp. 81–95). New York: Guilford Press.

Levy, D. (1938). Release therapy for young children. *Psychiatry, 1,* 387–389.

Lew, A., & Bettner, B. L. (1996). *Responsibility in the classroom.* Newton Center, MA: Connexions.

Lew, A., & Bettner, B. L. (2000). *A parent's guide to understanding and motivating children* (Rev. ed.). Newton Center, MA: Connexions.

Locke, D.C. (1998). Increasing multicultural understanding: A comprehensive model (2nd ed.). Thousand Oaks, CA: Sage.

Lowenfeld, M. (1950). The nature and use of the Lowenfeld world technique in work with children and adults. *Journal of Psychology, 30,* 325–331.

Lyness-Richard, D. (1997). Play therapy for children with fears and phobias. In H. Kaduson, D. Cangelosi, & C. Schaefer (Eds.), *The playing cure: Individual play therapy for specific childhood problems* (pp. 29–60). Northvale, NJ: Jason Aronson.

Mader, C. (2000). Child-centered play therapy with disruptive school students. In H. Kaduson & C. Schaefer (Eds.), *Short-term play therapy for children* (pp. 53–68). New York: Guilford Press.

Mahler, M. (1972). On the first three subphases of the separation–individuation process. *International Journal of Psychoanalysis, 53,* 333–338.

Marschak, M. (1960). A method for evaluating child–parent interaction under controlled conditions. *Journal of Genetic Psychology, 97,* 3–22.

Martinez, K., & Valdez, D. (1992). Cultural considerations in play therapy with Hispanic children. In L. Vargas & J. Koss-Chioino (Eds.), *Working with culture: Psychotherapeutic interventions with ethnic minority children and adolescents* (pp. 85–102). San Francisco: Jossey-Bass.

Marvasti, J. (1993). "Please hurt me again": Posttraumatic play therapy with an abused child. In T. Kottman & C. Schaefer (Eds.), *Play therapy in action: A casebook for practitioners* (pp. 485–526). Northvale, NJ: Jason Aronson.

Marvasti, J. (1994). Play diagnosis and play therapy with child victims of incest. In K. O'Connor & C. Schaefer (Eds.), *Handbook of play therapy* (Vol. 2, pp. 319–348). New York: Wiley.

Masur, C. (1991). The crisis of early maternal loss: Unresolved grief of 6-year-old Chris in foster care. In N. B. Webb (Ed.), *Play therapy with children in crisis* (pp. 164–176). New York: Guilford Press.

McNeil, C., Bahl, A., & Herschell, A. (2000). Involving and empowering parents in short-term play therapy for disruptive children. In H. Kaduson & C. Schaefer (Eds.), *Short-term play therapy for children* (pp. 228–255). New York: Guilford Press.

Mendell, A. (1983). Play therapy with children of divorced parents. In C. Schaefer & K. O'Connor (Eds.), *Handbook of play therapy* (pp. 320–354). New York: Wiley.

Mills, B., & Allan, J. (1992). Play therapy with the maltreated child: Impact upon aggressive and withdrawn patterns of interaction. *International Journal of Play Therapy, 1*(1), 1–20.

Mills, J., & Crowley, R. (1986). *Therapeutic metaphors for children and the child within.* New York: Brunner/Mazel.

Milos, M., & Reiss, S. (1982). Effects of three play conditions on separation anxiety in young children. *Journal of Consulting and Clinical Psychology, 50,* 389–395.

Mitchell, R. (2001). *Documentation in counseling records* (2nd ed.). Alexandria, VA: American Counseling Association.

Moustakas, C. (1953). *Children in play therapy.* New York: McGraw-Hill.

Moustakas, C. (1959). *Psychotherapy with children.* New York: Harper & Row.

Munns, E. (Ed.). (2000). *Theraplay: Innovations in attachment-enhancing play therapy.* Northvale, NJ: Jason Aronson.

Nemiroff, M., & Annunziata, J. (1990). *A child's first book about play therapy.* Washington, DC: American Psychological Association.

Nisivoccia, D., & Lynn, M. (1999). Helping forgotten victims: Using activity groups with children who witness violence. In N. B. Webb (Ed.), *Play therapy with children in crisis* (2nd ed., pp. 74–103). New York: Guilford Press.

Norcross, J. (1987). *Casebook of eclectic psychotherapy.* New York: Brunner/Mazel.

Norton, C., & Norton, B. (1997). *Reaching children through play therapy: An experiential approach.* Denver, CO: Publishing Cooperative.

Oaklander, V. (1992). *Windows to our children: A Gestalt approach to children and adolescents.* New York: Gestalt Journal Press. (Original work published 1978)

Oaklander, V. (1993). From meek to bold: A case study of Gestalt play therapy. In T. Kottman & C. Schaefer (Eds.), *Play therapy in action: A casebook for practitioners* (pp. 281–299). Northvale, NJ: Jason Aronson.

Oaklander, V. (1994). Gestalt play therapy. In K. O'Connor & C. Schaefer (Eds.), *Handbook of play therapy* (Vol. 2, pp. 143–156). New York: Wiley.

Oaklander, V. (2000). Short-term Gestalt play therapy for grieving children. In H. Kaduson & C. Schaefer (Eds.), *Short-term play therapy for children* (pp. 28–52). New York: Guilford Press.

O'Connor, K. (1986). The interaction of hostile and depressive behaviors: A case study of a depressed boy. *Journal of Child and Adolescent Psychotherapy, 3,* 105–108.

O'Connor, K. (1991). *The play therapy primer: An integration of theories and techniques.* New York: Wiley.

O'Connor, K. (1993). Child, protector, confidant: Structured group ecosystemic play therapy. In T. Kottman & C. Schaefer (Eds.), *Play therapy in action: A casebook for practitioners* (pp. 245–282). Northvale, NJ: Jason Aronson.

O'Connor, K. (1994). Ecosystemic play therapy. In K. O'Connor & C. Schaefer (Eds.), *Handbook of play therapy* (Vol. 2, pp. 61–84). New York: Wiley.

O'Connor, K. (1997). Ecosystemic play therapy. In K. O'Connor & L. M. Braverman (Eds.), *Play therapy theory and practice: A comparative presentation* (pp. 234–284). New York: Wiley.

O'Connor, K. (2000). *The play therapy primer* (2nd ed.). New York: Wiley.

O'Connor, K., & Ammen, S. (1997). *Play therapy treatment planning and interventions: The ecosystemic model and workbook.* Boston: Academic Press.

O'Doherty, S. (1989). Play and drama therapy with the Down's syndrome child. *Arts in Psychotherapy, 16,* 171–178.

Palumbo, A. (1988). Special puppet designs for profoundly handicapped children. *Journal of Rehabilitation, 54*(2), 41–45.

Pelcovitz, D. (1999). Betrayed by a trusted adult: Structured time-limited group therapy with elementary school children abused by a school employee. In N. B. Webb (Ed.), *Play therapy with children in crisis* (2nd ed., pp. 183–202). New York: Guilford Press.

Perls, F. (1973). *The Gestalt approach and eyewitness to therapy.* Palo Alto, CA: Science and Behavior Books.

Perry, L. (1993). Audrey, the bois d'arc, and me: A time of becoming. In T. Kottman & C. Schaefer (Eds.), *Play therapy in action: A casebook for practitioners* (pp. 5–44). Northvale, NJ: Jason Aronson.

Perry, L., & Landreth, G. (1991). Diagnostic assessment of children's play therapy behavior. In C. E. Schaefer, K. Gitlin, & A. Sandgrud (Eds.), *Play therapy diagnosis and assessment* (pp. 643–662). New York: Wiley.

Peyton, J. (1986). Use of puppets in a residence for the elderly. *Nursing Homes, 35,* 27–30.

Phillips, R. (1985). Whistling in the dark: A review of play therapy research. *Psychotherapy, 22,* 752–760.

Phillips, R., & Landreth, G. (1995). Play therapists on play therapy: I. A report of methods, demographics, and professional/practice issues. *International Journal of Play Therapy, 4*(1), 1–27.

Phillips, R., & Landreth, G. (1998). Play therapists on play therapy: II. Clinical issues in play therapy. *International Journal of Play Therapy, 7*(1), 1–32.

Piaget, J. (1952). *The origins of intelligence in children.* New York: International Universities Press.

Popkin, M. (1993). *Active parenting today.* Atlanta, GA: Active Parenting.

Price, J. (1991). The effects of divorce precipitate a suicide threat: Case of Philip, age 8. In N. B. Webb (Ed.), *Play therapy with children in crisis* (pp. 202–218). New York: Guilford Press.

Pumfrey, P., & Elliott, C. (1970). Play therapy, social adjustment and reading attainment. *Educational Research, 12,* 183–193.

Rank, O. (1936). *Will therapy.* New York: Knopf.

Rappaport, S. (1991). Diagnostic–prescriptive teaming: The road less traveled. *Journal of Reading, Writing and Learning Disabilities, 7,* 183–199.

Reid, S. (1993). It's all in the game: Game play therapy. In T. Kottman & C. Schaefer (Eds.), *Play therapy in action: A casebook for practitioners* (pp. 527–560). Northvale, NJ: Jason Aronson.

Richards, N. (1996). *Play therapy: Theoretical approaches 1909–1996.* Unpublished manuscript, University of Iowa, Iowa City.

Ridder, N. (1999). HIV/AIDS in the family: Group treatment for latency-age children affected by the illness of a family member. In N. B. Webb (Ed.), *Play therapy with children in crisis* (2nd ed., pp. 341–355). New York: Guilford Press.

Robinson, H. (1999). Unresolved conflicts in a divorced family: Case of Charlie, age 10. In N. B. Webb (Ed.), *Play therapy with children in crisis* (2nd ed., pp. 272–293). New York: Guilford Press.

Rogers, C. (1951). *Client-centered therapy: Its current practice, implications, and theory.* Boston: Houghton Mifflin.

Rogers, C. (1959). A theory of therapy, personality, and interpersonal relationships as developed in the client-centered framework. In S. Koch (Ed.), *Psychology: A study of a science. Study I. Conceptual and systematic. Vol. 3: Formulation of the person and social context* (pp. 184–256). New York: McGraw-Hill.

Rosenthal, L. (1956). Child guidance. In S. R. Slavson (Ed.), *The fields of group psychotherapy* (pp. 215–232). New York: International University Press.

Salo, M., & Shumate, S. (1993). *Counseling minor clients.* Alexandria, VA: American Counseling Association.

Salomon, M. (1983). Play therapy with the physically handicapped. In C. Schaefer & K. O'Connor (Eds.), *Handbook of play therapy* (pp. 455–469). New York: Wiley.

Saravay, B. (1991). Short-term play therapy with two preschool brothers following sudden paternal death. In N. B. Webb (Ed.), *Play therapy with children in crisis* (pp. 177–201). New York: Guilford Press.

Schaefer, C. (Ed.). (1993). *The therapeutic powers of play.* Northvale, NJ: Jason Aronson.

Schaefer, C. (1998). Play therapy: Critical issues for the next millennium. *Association for Play Therapy Newsletter, 17*(1), 1–5.

Schaefer, C. (2000, October). *Theories of play therapy: Eclectic/prescriptive play therapy.* Keynote address presented at the 17th Annual Conference of the Association for Play Therapy, New Orleans, LA.

Schaefer, C., & Carey, L. (Eds.). (1994). *Family play therapy.* Northvale, NJ: Jason Aronson.

Schaefer, C., & Greenberg, R. (1997). Measurement of playfulness: A neglected therapist variable. *International Journal of Play Therapy, 6*(2), 21–32.

Schiffer, M. (1952). Permissiveness versus sanction in activity group therapy. *International Journal of Group Psychotherapy, 2*, 255–261.

Shapiro, D. (1995). Puppet modeling technique for children undergoing stressful medical procedures: Tips for clinicians. *International Journal of Play Therapy, 4*(2), 31–40.

Shelby, J. (1997). Rubble, disruption, and tears: Helping young survivors of natural disaster. In H. Kaduson, D. Cangelosi, & C. Schaefer (Eds.), *The playing cure: Individual play therapy for specific childhood problems* (pp. 143–170). Northvale, NJ: Jason Aronson.

Slavson, S. R. (1943). *An introduction to group therapy.* New York: Commonwealth Fund.

Sloves, R., & Peterlin, K. (1993). Where in the world is . . . my father? A time-limited play therapy. In T. Kottman & C. Schaefer (Eds.), *Play therapy in action: A casebook for practitioners* (pp. 301–346). Northvale, NJ: Jason Aronson.

Sloves, R., & Peterlin, K. (1994). Time-limited play therapy. In K. O'Connor & C. Schaefer (Eds.), *Handbook of play therapy* (Vol. 2, pp. 27–59). New York: Wiley.

Smith, A., & Herman, J. (1994). Setting limits while enabling self-expression: Play therapy with an aggressive, controlling child. *International Journal of Play Therapy, 3*(1), 23–36.

Solomon, J. (1938). Active play therapy. *American Journal of Orthopsychiatry, 8,* 479–498.

Stiles, K., & Kottman, T. (1990). Mutual storytelling: An alternative intervention for depressed children. *The School Counselor, 37,* 337–343.

Stone, B. (2000). Managed care: "Mother may I?" *Association for Play Therapy Newsletter, 19*(2), 3, 5.

Strand, V. (1999). The assessment and treatment of family sexual abuse. In N. B. Webb (Ed.), *Play therapy with children in crisis* (2nd ed., pp. 104–130). New York: Guilford Press.

Sugar, M. (1988). A preschooler in a disaster. *American Journal of Psychotherapy, 42,* 619–629.

Sweeney, D. (2001). Legal and ethical issues in play therapy. In G. Landreth (Ed.), *Innovations in play therapy: Issues, process, and special populations* (pp. 65–81). Philadelphia: Brunner–Routledge.

Taft, J. (1933). *The dynamics of therapy in a controlled relationship*. New York: Macmillan.

Tait, D., & Depta, J. (1994). Play therapy group for bereaved children. In N. B. Webb (Ed.), *Helping bereaved children: A handbook for practitioners* (pp. 169–185). New York: Guilford Press.

Terr, L. (1983). Play therapy and psychic trauma: A preliminary report. In C. Schaefer & K. O'Connor (Eds.), *Handbook of play therapy* (pp. 308–319). New York: Wiley.

Terr, L. (1990). *Too scared to cry.* New York: Harper & Row.

Thompson, C., & Rudolph, L. (2000). *Counseling children* (5th ed.). Pacific Grove, CA: Brooks/Cole.

Tonning, L. (1999). Persistent and chronic neglect in the context of poverty—When parents can't parent: Case of Ricky, age 3. In N. B. Webb (Ed.), *Play therapy with children in crisis* (2nd ed., pp. 203–224). New York: Guilford Press.

Trottier, M., & Seferlis, N. (1990, June). *Using therapeutic metaphors in school counseling.* Paper presented at a conference of the American School Counselor Association, Little Rock, AR.

Van de Putte, S. (1995). A paradigm for working with child survivors of sexual abuse who exhibit sexualized behaviors during play therapy. *International Journal of Play Therapy, 4*(1), 27–49.

VanFleet, R. (1994a). Filial therapy for adoptive children and parents. In K. O'Connor & C. Schaefer (Eds.), *Handbook of play therapy* (Vol. 2, pp. 371–386). New York: Wiley.

VanFleet, R. (1994b). *Filial therapy: Strengthening parent–child relationships through play.* Sarasota, FL: Professional Resource Press.

VanFleet, R. (2000a). *A parent's handbook of filial therapy: Building strong families with play.* Boiling Springs, PA: Play Therapy Press.

VanFleet, R. (2000b). Short-term play therapy for families with chronic illness. In H. Kaduson & C. Schaefer (Eds.), *Short-term play therapy for children* (pp. 175–193). New York: Guilford Press.

VanFleet, R., Lilly, J. P., & Kaduson, H. (1999). Play therapy for children exposed to violence: Individual, family and community interventions. *International Journal of Play Therapy, 8*(1), 27–42.

Webb, J. (1995). Play therapy with hospitalized children. *International Journal of Play Therapy, 4*(1), 51–60.

Webb, N. B. (1991). Afterward: The crisis of war. In N. B. Webb (Ed.), *Play therapy with children in crisis* (pp. 437–444). New York: Guilford Press.

Webb, N. B. (1999). The child witness of parental violence: Case of Michael, age 4, and follow-up at age 16. In N. B. Webb (Ed.), *Play therapy with children in crisis* (2nd ed., pp. 49–73). New York: Guilford Press.

Williams, W., & Lair, G. (1991). Using a person-centered approach with children who have a disability. *Elementary School Guidance and Counseling, 25,* 194–203.

Williams-Gray, B. (1999). International consultation and intervention on behalf of children affected by war. In N. B. Webb (Ed.), *Play therapy with children in crisis* (2nd ed., pp. 448–470). New York: Guilford Press.

Winnicott, D. W. (1958). *Collected papers: Through paediatrics to psychoanalysis.* London: Tavistock.

Winnicott, D.W. (1971). *Playing and reality.* London: Tavistock.

Wojtasik, S., & Sanborn, S. (1991). The crisis of acute hospitalization: Case of Seth, age 7. In N. B. Webb (Ed.), *Play therapy with children in crisis* (pp. 295–309). New York: Guilford Press.

Wood, M., Combs, C., Gunn, A., & Weller, D. (1986). *Developmental therapy in the classroom* (2nd ed.). Austin, TX: Pro-Ed.

INDEX